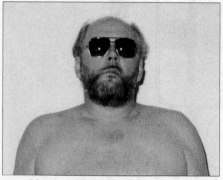

Mug shot of Richard Kuklinski on the day
of his capture, 1986.

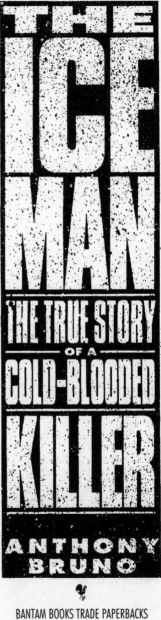

THE ICE MAN

THE TRUE STORY OF A COLD-BLOODED KILLER

ANTHONY BRUNO

BANTAM BOOKS TRADE PAPERBACKS
NEW YORK

Published in the United States by Bantam Books, an imprint of The Random House Publishing Group, a division of Random House, Inc., New York.

BANTAM BOOKS and the rooster colophon are registered trademarks of Random House, Inc.

Originally published in hardcover and in slightly different form in the United States by Delacorte Press, an imprint of The Random House Publishing Group, a division of Random House, Inc., in 1993, and subsequently in paperback by iUniverse in 2008.

Library of Congress Cataloging in Publication Data

Bruno, Anthony.
    The iceman : the true story of a cold-blooded killer / by Anthony Bruno.
        p. cm.
    ISBN 978-0-345-54011-9
    ISBN 978-0-345-54009-6 (eBook)
        1. Kuklinski, Richard. 2. Murderers—New Jersey—Biography.
    3. Serial murders—New Jersey—Case studies. I. Title.
    HV6248.K75B78 1993
    364.1'523'09749—dc20   92-44003

Printed in the United States of America

www.bantamdell.com

98765

Book design by Robin Arzt

In memory of all the victims of Richard Kuklinski,
both known and unknown

FOREWORD

by Jim Thebaut, producer and filmmaker of *The Iceman Tapes*

My involvement with the Iceman story started in 1986 when I first learned about Richard Kuklinski, a mass murderer who claimed to have killed scores of people while maintaining an outwardly normal, suburban lifestyle with a wife and three children. The police had nicknamed him "the Iceman" because he had frozen one of his victims for two years to see if he could disguise the time of death. Clearly this was not a run-of-the-mill killer. I was intrigued, but at the time I had no idea how deeply his story would affect my life. What a long strange trip it has been.

While serving as executive producer on *A Deadly Business,* a CBS Television dramatic special, a friend and adviser on that project told me that a dangerous killer had just been arrested in New Jersey, and he felt that this man's incredible story would make a great film. *A Deadly Business* delved into organized crime's involvement in the illegal dumping of toxic waste in the Garden State. The killer, Richard Kuklinski, had been apprehended on the quiet suburban street where he lived. My adviser, who at the time was the director of New Jersey's Organized Crime Task Force and later became a deputy attorney general of the state, told me that Kuklinski would have to be tried before I could approach any of the principal individuals in the case about doing a film, but he would help me get the cooperation of the police and prosecutors. Approximately two years later, in 1988 after Kuklinski's conviction, I started my quest to turn his story into what I hoped would be a powerful and successful motion picture.

What attracted me to this project was the opportunity to explore the dark side of human behavior. Kuklinski claimed to have killed more than 100 people. I wanted to know what created this monster. Was he born this way, or had his upbringing shaped him? I set about to secure the rights to the stories of the people who knew him best: his wife and children, as well as the federal undercover agent who had gotten close to him and secretly taped him talking about his crimes. After several months of negotiation, I was able to obtain options on those rights.

Shortly after, I received a call from the director of the New Jersey Division of Criminal Justice, who had prosecuted the case against Kuklinski, asking if I would be interested in interviewing Kuklinski at Trenton State Prison, where he was incarcerated. Naturally I accepted, with the understanding that at a later date I would be allowed to conduct an on-camera interview with him.

My initial meeting with the Iceman lasted two and a half hours. I was first struck by his size—six-foot-four, well over 250 pounds—and immediately recognized how intimidating he must have been on the street. We met one-on-one in a room reserved for lawyer/client conferences. I found him to be straightforward, cordial, and articulate. I felt that his dark story could potentially become a compelling, frightening, and unforgettable documentary, but first I had to see how forthcoming he would be and if he could cinematically sustain a one-hour program. I needed to discover what buttons, if any, I could push to elicit emotional responses on camera. When I asked him about his relationship with his son, he showed deep sadness, and tears came to his eyes. Later on, I realized this line of questioning might show the human being beneath the killer.

The very next day I pitched the idea to executives at HBO. I convinced them that Kuklinski was not just a thug with a gun and a chip on his shoulder. There was a real story here, I told them, an *impor-*

tant story. They felt my passion and agreed to move forward with the project.

My first meeting with Kuklinski at the prison laid the groundwork for our on-camera interview, which lasted a total of seventeen hours. In the early spring of 1991 I took a film crew to the prison and, over a three-day period, interviewed Kuklinski for fifteen hours. The prison gave us a room next to the execution chamber, which hadn't been used in fifteen years. Officials from the attorney general's office simultaneously taped the interview for their own use. Their hope was that Kuklinski would provide information regarding unsolved murders he was suspected of having committed. I met with them at the end of each day, and over pizza and wine we discussed what I would ask Kuklinski the next day. My challenge was to ask him questions that might provide factual information while making sure that his responses were visually compelling for the camera.

On camera, Kuklinski was sly but frank. He spoke of many murders, some at great length, but he was often stingy with the kind of specifics that might lead to new indictments. Perhaps he didn't want to go through another trial. I suspect he enjoyed the attention I gave him, and perhaps he feared that if he told me everything, I would lose interest in him. But his matter-of-fact retelling of his crimes was mesmerizing.

Several months later I went back into the prison with my film crew and a representative from HBO and conducted two more hours of interview, but something had changed. Unlike our previous experience, Kuklinski was uncooperative, and the effort was a waste of time.

I envisioned the Iceman project taking several forms—first, as a documentary, then as a book, then as a feature film—and I proceeded with this in mind. As it turned out, the first two stages of my plan were accomplished in relatively quick succession. *The Iceman Tapes: Conversations with a Killer* was first broadcast in the spring of 1992. The book, *The Iceman: The True Story of a Cold-Blooded Killer,* written by crime writer Anthony Bruno, was published in hardcover in 1993. Both were very successful. *The Iceman Tapes* became one of HBO's highest-rated documentaries and was nominated for a Cable Ace Award. The book stayed in print for many years, and foreign editions were published in the United Kingdom, Germany, and Japan. I felt confident that a movie deal would soon follow.

Unfortunately the toxic nature of the Kuklinski material seemed to infect the project itself. Success should have engendered further success, but instead it created greed, bruised egos, frustration, and enmity. The relationships I had worked so hard to build eroded around me. Suddenly I was seen as a "Hollywood producer" with all the negative attributes that phrase implies, and my motives became suspect. While my goal never changed and my intentions were exactly what they had been when I started, the tainted perceptions of others put obstacles in my path and kept me from making the film.

Perhaps I shouldn't have been surprised that the rights holders (the cops who investigated and arrested Kuklinski, the prosecutor who tried him, and Kuklinski's family) could not maintain the degree of solidarity I needed to make a feature film. I suspect the law-enforcement side wasn't comfortable being on equal footing with the family of a mass murderer, and those who had lived under Kuklinski's roof must have learned from him not to trust anyone. Securing options on their rights had been time consuming and labor intensive, requiring a great deal of legal wrangling. But it didn't take long before mistrust altered their thinking. They sought out attorneys and agents to protect their interests. Ironically, one member of the Iceman task force was represented by a former girlfriend of mine!

The rights holders were perfectly within their rights to seek representation, but as the saying goes, too many cooks spoiled the soup. "Hollywood" pockets are seldom as deep as most people think, but the rights holders failed to understand that. And none of them wanted to be paid less than anyone else. Rumors spread that HBO had compensated Mrs. Kuklinski handsomely, and the cops understandably felt the criminal's family had profited from his evil deeds. HBO's actions in effect stuck a large knife into my efforts. I did my utmost to secure funding to keep the project afloat, but as option periods ran out and agreements had to be renegotiated, the demands became unrealistic. Some of the principals went their own way and attempted to sell their rights to other producers. All *Iceman* and *Iceman*-related projects failed to get off the ground, including mine.

A lawsuit filed by Mrs. Kuklinski followed, which further hindered my efforts. It dragged on for years and was not settled until 1996. I couldn't help but think that Richard Kuklinski's noxious presence hovered over the project. While HBO executives reveled in his demonic qualities, I, like many members of the Iceman task force as well as his family, felt that we were poisoned by his influence. As silly as it might seem, anyone who came into contact with him was liable to be affected.

After many years of frustration, I turned my attention to other projects. My interests had taken me away from the dark side, and I focused on creating educational documentaries and implementing public policy regarding the evolving global water and sanitation crisis and its ultimate impact on international security. This became my passion.

The curse was broken in 2013 when Kuklinski's story finally made it to the big screen. The film, *The Iceman,* starring Michael Shannon as Richard Kuklinski and directed by Ariel Vromen, is based on this book and the seventeen hours of interviews I conducted with Kuklinski. It took more than twenty years, but my objective was finally realized.

Over the years a great deal of misinformation about Richard Kuklinski has circulated, most of it coming directly from Kuklinski himself. In interviews for two subsequent HBO documentaries and for another book, he spun tall tales and portrayed himself as the monster he thought the world wanted him to be. He was allowed to glorify himself. But he was enough of a monster on his own, unembellished, and all the more frightening because he didn't come from hell as he might have wanted the public to believe. He was the result of his upbringing. Under the right—or should I say, wrong—circumstances, any one of us could have grown up to become just like him. That's the real terror of his story.

I'm proud of my work on the Iceman project and how it contributed to this book. Our intent was to show the horrifying ripple effect of child abuse and the resulting post-traumatic stress syndrome, which took an aberrant turn in Kuklinski's case. The message I hope you come away with is that violence begets violence.

Read on and you will be fascinated and horrified by his strange tale. You will also become engrossed in the story of the brave men who came together to stop him. Read on and learn the truth about the Iceman.

INTRODUCTION

I remember when I first laid eyes on Richard Kuklinski's face. It was a weekday afternoon in 1992, and I was in my living room in front of the TV, a stack of VHS tapes piled on the coffee table. My agent had called me a few days earlier and told me that he had a possible book project for me. A producer named Jim Thebaut was making a documentary about a mass murderer from New Jersey nicknamed "the Iceman," and he wanted a book based on seventeen hours of taped interviews with the killer. He was looking for the right author, someone who could make the Iceman's story come to life and read like fiction. I had published several well-received crime novels at the time. And, born and bred in North Jersey, I knew the Iceman's territory.

To be totally honest, the project didn't sound like a winner to me. Kuklinski claimed to have killed more than 100 people, but I had never heard of him. Not surprising considering that his trial happened at a time when two other crime stories were eating up the headlines, the trials of Robert Chambers (the "Preppy Murderer") and Margaret Kelly Michaels, a teacher accused of sexually abusing thirty-three pre-schoolers. (She was convicted, but it was overturned on appeal.) I had been approached to do other books about criminals and I knew that for the most part in real life they aren't that interesting as people. They're rarely as clever and sophisticated as the murderers in novels, characters like "Hannibal Lecter."

So as I pressed play on the VCR, I intended to watch only as much as I needed to give a polite but informed "no thanks." But long past midnight I was still watching. The next morning I picked up where I'd left off and stayed with it until I'd viewed the entire seventeen hours. It was just Kuklinski, the camera focused on his face, Jim Thebaut off camera asking him questions. No supporting footage, no crime-scene photos, no family photographs, just him. But I couldn't stop watching.

There was something about him that riveted my attention. He wasn't a wild man or a snarling demon. There was a curious disconnect between his appearance and his manner. He was a huge man—bald, long face, hollow cheeks, full gray beard, small wary eyes. Sometimes when asked a question, he would pause and suck air between his teeth, waiting and making the moment uncomfortable. Other times he was affable, flashing a winning smile, and it became easy to see how he could fool people into thinking he was on the up-and-up and that he could get them whatever merchandise they wanted at a great discount, when in fact all he wanted was their money. And once he had it, he eliminated his customers.

He was totally blasé as he described killing after killing—mob hits, road-rage slayings, experiments in murder techniques, lethal scams. He was philosophical about murder, and he understood human greed better than any psychiatrist, using it subtly and seductively to lure his victims with promises of deals that were too good to be true. His victims brought money, he brought a gun—or in some cases, a small spray bottle of cyanide.

I called my agent as soon as I finished the tapes. I was hooked. I wanted to write this book.

Unfortunately Kuklinski wasn't as excited about me as I was about him. Though he had given Thebaut an extended on-camera interview, he refused to talk to me. Instead he sent me letters. Lots of letters, some of them quite long. Handwritten accounts of various murders. He also sent me newspaper articles with Post-it notes attached. The messages were cryptic: a place, the name of a restaurant, a gun-caliber, "pop-pop-pop like balloons breaking."

He gave me lists of names, many of them dead mobsters. Some were men he might have met through his association with Gambino soldier Roy DeMeo; others were puzzles. Was he bragging, implying that he had killed them?

He seldom took direct responsibility for any murder he described. His stories typically started, "There was a guy . . . ," but it was obvious that he was the guy.

Some of his claims were dubious. For example, he claimed he was part of the hit team that killed Gambino boss Paul Castellano in midtown Manhattan in 1985. It's highly unlikely that such an important assassination would have been entrusted to someone who wasn't a made member of the Mafia. As with all his claims, if I couldn't get some kind of corroboration from law enforcement, I didn't put it in the book.

When Kuklinski wrote me a letter in which he described in great detail the murder of a "man with a big mouth" in Detroit, it was clear that he was taking credit for the murder of Teamster boss Jimmy Hoffa. When I first read his account, I thought I had struck journalistic gold, but when I consulted investigators who knew the Hoffa case well, the details of Kuklinski's story didn't check out. I wondered why he felt he had to add extra value to his brand. Weren't the crimes he had actually committed enough?

Even though many of his stories didn't pass the smell test, these letters were nevertheless invaluable . . . and maddening. They kept coming—thirty in all—but he still refused to see me. I had been working on the book for a year and had completed a first draft when I finally got word from his wife that he would sit for an interview. On January 16, 1992, I spent five and a half hours with him, just the two of us locked in the "lawyer's room" at Trenton State Prison, no barrier between us, no guards in sight. Before letting me in, prison officials had me sign a release stating that I had no official business there and that if Kuklinski took me captive, no extraordinary measures would be taken to save me. I was on my own.

When we finally met face-to-face, he was jovial and even told me a joke to break the ice. But when we shook hands, I was very aware that the hand I was holding might have killed up to 100 people. As we entered the room, he immediately took a seat at the table with his back to the door. I realized later that this was a deliberate maneuver. He wanted to watch my eyes to see how often I looked for the guard through the small window in the door. I think he wanted to gauge my fear.

He told me little of substance in the first two hours. He kept his sunglasses on and evaded my questions. Finally I told him we weren't getting anywhere and started to pack up, putting away my tape recorder. That's when he started to talk. Perhaps the tape recorder spooked him. After all he had been burned by ATF Special Agent Dominick Polifrone's hidden tape recorder. But as he talked, I started scribbling on a legal pad, and the more he talked the quicker I scribbled. I have a feeling he got a kick out of having some control over me.

I had brought along the letters and newspaper clippings he'd sent and asked for clarification. He talked about many murders, some that he hadn't put in his letters, but I noticed that some of his descriptions were quick and cursory. When I pressed him for details, he'd just shrug.

But with other murders, he was expansive. When he told me how he had murdered pharmacist Paul Hoffman, he gave me all the particulars. I suspect he made Hoffman's murder his most complete story out of spite. He knew the police wanted to recover Hoffman's body because his widow was desperate to give her husband a proper burial. He told me every little detail about that murder except where the body was. He said he didn't know.

Some of his descriptions were so vivid I instinctively believed he had committed the crime. But the sketchier the description, the more I doubted. Some of his stories stood up to close scrutiny. Others remain mysteries . . . or just fiction.

One afternoon, months after my visit to the prison, Kuklinski called me at home. He asked how the book was coming along and said if I needed more murders to "spice it up," he might be able to come up with a few.

I just shook my head. "Richard," I said, "I have a feeling if I listen to you long enough, you'll tell me you shot President Lincoln."

He chuckled. "Yeah. You're probably right."

But despite his boasts and lies, Kuklinski was the real deal. He was without question one of the most prolific and deceptive killers ever encountered by American law enforcement. His story is unique, and my goal in writing this book was to present him without hype or enhancement. The reality of this man's life is horrible enough.

I was fortunate to have met many people in law enforcement who generously gave me their time and insights about Kuklinski. Several of those people became good friends, and I'm grateful to know these courageous professionals who stopped Kuklinski and undoubtedly saved the lives of people who would have become his victims.

The Iceman: The True Story of a Cold-Blooded Killer is a portrait of a life gone wrong, the one cell out of a million that becomes cancerous and grows to kill. Kuklinski's wife once pointed out that plenty of people grow up poor and abused in the projects—what gave Richard the "right" to become a killer? There's no good answer for that. He certainly seemed to enjoy killing, but it wasn't a psychosexual compulsion with him. Strictly speaking, he wasn't a serial killer. Still, were his deadly impulses beyond his control? Or was it something he did because, as he told me, "I found out murder was a way to solve my problems"?

The Iceman died in prison in 2006 at the age of seventy. To say the least, he was a complex individual—abused son, abusive husband, doting father, con man, killer. What you will read here are the facts of his life.

Anthony Bruno
February 2012

AUTHOR'S NOTE

All the people depicted in this book are real with two exceptions: "Captain Brealy" is a composite character representing several individuals who had little faith in Special Agent Dominick Polifrone's chances of getting close to Richard Kuklinski, the Iceman; "Mr. Butterfield" is a fictitious character created to illustrate Kuklinski's negative feelings for his neighbors in the Jersey City housing projects.

Richard Kuklinski would not reveal the name of his first victim, so I have called him Johnny.

The identities of some individuals have been changed for their own protection.

The dialogue presented in this book is based on the actual undercover tapes that were used to convict Richard Kuklinski, the trial transcripts, or the recollections of the people involved.

JERSEY CITY, NEW JERSEY—1949

The boy stood in the shadows, leaning against the brick wall, listening to the night. The distant clack of diesel engines from the Hoboken train yards filled the sky over the Sixteenth Street projects. Tugboats on the Hudson sounded their horns as they pushed garbage scows downriver, heading out to sea. The rumble of the incinerator on the other side of the brick wall vibrated the boy's back. It seemed like they burned garbage all the time around here. He looked up at the stars shining dully through the drifting smoke from the incinerator. For fourteen-year-old Richard Kuklinski, life was *all* garbage, and he just couldn't take any more. He'd had it.

The warm bricks heated his back as his breath turned to vapor on the cold air. Down by his side, he held the wooden closet pole. His hand was sweaty as his eyes darted into the darkness and he listened for the footsteps, for that voice. Johnny's voice.

He glanced up at the projects, the lights in the windows. His apartment was up there somewhere, but he wasn't sure which window was his. It didn't matter really. The apartments were all the same here, and they all stunk. The heavy wooden pole came from the hallway closet, the only closet in the whole apartment. It was stupid having a closet pole up there, the way he figured. There were hardly any clothes to move when he took it down. Just about the only clothes he and his little brother and sister owned were the ones they wore. Whenever something wore out and his mother could afford it, they'd just go downtown and replace it, wear it home stiff, sometimes with the tags still on. He felt his frayed shirtfront, ashamed of the way he had to go around. The other kids in the projects teased him all the time, but the most stinging remarks always came from Johnny. "Richie the rag boy." "Hobo Richie." "The skinny Polack."

His mother never listened to him. She always bought his clothes big so he wouldn't outgrow them too fast, she said. But he was a skinny kid, and he never grew into them. They just flapped around him as if he were some kind of a . . . hobo.

Might as well be a hobo, he thought. He spent all his time wandering the streets as it was, staying to himself. He didn't hang out in gangs the way other kids did. He didn't get along with those kids. He preferred his own company, walking around, seeing what there was to see, watching the sailors getting drunk and picking up whores over in Hoboken, watching the tired factory workers dragging themselves in and out of the Maxwell House factory just to make a buck, watching people arguing with shopkeepers up in Journal Square, going crazy to save a few pennies on a pound of potatoes.

It was all garbage. People going nuts just so they could grab a little piece of something for themselves. But it was all garbage. Couldn't they see that?

One time he was over on Henderson Street, just walking around, when he spotted this truck parked in front of the Manischewitz factory. The back of the truck was open, and it was stacked high with wooden crates. As he got closer, he could see that there were bottles in the crates, bottles of wine. There was writing stenciled on the crates, but it was all in that Jewish writing, just like in the window of that butcher shop over on Newark Avenue. There was only one word in English: "Kosher." Richie didn't know what that meant, but he'd heard that Jews used a lot of wine in their religious ceremonies and Jews had money. They probably didn't drink cheap stuff because they didn't have to, so he figured this wine had to be worth something.

He walked around to the front of the truck. The cab was empty. No one was around. His heart started to pound. It was right there for the taking. If he waited, the driver would come back, and then it would be too late. He looked all around as he went to the back of the truck. He let a couple of cars pass, then looked over at the loading docks at the Manischewitz factory. Nobody was there.

Suddenly all he could hear was his heart beating. He reached up to haul down a crate from the top of a stack, but it was heavy, heavier than he'd expected. His hand was on the crate, but the whole stack was teetering, and he was afraid to step up onto the tailgate to get it down. If someone spotted him *in* the truck, it would *look* like he was stealing. But he wanted the wine. He'd never even tasted wine, but he knew he wanted it because it was worth something.

With sweat beading on his forehead, Richie put his foot up on the tailgate, hoisted himself up just long enough to get the crate down without toppling the whole stack, and bounced back down to the pavement. The crate was heavy, very heavy. But he had it, and he was standing there at the curb with it, guilty as sin. He lifted it onto his shoulder and started to run with it, his back aching and his heart going crazy, thinking about the Paramount Theater downtown and the cowboy movies he'd seen there on Saturday afternoons, how the good guys always talked about catching the bad guys red-handed. That's what he was now. Red-handed with red wine.

He ran all the way back to the projects, straight to the incinerators, slamming the heavy metal door behind him. A window the size of an envelope on the face of the furnace sent a fiery glow into the dark room. Richie set down the crate and closed the door. Staring at the fire, he remembered the bullshit the nuns always told him in school about burning in hell. He didn't believe it. It was just something they tried to scare you with to keep you in line. He pulled out a bottle from the crate and examined it. The wine was so dark even the light of the fiery blast couldn't penetrate it. He took out the penknife he carried and tried to figure out how to get the cork out. His heart was still pounding, and the heat of the furnace flushed his face. He picked at the cork with the blade of the knife, hoping he could pry it out, but that didn't work, so he sliced the cork while it was still in the bottle and broke it into pieces. He dug out part of the cork, then jammed the rest into the bottle. His hand was shaking as he lifted it to his lips. The taste wasn't what he expected. It was thick and sweet, but not a good sweet. But maybe this was what his well-off uncle Mickey had meant when he said something was an "acquired taste." That meant it was really worth something even if it didn't seem that way. Richie spit out cork crumbs and took another swig. He wasn't sure whether he liked it or not. It must take time to acquire a taste, he figured. He drank as much as he could stand, then hid the rest of the crate under some old newspapers in a corner of the incinerator room.

That night he was sick, and he threw up purple. He didn't get drunk; at least he didn't think so. He was just sick—*worried* sick that the police would come to the door and take him away, worried that they knew it was him who took the wine.

His stomach bothered him for a week, but he didn't say a word to his mother. He couldn't eat, and he was afraid to go out, afraid that the police would snatch him off the street if he did. But nothing happened. It was two weeks before he finally convinced himself that he'd gotten away with it, and the wine was really his.

But when he went back to the incinerator room to check his stash, the crate was gone. Someone had found it and taken his wine. He figured it was probably Johnny trying to screw him up again.

A train clattered in the distance, crossing the concrete trestle on Newark Avenue, either heading for or coming from the Hoboken yards. Richie's father worked for the railroad. He thought his father was a brakeman, but he wasn't sure. The last time he'd seen his old man was when his little sister was born three years ago. The old man had run off when Richie was just a little kid, but he'd show up out of the blue every now and then like a sailor home from the sea. It was no treat when he came around. He had a bad temper, and he liked to beat his oldest son just for the hell of it. He'd come storming into the kids' room, stinking drunk, yelling and screaming about something, already pulling the belt out of his pants. It wasn't so bad when his mother was home. She'd try to stop it, yelling and screaming herself, and the beating usually wouldn't last too long. Richie had figured out that his old man was like anyone else. All he really wanted was a little attention. That's why Richie knew that whenever his mother was at work, the old man would take off that belt and do his worst, and there was nothing Richie could do or say that would change his father's mind because the guy was just looking for attention. All Richie could do was take it and try to think about something else while it was happening.

Of course, his mother beat him, too, with the broom handle, but she never seemed to have as much energy, so it didn't hurt half as bad as the belt. She put in so many hours at the Armour meat plant she hardly had the time to beat her kids. She had other ways of making you feel bad, though. Better ways. She did it with words and attitude, comments that stung and cut and left you feeling like shit, feeling that her disappointment with life was all *your* fault, that you should do something to fix it. But whatever you did just made her more miserable. Yeah, she could be much worse than the old man.

But taking crap from your parents was one thing; taking it from another kid was something else. You couldn't do anything about your parents, but someone else giving you grief you were *supposed* to do something about, the way the cowboys did in the movies. And now, standing under the smoky night sky with his back to the warm bricks, the closet pole in his hand, he was ready to do something about it. He was ready to go to war.

Johnny didn't just taunt Richie. The bully liked to beat him up, too. He lived downstairs from Richie, and he had his own gang, six other kids who lived in the Sixteenth Street projects. Johnny always smacked Richie around when his gang was there. It made him look like a big man. It made him the leader. In the beginning Richie had tried to fight back, but whenever he raised a hand to Johnny, the other kids would gang up on him and get their licks in, punching and kicking. After a split lip and a dull pain in his side that took a month to go away, Richie learned that it was better just to take it and get it over with, the same way he took his father's beatings. But it was hard to take it from Johnny. The boy's incredible arrogance just got to him, and the humiliation of hearing the gang laughing at him gnawed at his gut.

Richie shuddered with pent-up hate just thinking about Johnny and his stupid gang. He tapped the end of the pole on the asphalt pavement, nervously waiting. No. He'd really had it now. He wasn't going to take any more.

Footsteps came into the dark courtyard, and Richie's heart stopped. Someone was coming this way. Richie gripped the closet pole and started to raise it over his head. His arms were shaking. His legs were like lead.

The footsteps came closer.

Richie wished he could stop shaking. He wanted to run, but he didn't want to run, not anymore. He wanted to teach Johnny a lesson, show him that he couldn't pick on Richard Kuklinski anymore. Richie just wanted to get Johnny off his back so he could live in peace. Richie just wanted to be left alone.

The footsteps were within reach when he saw a face squinting out of the gloom.

"Richie?"

He dropped the pole to his side and hid it behind his leg when he saw who it was, Mr. Butterfield from down the hall. The man had a quart bottle of Rheingold in his hand, and Richie could tell this wasn't his first quart of beer tonight. Mr. Butterfield was a drunk, and he beat his kids, too.

"Your mother know you're out this late?"

Richie shrugged. "She don't care." She had fallen asleep listening to the radio, same as every other night.

"You better get in. It's late."

Butterfield took a swig from his quart and moved on.

Richie chewed his fingernail as he glared at the man. The bastard didn't give a shit about his own kids, and here he was making believe he cared about someone else's kid. Listen to him: "It's late." Goddamn hypocrite.

But Richie wondered how late it really was. He didn't own a watch, not one that worked. Suddenly he remembered his confirmation day, three years ago, and that burning humiliation attacked him again. It blinded him with rage whenever he thought about it.

Johnny had worn a new blue suit, white shirt, silver tie, and the lily white satin armband on his bicep. He looked more like a young hood than a kid going to his confirmation. He must've stolen the damn clothes because he was as poor as everyone else in the projects. But there he was that day, cockier than ever, strutting down the church steps after the ceremony, a new soldier in the army of Christ. More bullshit and hypocrisy from the nuns. Why would God want an asshole like him in His army? Why would they even allow someone like Johnny to be confirmed? Why? Because he had a nice suit? Bunch of goddamn hypocrites, all of them.

Richard had been confirmed that day, too, but he wore the same baggy clothes he wore every day: the brown pants, a worn striped shirt, and his navy blue wool peacoat. It was April, but he had to wear his winter coat because it was all that he had, and his mother had insisted. He remembered working the armband up the sleeve of his coat, hoping the elastic wouldn't snap, wishing his mother had put it on for him. But she had to work that day; she got time and a half on Sundays. His little brother and sister stayed with one of the neighbors.

Richie had gone to church by himself that day, and he did what the nuns told him to do, kneeling at the altar with the others as the priest came down the line, mumbling in Latin, dipping his thumb in holy oil and anointing each forehead, tapping each cheek with the blow of humility before he moved on to the next inductee. Richard floated through the whole event, feeling blank and empty, and after it was over and the other kids ran to their waiting families, he just started for home, intending to fix himself a sandwich for lunch if there was anything to eat in the icebox.

But as he came down the steps, he spotted Johnny with his family. They were making a big fuss over him. Johnny was smiling, holding up his wrist for everyone to see. Richie could hear Johnny's mother cackling, "Say thank you to your uncle Mario, Johnny. Say thank you." Johnny had a new watch. It was gold with a gold stretch band. Johnny always bragged that he had a rich uncle who gave him things. Until Richie saw that watch, he had never believed it. His mother hadn't even bothered to tell his uncle Mickey that he was getting confirmed.

As he pushed his way through the crowd, he noticed other kids holding up their wrists, showing off new watches. Even the girls had watches, those tiny little watches so small you could barely read the time. Everybody had gotten a new watch except him.

The next day after school he went to the corner candy store, determined to buy himself something for his confirmation. He'd seen wristwatches there, pinned to a sheet of cardboard hanging over the cash register. He had almost a dollar in change. The watches cost seventy-nine cents each, and his heart raced as he counted out the coins on the counter. The man took down the cardboard and let him pick the one he wanted, even though the watches were all the same. He picked one, and the man wound it for him, set the time, and said, "Good luck, kiddo." Richie strapped it to his wrist and admired it.

The next morning when Richie woke up, he noticed that the watch had stopped. He tried to rewind it, but the stem came out in his hand. He went back to the candy store, but the man refused to take it back.

Richie wore it anyway, just so he wouldn't be the only one without a new watch. But in his daydreams he dreaded the moment when Johnny would notice that his watch did not have the right time and the stem was missing, that the cheap band was cracking and left brown stains on his skin. He could hear what Johnny would say, how he would say it, how it would probably lead to another beating if his gang were around. Richie's heart was thumping, his jaws clenched in fear and anger just thinking about it.

Johnny and his gang had been bothering him for years. But that was going to stop. He was going to show them that he couldn't be pushed around anymore. Not anymore.

Richie stared hard into the dark shadows across the courtyard. He was staring at the corner of his building, the corner where Johnny would be coming from. Lately Johnny had been coming out here every night to call up to his gang members and taunt them into coming down so they could smoke and joke and yell up to the girls they knew and say dirty things about them. Sometimes Johnny would call up to him. "Hey, Polack, you sleeping up there? Or you just making believe so your mother won't know you're jerking off?"

Every night this went on. But it was going to stop.

Suddenly he saw something in the shadows. He squinted to see better. A glowing orange pinpoint was rounding the corner of the building, coming this way. It was a burning cigarette. Richie clung to the wall, the pole tight in his fist, close to his leg. His eyes were wide, and he wasn't breathing. His pulse was racing. He didn't have the urge to run this time. He wanted to get this over with. He wanted to show Johnny. He wanted to hurt him and teach him a lesson once and for all.

The face behind the orange glow emerged from the dark. The small dark eyes, the wise-ass smirk. It was him. Cigarette smoke trailed off behind Johnny as he stepped closer, surprised to see Richie out there, but also pleased to see him, pleased to have his favorite target right there out in the dark courtyard, alone.

Johnny stopped a few feet away from Richie, took a long drag off his cigarette, and just stared at him for a moment. "What the hell you doin' out here, Polack? You looking for trouble or what?" He coughed up a laugh.

Richie didn't answer. He couldn't.

"Hey, I'm talking to you, Polack. I asked you what you think you're doing out here."

That vicious bark of his made Richie blink. It always did.

"Answer me, Polack, or I'll kick your fuckin' teeth in."

Johnny stepped closer, and automatically Richie raised the pole.

Johnny backed off but then laughed at him. "What the fuck you gonna do with that?"

Richie was mute, both hands wrapped around the heavy pole.

"Whattaya, playing stickball out here, Polack?"

Johnny reached for the pole to take it away from him, but Richie pulled it back out of his reach.

Johnny's face turned mean. "Gimme that." He lunged for the pole.

Richie swung on impulse. It caught Johnny on the cheek, not hard, but it did hit him. It shocked Richie more than it did Johnny. Richie wanted to run, but he couldn't move his legs. In his heart he didn't want to run. He wanted to go through with this. He wanted to show Johnny that no one could mess with him anymore.

Johnny glowered at him, his hand on his cheek. "You son of a bitch," he whispered. "You little son of a bitch," he repeated as he went for the pole again.

But this time Richie swung hard. Johnny raised his hand to block it and took the full impact on his forearm. The boy yelped and cursed, holding his smarting arm and curling into himself.

Richie stepped forward and hit him again, this time over the head.

"Hey! Stop!"

Richie hit him again, harder. Johnny yelled louder. Johnny was pleading with him to stop. Richie hit him again, raising the heavy pole over his head and swinging it down onto his tormentor's back as if he were trying to ring the gong at a carnival. Richie wanted him to shut up. The rest of Johnny's gang would hear him, and they'd come down to help him. Richie kept hitting him. He wanted Johnny to be quiet.

"Shut up," he grunted through clenched teeth.

But Johnny didn't shut up. He was screaming like a girl now, and Richie bashed him again and again, swinging as hard as he could with each blow. Johnny finally quieted down, and Richie felt something he'd never felt in his entire life: *power*. He gained strength with each new blow as he saw Johnny fall down on his knees, getting weaker and more helpless. The rush of total control flew through his veins like a drug. It felt good. It felt great. He kept swinging, pounding Johnny sideways now, hammering his head the way Ted Williams hammered home runs. He couldn't stop. He had to hurt Johnny. He had to show him. He was Richard Kuklinski, and no one messed with Richard Kuklinski. No one. *No one.*

When he finally stopped, Johnny was flat on the ground, and it was hard to get a good whack at him in that position. Richie stood over him, breathing hard, waiting for him to get up so he could hit him again. He was out of breath, but he felt so good. He was exhilarated, in control, powerful. He'd shown Johnny. The whole gang would know not to mess with him anymore. He'd shown them.

He climbed the stairs back up to his apartment and hung the pole back in the closet, then got into bed. He lay awake for a while, reliving the excitement of his triumph, then fell into a deep sleep.

The next morning Richie's mother yelled from the bedroom door, telling him to get out of bed or he was going to be late for school. He'd been sound asleep and he didn't want to move, but the sound of men's voices coming from outside drew him to the window. Police cars were parked in the asphalt courtyard. At least a dozen men were clustered around the spot by the incinerator wall where he'd left Johnny the night before. There were a lot of people from the projects down there, too, the usual busybodies trying to find out what was going on. Some of the kids from Johnny's gang were talking to the cops, one kid sticking out his bottom lip and frowning, shaking his head no.

"Richard, you're gonna be late!" his mother yelled from the kitchen.

"What's going on outside?" he yelled back.

"What?"

"Outside. Down by the incinerator."

"You know that fresh boy Johnny from downstairs? Somebody killed him last night. Now hurry up and get dressed, or you can forget about breakfast."

Richie's fingers were numb as he stared down at the courtyard. Johnny was dead? He hadn't meant to do that. He'd just wanted to teach Johnny a lesson. That's all. He hadn't meant to *kill* him.

"Richard! Are you dressed yet?"

His stomach started to ache as he stepped back from the window, afraid that the cops would look up and see him. He went out into the hallway and opened the closet door. He inspected the pole, turning it around and around on its brackets. There was no blood that he could see. Maybe he *hadn't* killed Johnny. Maybe someone else did it after he left. Maybe someone else found Johnny unconscious down on the ground and took the opportunity to get rid of him. It was possible. He did bully other kids, too. But somehow Richie didn't really believe it. He knew he was the one.

The cramps in his stomach got so bad he doubled over in pain. His mother kept yelling for him to get dressed and get to school. It was an ordeal getting his clothes on. Thank God, she had already left for work by the time he finished. She'd put some cereal and milk out on the table for his breakfast, but the sight of it nauseated him, and he threw up in the kitchen sink. He leaned on the edge, waiting for more to come up, and through the closed kitchen window he could still hear the police down in the courtyard. He decided to skip school and stay home.

He was afraid to go out, afraid to go to the windows, afraid they'd find him and take him away. He lay in bed, imagining the worst. The other kids in Johnny's gang would tell the police that he was the one who probably had done it, that he hated Johnny because Johnny picked on him. Maybe Mr. Butterfield hadn't been that drunk last night. Maybe he'd seen Richie holding the pole and told the police about it. They'd come up to the apartment, beat the door down, and drag him away. He wondered what they did to kids who killed other kids. Did they throw kids in jail? He'd heard about reform schools, but he didn't really know what they were. He'd *killed* Johnny. Maybe they'd kill him. Strap him to the electric chair and pull the switch, same as they did to adult killers.

Richie bounced off his bed and ran to the closet. He threw the few clothes that were hanging onto the floor and pulled the pole down again. In the bathtub he ran hot water and scrubbed the pole with a washcloth, just in case, then dried it with a towel and put it back.

It wasn't enough, though. He paced the apartment long into the afternoon, wondering what the police knew, what kind of evidence they could have, when they'd come for him. He shivered and his teeth chattered as he lay in bed, staring at the ceiling, wondering when they'd finally come. The pillow was soaked with sweat when he finally passed out as if in a fever.

When his mother returned that night after picking up his four-year-old brother and three-year-old sister from the neighbor who watched them, Richie pretended that he'd gone to school, that everything was normal. His mother didn't mention Johnny. As usual, she was too exhausted to talk about anything. For a while that afternoon he'd thought maybe he could tell her and get it off his chest. But now he knew he couldn't do that. He couldn't tell anyone.

That night he couldn't sleep. He kept hearing Johnny's voice out in the courtyard. That, and the whomp of the closet pole as it kept hitting Johnny's head.

The next morning Richie lingered in bed and deliberately made himself late, intending to stay home again. He was never going to go back to school. He was never going to leave the house. He was going to die here. He was going to starve to death because he couldn't eat and he couldn't stop throwing up.

All he did was lie in bed, thinking about Johnny, thinking about that moment when the cops would break down the door.

But that moment didn't come.

He stayed home for the rest of the week, worrying, pacing, sweating.

But nothing happened.

The nuns notified his mother that he hadn't been to school all week and asked why she hadn't sent a note if he was sick. She got so mad she beat him with the broomstick and told him that he was going to school on Monday and that he'd better not try to pull a stunt like that again. She also made him go to church on Sunday, and the sweat poured off him as he sat through Mass, glancing at the pews all around him, looking for the one boy in the gang who would point at him and yell out that Richard Kuklinski was the one who had killed Johnny.

But that didn't happen.

On Monday morning he told his mother he was sick for real, but she didn't buy it, and she made him leave the apartment with her. Walking to school, he tried not to be obvious, but he couldn't help looking back whenever he heard a car coming up from behind. He kept expecting a police car to come and take him away.

But that never happened.

In school he couldn't pay attention, and the nun who taught his class scolded him several times for daydreaming. If anyone would finger him, she would, he thought. Nuns can spot sinners a mile away. He kept waiting for her screeching accusation, followed by the cops coming into the classroom to haul him away.

But that never happened.

Nothing happened.

It had been almost two weeks since that night in the courtyard, and nobody had bothered with him. No cops, none of the kids in the gang, no one in Johnny's family, not even Mr. Butterfield. No one at all.

But this was a trap, he thought. They were all pretending. The police were just waiting for the right moment when they could pounce. This was a trap.

It occurred to him that maybe Johnny wasn't even dead, that one of these days he'd be walking down the street and Johnny would pop out of nowhere, back from the hospital where the police had been hiding him. He'd point his finger at Richie and tell the police, "That's him. The skinny Polack is the guy who tried to kill me."

Richie couldn't eat; he couldn't sleep. He dreaded going out.

But nothing ever happened. Nothing.

Gradually he started to calm down. Maybe no one knew. Maybe he was safe. Then one day he caught himself smiling, and he realized that he hadn't thought about Johnny for a whole day. He started going out on the street more, and eventually he stopped worrying about police cars. He still thought about Johnny, but he wasn't worried about him anymore. He still felt bad about it, but in another way he also felt good about it. The bully was gone, and no one was bothering him. He'd solved his problem. When you hurt people, they leave you alone.

As the months passed, he'd see detectives down in the lobby of his building every once in a while, talking to the neighbors about Johnny, checking to see if there was any new information they could pick up. Richie would walk right by them and head for the stairs, biting his grin until he rounded the corner and no one could see him. He knew who killed Johnny, but no one else did. It was his little secret, his alone. It was something no one else in the whole world had except him, and it made him valuable. It made him special. It made him someone.

JULY 1986

The doorbell chimed. Richard Kuklinski, age fifty-one, looked up from the TV set and frowned. His wife, Barbara, was out shopping with their daughters, Merrick and Christen, but his son, Dwayne, was around someplace. Kuklinski never answered the door himself, so he ignored it and returned to the movie on TV. Dwayne would get it.

The doorbell chimed again, and Shaba, the family dog, stirred from his nap. The Newfoundland was all black, shaggy, and as big as a small bear. Shaba had been near death when Kuklinski found him in a Dumpster. The puppy had been abandoned along with two female pups that were already dead when Kuklinski heard the pathetic yelps coming out of the garbage. The dog's name was Polish for "little frog." They'd named him that because when Richard Kuklinski first brought him home, he had big webbed feet, and before he could run, he hopped around the house like a frog.

The doorbell chimed again, and the big dog opened his eyes and growled.

Kuklinski called out to his son, "Dwayne! Get the door." He reached down and scratched the growling animal's head. "It's all right, Shaba. It's all right."

But the bell chimed again, and Kuklinski scowled. The dog got up and barked as he trotted to the front door. Kuklinski ran his hand over his bald head and scratched his beard. "Dwayne?" But Dwayne didn't answer. He must have gone out.

The dog was barking at the front door. "Shut up, Shaba," Kuklinski grumbled, trying to pay attention to the movie. But the dog kept barking.

The doorbell chimed once more, and the dog barked louder, becoming more frantic.

"Shit," Kuklinski mumbled as he hauled himself up from the sofa in the den and unfolded his six-foot-four, 270-pound frame.

"Shaba," he called out as he went to retrieve the dog, "shut up."

The dog didn't listen, which wasn't unusual, but Kuklinski was mad now. Must be goddamn Jehovah's Witnesses, ringing the bell like that. He'd make them sorry they'd ever got up this morning, the bastards.

He climbed the stairs of the split-level house to the front door and grabbed Shaba by the collar as he turned the bolt and opened the front door a few inches.

"Whattaya want?" he snarled into the crack. Shaba strained at the collar and barked by his side.

Two broad-shouldered men in jackets and ties were at the door. One was holding up a badge. "Mr. Richard Kuklinski?"

Kuklinski opened the door a little more and squinted at the badge. "Yeah? Can I help you?"

"I'm Detective Volkman, New Jersey State Police. This is Detective Kane. We'd like to ask you a few questions."

Kuklinski tilted his head back. "About what?"

"Several murders."

"I don't know anything about any murders."

Shaba growled and thrashed his head to get loose from Kuklinski's grip.

"Did you know an individual by the name of George Malliband, Junior?" Detective Volkman asked.

Kuklinski shrugged and shook his head.

"Did you know an individual by the name of Louis Masgay?"

"Nope."

The other cop, the younger of the two, just stared at him. Detective Kane didn't say a word, just tried to look mean. Kuklinski knew the routine. They weren't the first cops to come around asking questions. Volkman, the talker, was going to be the friendly guy; Kane was going to be the hard ass. Kuklinski wanted to laugh in their faces. Who the hell did these guys think they were? Better yet, who the hell did they think they were dealing with?

"How about Paul L. Hoffman?" Volkman asked. "Did you know him?"

Kuklinski shook his head.

"Gary Thomas Smith?"

"Nope."

"How about Daniel Everett Deppner?"

Kuklinski yanked up sharply on Shaba's collar to silence the barking. "Never heard of him either." He had his hand on the edge of the door, ready to close it.

Detective Volkman's glance slid toward his partner. "Well, if you don't know these men, Mr. Kuklinski, then I don't suppose you know anything about a Mr. Roy DeMeo."

Kuklinski squinted at the detective as his grip tightened on the dog's collar. He wanted to know how the hell they'd gotten that one.

"Roy DeMeo," Detective Kane snapped. "He was a soldier in the Gambino crime family. Until he was murdered."

Kuklinski flashed a cordial smile. "Why don't you boys come in? Let's not talk out here." He opened the door all the way and showed them in. Shaba was agitated, sniffing at their pants, but the dog had stopped barking.

Kuklinski led them up the short flight of stairs to the living room. "Have a seat," he said, indicating the couch, as he got comfortable in his favorite chair in the house, the beige leather easy chair next to the fireplace, his "throne." The shaggy Newfoundland flopped down on the floor at his feet. He took the dark amber-tinted prescription glasses out of his shirt pocket, put them on, and tilted his head back. He stared at the two detectives and let the silence get uncomfortable. He wanted them to make the first move to see how much they really knew.

Detective Volkman, the talker, finally spoke up. "Are you sure you don't know any of those men, Mr. Kuklinski?"

Kuklinski shook his head.

"You didn't know George Malliband?" Kane asked.

"I don't believe so."

Volkman opened a small notepad. "On March 31, 1980, Mr. Malliband told his brother that he was going to a meeting with you to conclude a business deal. That was the last time he was seen alive."

Kuklinski shook his head and shrugged. "Sorry. I have no recollection of such a person."

He scratched Shaba's head. He remembered George Malliband. A big mother, three hundred pounds easy. Barely fit into the barrel.

Detective Volkman consulted his notes. "On July 1, 1981, Louis Masgay was supposed to be meeting you in Little Ferry to buy blank videotapes. He was carrying a large amount of cash. His body was found two years later in Orangetown, New York."

Kuklinski raised his eyebrows and smiled. "I've already told you, Detective. I don't know these guys."

He stroked the dog's black fur. Almost a hundred grand. Frozen solid, stiff as a board. Made the cops look like a bunch of jackasses.

Volkman flipped to another page in his notepad. "Paul Hoffman. A pharmacist from Cliffside Park. He left his home on April 29, 1982, supposedly to meet with you to conclude a business transaction. Again, he also had a large amount of cash with him."

Kuklinski sucked his teeth. "Don't know him."

He glanced down at the dozing Newfoundland. A real pain in the ass, that guy. Hardly worth the twenty grand for all the trouble he caused.

Detective Kane, the hard ball, piped up. "You gonna tell us you didn't know Gary Smith and Danny Deppner either?"

Kuklinski stared at him through his dark glasses, then turned to Volkman. "Why doesn't my friend Mr. Kane here like me?"

"Just answer the question please," Kane insisted.

"I already told you, Detective. If I said I didn't know them, I didn't know them."

Shaba lifted his head and growled. Kuklinski scratched the dog's ears to quiet him down. Smith and Deppner had to go. They couldn't be trusted anymore.

Kane glared at him, sitting on the edge of the couch as if he were going to jump up and do something. "Mr. Kuklinski, we have reliable information that you were well acquainted with Gary Smith and Danny Deppner, that they worked for you." Kane spit out the words, challenging him.

"And who is this reliable person who says I knew these two fellas?"

"I'm not at liberty to divulge that person's name."

"And why is that, Detective? I thought this was America. I thought you were supposed to know who your accusers are. Or maybe I just watch too many TV shows, Detective. Could that be my problem, Detective?"

Shaba growled deep in his throat.

Kuklinski glared at Kane through his dark glasses. He had a pretty good idea who their "reliable" source was. Frigging Percy House and that bitch of his, Barbara Deppner, Danny's ex-wife. He knew he should've taken care of those two a long time ago. Just like Gary and Danny. But if Percy House was talking, he wasn't saying much—at least not yet—because these two from the state police didn't know shit. If they did, they wouldn't be sitting here playing games with him. They'd have an arrest warrant. These fools didn't know shit.

"How about Robert Prongay?" Kane pressed. "Did you know Bobby Prongay?"

"Nope."

"Think hard. Maybe you just forgot. He used to drive a Mister Softee ice-cream truck in North Bergen. He kept that truck in a garage right across from a garage you used to rent. Is it coming back to you now, Mr. Kuklinski?"

Kuklinski stared at him for a moment. Then he spoke softly. "I don't care that much for ice cream, Detective."

"That wasn't what I asked, Mr. Kuklinski. I asked if you knew Robert Prongay."

"No. I didn't know him either."

Kuklinski kneaded the dog's neck. Mister Softee. Dr. Death.

Volkman ruffled some pages to break the tension. He was supposed to be the "good cop" after all. He was supposed to make things nice. "How about Roy DeMeo, Mr. Kuklinski? Did you know him?"

He was silent for a moment. "I don't know. I don't think so."

"Have you ever been to a place called the Gemini Lounge, Mr. Kuklinski? On Flatlands Avenue in the Canarsie section of Brooklyn."

"I don't think so."

"Are you sure, Mr. Kuklinski?"

"That sounds like some kind of gin mill, Detective. I'm a family man. I don't go to places like that."

Kane fidgeted in his seat. He looked like he was about to say something, but a glance from Volkman kept him quiet.

"Roy DeMeo was a made member of the Gambino crime family," Volkman said. "He was into pornography, among other things. Weren't you also involved in the pornography business at one time, Mr. Kuklinski?"

Kuklinski felt the blood rushing to his face. "Pornography? No, Detective. I told you, I'm a family man."

Shaba whimpered as he dug his fingers into the dog's neck.

Unwanted memories drifted back. The office on Lafayette Street in Manhattan around the corner from the film lab. Roy's crazy crew. The apartment behind the Gemini Lounge where Dracula lived. Sausage and angel hair. The sharks off Long Island. Unconsciously Kuklinski touched the scar high on his forehead.

Volkman continued. "DeMeo's body was found in the trunk of his own car in January 1983."

"Yeah? So what?"

"Something was found on top of his body. You wouldn't have any idea what that item might be?"

Kuklinski didn't say a word. He just stared and let the moment stretch. Then he smiled. "Are we playing games here, Detective?"

Kane barked. "No, Mr. Kuklinski, we are *not* playing games."

"Then what are you doing here? I told you already. I don't know any of those guys you're talking about."

"We have a reliable source who says you—"

"Would you like me to tell you what you can do with your 'reliable source,' Detective Kane?"

He pictured Percy House's big ugly face. Rat bastard.

Detective Kane was fuming. He looked like he was having a hard time just keeping himself on the couch. Kuklinski grinned at him.

Volkman flipped some more pages. "Now just to be absolutely sure, Mr. Kuklinski, let's go over the names one more time. Okay?"

Kuklinski shrugged. "Whatever'll make you happy."

"George Malliband, Junior. You say you didn't know him?"

"I don't believe I ever met anyone by that name. No."

"And did you know Louis Masgay?"

"Nope."

"Paul Hoffman?"

"Don't know him."

"Robert Prongay."

Kuklinski shook his head.

"Gary Smith."

"Don't know him either."

"Danny Deppner."

"Never heard of the guy."

Kane was squinting at him. He looked very skeptical. "If you don't know any of these men, Mr. Kuklinski, then why are you grinning like that?"

Kuklinski's grin broke out into a toothy smile. "I guess I'm just a happy guy, Detective."

"Why do I have a feeling you know more than you're saying, Mr. Kuklinski?"

Richard Kuklinski just grinned at him.

He ran his fingers through Shaba's thick coat as the two detectives looked at each other, trying to figure out how to walk away from this without looking like a couple of assholes. But these two jokers came in here with nothing, Kuklinski thought. That was their first mistake. They were on a fishing expedition. But they had nothing, and they *were* nothing. The way Richard Kuklinski figured it, they were a couple of two-bit state cops, struggling with their mortgages and their car payments, scraping to get by, looking forward to nothing more than getting their twenty years in so they could get their shitty little pensions. They were losers. They knew nothing and they had nothing.

But Richard Kuklinski, on the other hand, had everything.

The big man adjusted his glasses and grinned with satisfaction. "Now is there anything else I can do for you, gentlemen?"

AUGUST 1986

The duck pond in Demarest, New Jersey, was Barbara and Richard Kuklinski's special place. They would come here two, three times a week after breakfast just to sit and feed the ducks and Canada geese. Richard would go across the street to the deli and buy a loaf of bread, and they'd while away the morning, tearing up slices and throwing the pieces into the water. It was very peaceful here, and Richard always said this place calmed him down. But sitting next to him on their usual park bench this morning, Barbara Kuklinski could tell that her husband wasn't calm—not really—and that made her very nervous.

Out of the corner of her eye, Barbara could see her husband glancing back at the pay phone at the edge of the parking lot again.

Richard tossed out the bread in his hand and looked at her. "You want me to get the blanket from the car? To sit on."

"No, thanks. I'm fine."

"You sure? I'll go get it."

"No, I'm fine, Rich."

"Okay." He was looking at the pay phone again.

ANTHONY BRUNO

Smoothing the short blond hair at the back of her head, Barbara tried not to let on that she thought anything was wrong. But there was definitely something the matter today. Not that Richard couldn't be genuinely sweet. Most of the time he was very attentive to her and courteous to a fault. He really worried about her, and he cared about her, and sometimes no gesture was too extravagant to make her happy.

When they first met, she had been working as a secretary at a trucking company and he was working on the loading dock. For him, it was practically love at first sight, and he pursued her relentlessly, sending her flowers every single day until she agreed to go out on a date with him. Barbara was thrilled by the attention, but she was afraid to get involved with him. She knew that her Italian-American parents would not approve of him simply because he wasn't Italian. But Richard could not be dissuaded, and the flowers kept on coming, every day a new bouquet on her desk. Eventually she gave in and agreed to go out with him on a double date, but the first time she brought Richard home, she told her parents he was Italian and made him use an Italian name. Richard played along with the ruse because he said he loved her. It was months before Barbara confessed to her parents that Richard's real name was Kuklinski.

Tossing pieces of bread into the water, Barbara smiled to herself, thinking back to those days when Richard was thin and bashful and always so sweet and thoughtful.

She also remembered when Merrick, their oldest daughter, was born and how sick she had been. The baby had developed a kidney infection, and Richard stayed up all night, night after night, sitting next to the crib with his hand on Merrick's back to keep her warm, watching her breathe, cleaning up her spit-up, changing her diapers.

Barbara brushed away a tear from the corner of her eye. She had a lot of precious memories of her life with Richard. They'd had some very good times together. She sighed, and then her smile started to fade. They'd also had some not-so-good times. . . .

There were the times when things weren't going Richard's way, times when he could be a major bastard. After twenty-five years of marriage Barbara knew instinctively when things weren't right with Richard. She could *smell* it on him. In her mind there were actually two Richards—the good Richard and the bad Richard— and she had a terrible feeling that she was sitting here with the bad one.

Today it wasn't obvious which Richard he was. Of course, it never was—not until it was too late. Even the children could be fooled sometimes because he was tricky. He hid his moods. He could be furious about something, and you'd never know it. He would sit on his anger for weeks; then suddenly, out of the blue, he would fly into a rage, scream and yell for hours on end. And when the bad Richard went into one of his tirades, the best thing to do was to stay out of his way. But that never worked well for Barbara. The children were generally spared the full treatment, but with her it was different. Whenever he got started, she had to sit and listen and take it. Or else. She knew firsthand what the consequences of walking away from him could be.

Barbara blinked and touched the bridge of her nose, recalling the third time it was broken. She quickly removed her hand and took a slice of bread out of the bag and started to tear it, fearing that he might figure out what she was thinking.

Over the years she'd tried to forget or at least rationalize the awful things the bad Richard had done to her, but she couldn't bring herself to live a lie. It was hard to forget scars you saw in the mirror, hard to forget waking up from a sound sleep in the middle of the night with a pillow held over your face, hard to forget coming out of the shower and finding your husband crouched in the bedroom, holding a gun on you. No, she could never forget, and she could never rationalize. But by the same token she'd never bring any of these things up again. She didn't dare.

It was like asking Richard what he did for a living. She knew he was into currency exchange because calls came into the house at all hours from all over the world. She knew he had business associates here and there because he'd leave the house to go meet with them. But she didn't know any of the particulars, and she didn't want to. If Richard got up at three o'clock in the morning, put on his shoes, and went out, she pretended to be asleep. If he told her anything about any of the people he was involved with, fine. But she didn't ask any questions. She never did. She knew better. She knew her husband was no angel, but he did provide for his family, so she didn't ask questions. You were just asking for trouble from the bad Richard if you did.

She tossed more bread into the water and sneaked a glance at her husband. He was looking over his shoulder at the pay phone again. He was making sure that no one used it in case someone beeped him and he had to make a call. God only knew what he would do if some poor bastard came along and tried to use *his* phone.

Suddenly Richard's beeper went off, and the startled ducks at Barbara's feet darted back into the water. Richard unclipped the beeper from his belt and looked at the readout. This toy was his latest fascination. He'd been unhooking the answering machine at home ever since he'd gotten the beeper, and he never went anywhere without it. He even wore it around the house.

Richard got up from the bench and started for the pay phone.

"Who is it?" she asked. She really didn't care who it was. She just wanted him to stay with her and feed the ducks, the way they used to.

He looked down at her. "It's John." He was wearing his dark glasses.

"Oh." She nodded, then turned back to the ducks as he went off to make his phone call.

Richard never used to make phone calls from here. The duck pond used to be sacred. It was their time together, the place where the good Richard could recharge his batteries. At one time they used to come here every day, it seemed. They'd go out to breakfast, then come here, hold hands, feed the ducks, not talk. It was always calm and serene, and Richard was always at his best when he was here, always so polite, so considerate. When the weather turned chilly, he'd put out a blanket for her to sit on, another one for her lap, and a pillow for her back. He did worry about her. He really did. He worried about her too much. That was the whole problem.

Richard was obsessed with her. He wanted to know where she was at every moment. He wanted her home with him. For the past few years she'd worked at Dial-America, a telemarketing company. At first it wasn't much of a job, but she'd worked her way up to supervisor, and she was really enjoying it. It was the first job she'd had since she was single, and she felt good about herself again. But Richard hated her having that job. He told her to quit, tried to browbeat her into giving notice. He snooped around the building and spied on her through the windows. Then one night, when he picked her up from work, he happened to see one of her co-workers walking out of the building with her. The man meant nothing to her, he was just someone she worked with, but when she got into the car, Richard was wearing his dark glasses. If she didn't quit the job immediately, he stated flatly, something bad would happen to her "friend." She knew he meant it, so she gave notice the next Friday. That had happened six weeks ago.

It was hard for her to decide whether this insane jealousy came from the good Richard or the bad Richard. It was probably a little of both, she suspected. He did love her—she had no doubt about that—but it was a warped kind of love.

Richard wanted perfection in everything, and he demanded that his family be the perfect American family. Nothing made him happier than a family outing, everybody getting dressed up and going out to a nice restaurant for a meal together. He was in his glory at times like that. But the kids were older now—Merrick was twenty-

one, Christen was twenty, and Dwayne was a senior in high school
—and they had their own lives. They wanted to be with their
friends, not with their parents—at least not all the time. But Richard couldn't understand that, and it genuinely hurt him when one
of the girls refused to watch television with him because she had
something else to do. He couldn't understand the children wanting to grow up and go off on their own. Barbara dreaded the day
one of them decided to leave the nest. It wouldn't be an easy
parting.

But he had never hurt them, at least not physically. Verbally,
psychologically—that was something else. Whenever report cards
came home, he would never praise them for the A's. He'd berate
them for the B's. But that was Richard's whole philosophy of life:
The glass was always half empty, and no matter what, things were
never good enough. Not for him.

That's why money was so important to him. "It's the green that
counts, babe," he would always tell her. Money was the only thing
that made him happy—money and what it could buy. He loved to
shop, loved to buy things for her and the kids. Christian Dior suits
for her, spur-of-the-moment vacations, diamonds and gold jewelry
for the girls, ridiculous toys for Dwayne—like the hunting bow
that was never used. You could kill a bear with that thing, but it
just ended up hanging on the wall over the window in Dwayne's
room, collecting dust. But that was Richard. He thought nothing of
spending four, five, six hundred dollars on a single meal. When it
came to his family, price was no object.

Every six months they had new cars, and Richard was crazy
about cars. He'd bought Dwayne the blue Camaro they had now.
The thing was so souped up Dwayne had to call home from a pay
phone the first time he took it out. He couldn't control the thing, it
was so powerful. Richard had to go pick him up and drive the car
back. Now Richard was telling Dwayne he was going to buy him a
Lamborghini Excalibur, asking him what the priests at school
would say if they saw him driving up in one of those.

Barbara just shook her head. There was no reasoning with Richard when it came to possessions. If he decided they had to have something, they had to have it. Case closed.

It was money and the things money bought that made him feel like he was someone. When he was a poor kid in Jersey City, he felt that he was a nobody. Now he had money, and that made him a somebody. She knew that was the way he saw it. You were worthless unless you had a roll of bills in your pocket, unless you drove a Cadillac, unless you could buy whatever you wanted whenever you wanted it. That was what made you a somebody in Richard's estimation.

Money. That was the problem. It was the trigger that brought out the bad Richard. Whenever the money started running low, the bad Richard started coming out. And even though she'd never dream of asking, she knew the money must be running low now. She could smell it.

Where the money came from, she didn't want to know. Some of it came from Richard's currency exchange business, the Sunset Company, named after the street in Dumont where they lived. Richard traded foreign currencies, and his business often took him to England and Switzerland. As far as she knew, that was all legitimate because Richard filed tax returns and declared that income. In June he'd gone to Zurich to conclude a deal to sell a large sum of Nigerian currency. He'd had high hopes for this deal because he was talking about buying a house in ultrarich Saddle River that he'd become fixated with, a million-dollar home right around the corner from former President Nixon. But when he came back from Switzerland, he was in a foul mood. The deal had fallen through at the last minute. They'd screwed him, he kept muttering. The house in Saddle River wasn't mentioned anymore after that.

But currency exchange wasn't his only source of income. There was other money, money that was off the books. There *had* to be, considering the way they lived. But Barbara didn't ask.

She tore off another piece of bread and dropped it in front of her feet, enticing the ducks to come closer. She remembered times when they'd had to borrow food from the neighbors, they were so broke, and it wasn't that long ago. From borrowed cans of Campbell's soup to extravagant meals at fancy French restaurants—that was their life. To call it a roller coaster would be an understatement. There were ups and downs, and the thrills could be very thrilling; but unlike an amusement park ride, the scary parts were for real.

She glanced over her shoulder at Richard on the phone and sighed. He was talking to John Sposato. A year ago Richard had had high hopes for John Sposato. They were going to make a lot of money together, he'd told her. At what he didn't say, but from what she'd gathered, that big payoff hadn't happened yet.

John had had something to do with the currency deal that fell through in Zurich, and Barbara had a feeling that Richard was just trying to recoup his losses with Sposato now. She remembered the time last summer when she got a call from New Jersey Bell in the middle of the month asking for a down payment on their monthly bill. Why? she asked. Because your charges for the current month are already over seven thousand dollars, the woman from the telephone company said. Barbara nearly fainted. The calls were mostly third-party calls, long distance to Europe, made by Sposato from his place down in south Jersey.

She'd told Richard about it, expecting him to go through the roof, but he didn't. It was business, he'd said. He had faith in Sposato. John Sposato knew what he was doing, he'd said. Barbara didn't believe it, and she had a feeling Richard really didn't either. Richard rarely trusted anyone that much.

Her doubts about Sposato were confirmed when she finally met him. The fact that Richard let her meet him said a lot in itself because he was very strict about keeping his business life separate from his personal life. Even though at the time Richard never said it directly, she knew that he wanted her opinion of this new partner—and if he wanted her opinion, that meant he had doubts about the man.

She remembered when she first set eyes on Sposato in the parking lot of a truck stop on Route 80 in central Pennsylvania. To call him a big fat slob would be putting it nicely. His hair was long and stringy and looked as if it hadn't been washed in a month. His last few meals were all over his shirt. He came with his wife and three children, and the toddler screamed and fussed the whole time. The woman gave the poor thing a box of Cap'n Crunch cereal to keep it quiet. They never bothered to feed any of the kids a real meal, and repeated hints that the toddler's diaper needed to be changed were ignored by both parents.

Richard was thinking about buying into the truck stop with Sposato, and they were here to check out the place. At first Barbara assumed this would be a legitimate investment; then she met Richard's partner in the flesh. But Richard was high on Sposato in those days, so she didn't dare spoil it by expressing her gut feelings about him.

The day after they returned from Pennsylvania, Richard made an appointment with a real estate agent to see houses in Saddle River. She was the agent who showed them the house he'd wanted so badly. Barbara watched Richard's face from the backseat of the agent's car as they drove through the neighborhood. Richard's eyes narrowed when he spotted a video camera mounted on a high pole in the driveway of one grand home. There was another camera sticking out of the mailbox. She knew he wouldn't like this. Richard insisted on privacy.

But when the real estate agent told him that this was where Richard Nixon lived, his face changed. Barbara knew exactly what he was thinking. Living in the same neighborhood as a former president of the United States meant prestige. Richard liked that. From a dirt-poor kid in the Jersey City projects to back-fence neighbors with Tricky Dick. That would really be something for Richard. That night after dinner he kept joking about what it would be like taking Shaba out for a walk in that neighborhood, running into Nixon out walking his dog.

Barbara closed her eyes and sighed.

"No! Just shut up about that!" Richard yelled.

The ducks scattered in fright. Barbara glanced over her shoulder and saw Richard scowling into the pay phone as his voice boomed across the pond. The ducks paddled across to the other side.

Richard was jabbing his finger into the air, lecturing the phone as if Sposato were right there in front of him. She couldn't make out what he was saying now, but his tone was clear, and the anger in his face confirmed it. What little patience Richard had was wearing thin. She wondered whether Sposato realized how close to the edge he was skating. From what Richard had said, Sposato was supposedly a smart guy. For his sake she hoped he was smart enough to stay on Richard's good side.

Richard banged the phone down, then picked it up again and punched out another number. She strained to hear who he was calling now.

"Hello, Lenny? It's Rich." All of a sudden the anger was gone. He was smiling into the phone.

Barbara turned back to the pond. She didn't want to hear.

On the other side of the water the ducks were cowering in a huddle, their wings pulled in tight. She tore up what was left of the loaf and scattered it on the bank, then folded the plastic bag and got up from the bench. There was no use hanging around any longer. The birds were too scared to come back. The day was starting to get hot anyway. You could feel the humidity rising already. She walked across the grass to go wait in the car. It was going to be another wicked day.

TUESDAY, SEPTEMBER 2, 1986

Special Agent Dominick Polifrone of the Bureau of Alcohol, Tobacco, and Firearms had a lot on his mind as he parked the Shark, his long black Lincoln Continental coupe. Backing into a space on the busy north Jersey road, watching for cars coming up from behind, he was thinking about his family. Today was the first day of school for his kids, and his wife, Ellen, was overjoyed. The boys, Drew and Matt, had moped around all weekend, complaining that the summer had been too short, driving their mother nuts. His daughter, Keri, couldn't wait to get back and start eighth grade. She was thirteen, and she and her girlfriends were boy-crazy all of a sudden. Dominick wasn't sure if he was ready to have boyfriends hanging around the house. Keri wasn't even in high school, for God's sake. But right now he had to stop worrying about all that because he wasn't Dominick Polifrone now.

Agent Polifrone got out of the car, locked the door, and flipped up the collar of his black leather jacket against the rain as he glanced across the city avenue at the ordinary-looking storefront on the first floor of the three-story brick building, the place that had no name and was known simply as "the store." When he stepped into "the store," he would be "Michael Dominick Provenzano," "Dom" to those who knew him, a "connected" guy currently in the market for guns. Unlike Dominick Polifrone, Michael Dominick Provenzano didn't give a shit about wives, report cards, and Little League games. Provenzano's main interest was in making deals and making money. That was the mind-set that Special Agent Dominick Polifrone had to put himself in as he waited for a break in the traffic so he could cross the street.

Tires hissed on the wet pavement as he started across. He looked through the plate glass window of the greasy spoon luncheonette next door to "the store" to see if he recognized any faces. Thank God he'd already had lunch. You took your life in your hands eating in that place. Even the coffee was treacherous. But sometimes having coffee there was a necessary risk. It was where the clientele from "the store" went when they wanted a little privacy to discuss a deal.

The narrow driveway next to the store was jammed with big cars —Caddys and Lincolns. The end of the drive was blocked by an idling police cruiser with its front end hanging out into the street. The trunk was open. A cop in uniform had a cardboard box on his shoulder, which he was carrying in through the side door. Dominick followed him up the steps. The cop glanced at him around the edge of the box and avoided eye contact, but once they got inside the doorway and no one challenged Dom's presence there, the cop smiled and nodded.

"Need any umbrellas?" the cop asked, lowering the box off his shoulder. It was full of brand-new umbrellas, the tags still on them. Dominick had no doubt that they'd just "fallen off the truck."

Dominick stroked the ends of his bandito mustache as if he were thinking about it. "Nah. Can't move stuff like that."

The cop shrugged and dropped the box. He kicked it into a corner and looked around for another taker.

Dominick scanned the room. It was nothing to look at. The floor was littered with cigarette butts, the walls hadn't seen paint in twenty years, and there was hardly a place to sit, but "the store" was a virtual K mart of criminal activity.

A dozen men or so huddled in twos and threes under clouds of cigarette smoke, buying and selling stolen property, making connections, planning hijackings and burglaries, bragging and bullshitting. Dominick noticed a short, wiry guy in a maroon silk shirt and a burgundy leather sports jacket scribbling in a notepad as he nodded and smiled and talked to a heavyset guy in his forties whose hairline nearly touched his eyebrows. They didn't know Dominick, but Dominick knew who they were. The hairy guy had a methamphetamine factory somewhere out in Pennsylvania. The little guy was a loan shark associated with one of the New York Mafia families. It looked like the hairy guy was taking out a loan, perhaps to expand his speed business. Dominick made a mental note, so he could pass it on.

At a wobbly kitchen table with mismatched chairs, a scruffy-looking character with a ragged red beard dealt out cards to three meticulously groomed older gentlemen who all wore sheer nylon socks and lots of gold jewelry.

A fat man with three chins and a wart on the side of his nose was coming down the back staircase, peering over his belly and stepping carefully as if he were crossing a stream on slippery stones. He looked happy. No wonder. A pair of prostitutes had their own boutique up on the third floor.

A smudged glass counter near the front door held a small electric fan, a few cheap Korean cameras, and a set of aluminum pots and pans. The merchandise was just there for show. It was covered with dust and hadn't been touched in the seventeen months Dominick had been coming here. Except that there used to be two fans. Dominick recalled the first hot day of the summer when a little old Italian lady came in wanting to buy a fan. Everything stopped when the regulars finally noticed her. They stared at her as if she were from the moon. Someone grabbed one of the fans and gave it to her for nothing, then told her to get the hell out. The poor old lady was still good for a laugh now and then. She had become something of a legend at "the store"—the first and only honest person ever to walk into this place.

Over by the pay phone on the wall, Lenny DePrima, one of the regular fixtures here, was talking to the crooked cop with the umbrellas. Dominick had to talk to DePrima. But before he could make it across the room, someone grabbed his sleeve.

"Hey, Dom."

Walter Kipner peered over his tinted aviator glasses and grinned up at Dominick. Thick ropes of gold chain mingled with his gray chest hairs. His silver gray mane was perfect.

"Hey, what's up, Walt?" Kipner always had something going.

"C'mere. I wanna show you something." Kipner led Dominick over to a secluded corner. He had a Bloomingdale's shopping bag in his hand. He opened the bag and let Dominick take a peek. It was full of five-dollar bills, bundles of them bound with rubber bands.

Kipner pulled a loose bill out and handed it to Dominick. "Made in England. The best. You can't tell the difference, can you?"

Dominick rubbed the counterfeit bill between his fingers. "Yeah, not bad." Frigging Kipner. He was into everything.

"If you take half a mil, you can have 'em for twenty cents on the dollar." Kipner was slathering like the wolf who ate Grandma.

Dominick pressed his lips together and shook his head. "I dunno, Walt. Fives. Who the fuck wants fives? Twenties, sure. But fives? Gimme a break. You gotta walk around with a fucking suitcase with these things."

Kipner looked deeply hurt. "Whattaya talkin' about, Dom? Fives are perfect. Who the fuck bothers to check out a five? You tell me. Big bills they check. But they don't check little stuff. Never. That's why they're perfect."

Lenny DePrima was still over by the phone, but the cop was gone. Dominick really had to talk to him.

Kipner lowered his voice. "You take a mil and I'll give 'em to you for *fifteen cents*. Just for you, Dom."

Dominick kept his eye on DePrima. He had to get rid of Kipner and his phony fives so he could talk to him, but he'd write this up later in his daily report. Kipner was a real piece of work. In the last year he'd tried to sell Dominick everything—silencers, rocket launchers, plastic explosives. This was the first time with counterfeit money, though. If this guy only knew what a pass he was getting. It had been decided from the beginning that they weren't going to bust any bad guys Dominick found out about and risk blowing his cover. For the past seventeen months he'd had just one target and that was all he was supposed to focus on. His assignment was to get close to Richard Kuklinski—that's all. But now, almost a year and a half later, he was no closer to Kuklinski than he had been when he started this undercover. That's why he and Lenny DePrima had to have a little talk. DePrima had to start doing more.

Dominick suspected that Lenny DePrima was jerking him around now. Between the New Jersey State Police and the New Jersey Division of Criminal Justice, they had more than enough on DePrima to make his life miserable. He was a known fence with a lengthy criminal record, and they could easily put him away for receiving stolen property. They could also prosecute him for a number of auto thefts, burglaries, and hijackings he'd sponsored. This was how people in DePrima's business ordered their wares. If there was something you knew you could sell, you hired somebody else to steal it for you. Cars, jewelry, fur coats, TV sets, sewing machines, watches, canned goods, whatever. Dominick remembered when a hijacked truckload of Maine lobsters had appeared a couple of days before New Year's. DePrima figured he could unload lobsters easy for the holiday, so he'd put in an order.

But DePrima wasn't getting a free ride from the state for nothing. Dominick had several informants who said they knew Richard Kuklinski and were working to get him an introduction, but DePrima was the one who claimed to be Kuklinski's old buddy. When they first started leaning on DePrima, he had promised to introduce Dominick to Kuklinski and vouch for him, no problem. But in seventeen months Kuklinski hadn't come into "the store" once, and whenever Dominick asked why, DePrima just shrugged and said Big Rich must be spooked or something. The state wanted to pack it in with Dominick and his informants and try something else. But Dominick had a feeling DePrima wasn't giving this his best effort, and he was getting tired of the bullshit. He wanted that introduction, and he wanted it soon. DePrima had to start doing more.

Normally Dominick might have been more patient. He knew from experience that these things took time, that in deep cover it often took years to establish yourself. But this wasn't a normal assignment. This one was different. It was a joint effort, state and federal, combining the U.S. Bureau of Alcohol, Tobacco, and Firearms, the New Jersey Attorney General's Office, and the New Jersey State Police. A cooperative effort like this was almost unheard of in law enforcement, but Richard Kuklinski was a very unusual kind of criminal. He was deadly, crafty, and efficient, a mass murderer who set no pattern and left no traces. Everybody had had high hopes when Dominick started out on this undercover assignment, but now he was hearing rumblings from the state side. People were getting impatient and beginning to have doubts about Dominick's ability to succeed.

Maybe if he hadn't come into this operation with such a fanfare, they wouldn't be so disappointed with his slow progress. Ed Denning and Alan Grieco, his old buddies from the Bergen County Homicide Unit, where Dominick had worked before he became a fed, had recommended him for the job. He could imagine the buildup they must have given him. Captain Denning, poker-faced, squinting behind the perpetual veil of cigar smoke, stating the facts as if they were carved in stone, and there must be something wrong with *you* that you didn't already know this: *Dominick Polifrone is the best, period*. And Alan Grieco, he looked so honest and sincere he could sell snow to an Eskimo.

Dominick could just hear the two of them: "Oh, Dominick's the guy you need for this job." "Dominick put John Gotti's little brother Vinny away—the one nobody ever hears about because Dominick put him away for a long, long time." "Dominick? He's got balls like a frigging elephant. One time he went undercover on location in New York where Frank Sinatra was making a movie and he busted some guy on the crew who was dealing coke." "Dominick's got a scrapbook full of wiseguys he's put away over the years that would make Dick Tracy jealous."

It was all true, of course, but Dominick knew how Grieco and Denning operated. They must have made him out to be Superman. And Grieco was his best friend. Three times a week he and Dominick went jogging together. No one could ever live up to whatever those two had said about him.

Of course, when you consider who they were giving their sales pitch to, the hype job wasn't so surprising. Pat Kane of the state police had been dogging Kuklinski since 1980 and all by himself for most of that time. Catching Kuklinski had practically become his mission in life. So when a pharmacist in Bergen County was reported missing and the last person this man was supposed to have been with was Richard Kuklinski, Pat Kane made a beeline for the Bergen County Homicide Unit and asked that they not pursue this suspected homicide but leave it to the state police instead.

It never sits well with the locals when other agencies try to horn in on their territory, but when Captain Denning and Lieutenant Grieco heard about all the killings that were linked to Kuklinski, they decided not to argue with Detective Kane over jurisdiction. Wishing out loud, Kane said what they really needed to flush Kuklinski out was a good undercover man, and a single lightbulb went on over Denning's and Grieco's heads: Dominick Polifrone. If they got Dominick involved, they could cooperate with the state police and still keep it in the family, so to speak. Even though Dominick was a fed now, he was still one of them. They told Detective Kane that Dominick Polifrone was without a doubt the one man for this job, and when Kane objected that Dominick was a federal agent and probably couldn't get involved in a homicide investigation like this, Denning puffed on his cigar and said one word: "Guns." Selling guns was part of Kuklinski's extensive criminal portfolio. As long as there were guns involved, an ATF agent could be brought in.

Pat Kane bought their pitch and called Dominick that very afternoon. It wasn't long before Dominick was on the job as "Michael Dominick Provenzano."

But that had been seventeen months ago, and even though certain people from the state might not be saying it out loud, Dominick could feel that they were getting antsy. Frankly so was he. In the past year and a half he'd heard a lot of stories about Kuklinski and the things he was supposed to have done, stories from both sides of the law. At "the store" they referred to him as "the one-man army" and "the devil himself." If half of what Dominick had heard was true, these names were well deserved.

Dominick could understand Pat Kane's relentless devotion to this case. There was something about Kuklinski that was so insidious, so arrogant. Kuklinski's face had become the last thing Dominick pictured before he went to sleep at night, and it was right there staring at him when he woke up in the morning. There was no question about it anymore. The bastard had to go down; he *had* to. Everyone understood that. But even though Dominick hadn't gotten the kind of results he'd hoped for at this point, no one else had gotten any closer to Kuklinski than he had. Besides, Dominick had put too much time into this to let the state pull the plug on him now. He could smell Kuklinski. He could feel his presence in everyone who'd ever met him. In his gut he *knew* Kuklinski. The introduction was only a matter of time.

Walter Kipner had moved over to the poker table to peddle his phony fives. He must have been desperate for a sale because he was handing out freebies now, inviting comparison with the real bills that were scattered on the table. Other bad guys flocked to the table, eager to get a free fin. Dominick noticed that DePrima was by himself. He decided to take advantage of the distraction.

"Hey, Lenny, what's happening?" Dominick put his hand on the wall and corralled DePrima.

"Hey, Dom, *che se dice?*" DePrima made like he'd just noticed Dominick.

Dominick gave him a dirty look.

DePrima shrugged. "What can I tell you?" he said under his breath. "I'm doing what I can."

"When, Lenny? When?"

"I'm trying, Dom. I'm trying. I've been calling the big guy up, just like I told you. I told him I got this guy here who's looking for guns in quantity. I offered to set up a meet, the whole bit. But he ain't biting."

"Why not?"

"You don't understand, Dom. You don't push the Polack. Not unless you're looking for big trouble."

"Did you tell him I was okay?"

"Whattaya think? Of course, I said you were okay. I told him we did some deals before. I gave you my Good Housekeeping Seal of Approval, Dom. I swear."

"Did you tell him I was connected?"

"Yeah."

"Did you tell him I had a customer who wanted to put in a big order? A *real* big order?"

DePrima nodded.

"Then what the fuck is this guy's problem, Lenny?"

"Like I told you, Dom. You don't push the Polack. He does

what he does when *he* decides he's gonna do it, and you do not ask why."

Dominick glanced at the poker table. Kipner was throwing his fives around as if they were confetti. Everybody was getting a big kick out of it, especially the crooked cop. Dominick turned his gaze back to DePrima. "I think you're jerking me around here, Lenny. You been bullshitting me from day one. You haven't been calling him. You're fulla shit. I'm gonna pull the fucking plug on this whole deal and let you take your chances with the—"

The pay phone rang. DePrima reached for the receiver. "One minute, Dom. Just take it easy and calm down. Okay?"

If he weren't undercover, Dominick would have made the little bullshitter eat the goddamn receiver.

"Hey, how ya doin'?" DePrima rolled his eyes to Dominick and nodded toward the phone. "You mean Dominick Provenzano? Yeah, he's still coming around. Why?"

Dominick furrowed his brows. What kind of bullshit was this? Did DePrima really expect him to believe that this was Kuklinski on the phone?

"Well, yeah, he did tell me he could get anything you might want along those lines, Rich." DePrima was looking Dom in the eye. He looked a little uneasy. "Yeah, sure, I believe him. I know guys who done stuff with him before. He's solid."

If that really was Kuklinski on the phone—and Dominick wasn't convinced that it was—the fish was nipping at the hook. Dominick waited and listened. It was out of his hands now. It was all up to the fish.

"Hey, all I can tell you, Rich, is that he's always done right by me. We made some good money together, and that's all I give a shit about. You wanna meet him, you meet him. You want the guy's fucking résumé, I can't help you out."

Dominick drummed his fingers against the wall, waiting for DePrima to get off the phone.

DePrima was shaking his head. "That I can't tell you, Rich. He says he can get anything. I don't know if he can or he can't." He looked at Dominick. "He's here right now, Rich. Why don't you ask him yourself?"

Dominick gave him an evil look. If this was some kind of bullshit stunt, he *would* make DePrima eat the phone.

"Well, it's up to you, Rich. Whatever you want . . . Right . . . Okay. Take it easy." DePrima hung up the phone.

"Who was that? Richie, I suppose."

DePrima lowered his voice. "I swear on my mother's grave, Dom. That was him. He wants to meet you. Right now. The Dunkin' Donuts over by the Shop Rite. He says he needs something, and I told him you could get it for him."

Dominick was suspicious, but he wanted to believe it. "So what's he need?"

"Cyanide."

A warm breeze blew through the Shark's open window as Dominick Polifrone cruised across the old steel girder bridge and crossed the river. The sun was peeking through gray clouds, and the sky was blue on the horizon as the rain tapered off. The hiss of tires on the wet blacktop came in through the open window, but Dominick was oblivious to the sound. He was thinking about Richard Kuklinski, focusing on his mark, trying not to outpsych himself for the meet, just trying to be himself. That was the key to good undercover work: Just be yourself.

Dominick had learned from experience that elaborate cover stories and aliases just get you into trouble on an undercover. You can't hesitate when you're in with bad guys. If it takes you a second to answer to your cover name, they may get suspicious. And bad guys seldom sit on their suspicions. You slip up once, you can get hurt. You slip up with the wrong people, it could mean your life.

That's why Dominick Polifrone wasn't that different from his cover, "Michael Dominick Provenzano." He'd told the guys he'd met at "the store" that some of his wiseguy connections in the city knew him as Sonny, but he told everyone just to call him Dom.

The address on his driver's license was a huge high rise in Fort Lee, and that, he'd say, was his girlfriend's apartment, his *goo-mata*'s place.

Michael Dominick Provenzano was a tough kid from a lower-middle-class section of Hackensack, New Jersey. So was Dominick Polifrone.

Michael Dominick Provenzano ran numbers when he was a kid. So had Dominick Polifrone.

Dominick Polifrone might have ended up being just like Michael Dominick Provenzano if he hadn't gotten a football scholarship to the University of Nebraska. Not that football or the Midwest turned his head around. Far from it. Dominick blew into Nebraska like an Italian-American twister. Coming from the East, he was easily the hippest guy on campus. He wore bell-bottoms before the farm kids even knew they were the fashion. Whenever he returned from school vacations, he brought back a suitcase full of the latest albums, stuff that wouldn't be in the stores in Nebraska for weeks. If Dominick was cocky in Hackensack, he was a wild man in Nebraska. By his sophomore year trashing bars on Friday nights had become his weekly ritual, and spending the night in jail was starting to become part of that ritual. That's when a sergeant on the Omaha police force took a special interest in this young pain in the ass from New Jersey and hauled him back to campus to have a little talk with Dominick's coach. It was that meeting with the coach and the sergeant that turned Dominick's head around. They put it to him straight: Either you calm down and start acting like a civilized human being or go back to Hackensack for good. The sergeant, however, felt that the warning by itself wasn't enough, so he strongly suggested that Dominick drop his current major, physical education, and take up a new one, law enforcement. The coach concurred. That Saturday afternoon meeting in the coach's office set Dominick's life in a new direction.

He still raised hell now and then, and he continued to play football and box with a vengeance, winning the Southeast District Heavyweight Golden Gloves Championship in 1969. But in his mind he knew who he was now. The bad guy in training was gone. Dominick Polifrone thought of himself as one of the good guys now.

And that was what made him so outstanding as an undercover agent. He could talk like a bad guy, look like a bad guy, and act like a bad guy because that was all a part of him, but deep down he knew he was one of the good guys.

That's why Dominick wasn't concerned with his undercover image as he drove across that bridge, heading for the Dunkin' Donuts. He knew he was convincing. What he was concerned about was meeting Richard Kuklinski by himself without any backups.

The situation had come down too fast to call in for help. Kuklinski was supposedly waiting for him. It was a five-minute drive to the doughnut shop from "the store." If he took too long getting there, Kuklinski wouldn't wait, he was sure of that. The guy was cautious to a fault. If anything made Kuklinski suspicious about Dominick, he would disappear, and Dominick could forget about ever meeting him again. That's why this first meeting was important. Dominick would know in the first five minutes whether he could pull this off or not. The important thing was control. He was a bad guy, and he wanted something. No matter how much he wanted to get close to Kuklinski, he could not kowtow to him. It would destroy his credibility as a player. And if Kuklinski thought he was bullshit, he'd have nothing to do with him.

Dominick reached into his pocket and felt the butt of his gun, a Walther PPK 380 automatic. Despite the balmy temperature, Dominick wore the leather jacket. It was part of his undercover uniform and served to conceal the bulge of his weapon. Considering Kuklinski's reputation, he planned to keep his hand in his pocket with his finger on the trigger.

Kuklinski was reputed to have taken part in dozens of murders, but the police had never been able to come up with enough evidence on any one crime to arrest him. Dominick had a gut feeling that the killings they knew about were only a fraction of Kuklinski's total body count. From all indications he was just too proficient at killing.

Sometimes Kuklinski killed alone, and sometimes he brought help. Sometimes he worked as a killer for hire; sometimes the killings were his own doing. Sometimes it was business; sometimes it was just blind rage. He was known to have used weapons as small as a two-shot derringer and as large as a twelve-gauge shotgun. On at least two occasions he'd killed with hand grenades. He'd used baseball bats, tire irons, rope, wire, knives, ice picks, screwdrivers, even his bare hands when necessary. And for some reason that no one could quite figure out, he kept one of his victims frozen solid for over two years before he dumped the body, which earned him the nickname Iceman in New Jersey police circles after he became the prime suspect in that murder. But according to state police reports, one of Kuklinski's favorite methods was cyanide poisoning. Dominick knew from sixteen years of working undercover that you never take any criminal lightly, but Richard Kuklinski was unlike any other bad guy he'd ever encountered. He was not a demented serial killer; killing apparently did not satisfy any kind of psychosexual need for him. Sometimes he killed weeks apart; sometimes he waited years before taking his next victim. He didn't smoke, drink, gamble, or womanize. He fitted no easy pattern, and there was no single word to describe what he was—except *monster*. Dominick let out a slow breath and took his hand out of his pocket.

A traffic light up ahead turned red, and Dominick quickly pulled the long black Lincoln into the left lane and stopped behind a white police car. He noticed the cop behind the wheel looking at

him in his side mirror. Dominick glanced ahead at the Dunkin'
Donuts on the other side of the intersection. A paranoid chill crept
through his stomach. What if these two cops decided to pull him
over? He hadn't signaled when he pulled into the left lane. What if
he fitted the description of some other meatball they were looking
for? Kuklinski was supposed to be waiting for him at the Dunkin'
Donuts. If Kuklinski saw the cops questioning him, he'd probably
scram. Worse than that, it would lower Dominick in Kuklinski's
eyes, make him seem like a street hood, some jerk the cops could
push around just for the hell of it. Kuklinski wasn't interested in
little guys, and Dominick had gone to great lengths to establish
himself as someone with solid connections to the mob families in
New York. After seventeen months of hard work, rubbing elbows
with some of the worst scum imaginable, he didn't want to blow
his one chance to finally meet the Iceman, not like this.

The cop behind the wheel kept looking at him in the side mirror, and his partner was turning around now, staring at Dominick
through the security grille that separated the unit's front and back
seats.

Dominick gritted his teeth. *Not now, guys. Please, not now.*

The light turned green. The cars in the right lane started to
move, but the police car didn't budge. The driver was staring at
him.

Christ Almighty, not now. Dominick glanced at the orange, pink,
and white Dunkin' Donuts sign across the intersection. He stared
at the unit's brake lights.

Please.

Dominick considered going around them, but that could have
been what they were waiting for. Maybe they wanted to get a look
at his profile as he passed, then they could pull him over. Goddammit. He knew he had to do something. He couldn't just sit here
acting suspicious.

But just as he was about to go around the cruiser, its brake lights
suddenly blinked off and it started to move forward. Dominick let

out a long breath as he pressed the accelerator and went through the intersection. He switched on his left directional. The doughnut shop was just ahead.

There were only three vehicles in the Dunkin' Donut's small parking lot: a black Toyota pickup truck with hot pink Oakley windshield wipers, a beige VW Rabbit with a bashed-in fender, and a blue Chevy Camaro, at least six or seven years old. Dominick pulled up next to the Camaro. From what he knew about Kuklinski's size, Dominick had a feeling his target wouldn't be coming in an imported compact.

Dominick cut the engine and looked to his right. A large, heavyset man was sitting behind the wheel of the Camaro, perusing the newspaper propped on the steering wheel. He was bald except for the longish gray hair on the sides, which was carefully combed up and over his ears. He wore a trim full beard and mustache, mostly gray now, though his dirty blond coloring was still in evidence. Oversize windowpane sunglasses covered his eyes. The man turned his head slowly and looked at Dominick. Dominick knew the face very well from the dozens of surveillance photographs he'd seen. It was him, the Iceman.

Dominick had to force himself from putting his hand in his pocket. The Iceman was sizing him up, and Dominick knew it, but he met Kuklinski's gaze with his own unconcerned stare. He had to establish control right off the bat, before they even exchanged a single word. You give a guy like Kuklinski the upper hand and he'll eat you alive.

Kuklinski closed his newspaper, folded it in half, and got out of the car. Dominick opened his door and got out of the Lincoln, and it was only then, looking over the roof of his car, that he realized just how big Kuklinski really was. At six feet even, Dominick had certainly never thought of himself as small or even medium, but compared with Richard Kuklinski, a thoroughbred would have looked small. The physical descriptions in the reports didn't do the man justice. "Six-four, 270 lbs" didn't convey the whole truth of the matter. The man wasn't just big, he was BIG.

"Richie?" Dominick asked.

Kuklinski nodded, no expression. He put the newspaper under his arm. "You wanna coffee?"

"Sure."

Kuklinski walked around the back of the Shark and extended his hand to Dominick.

Dominick shook his hand, deliberately keeping his face expressionless so his true feelings didn't show. He was shaking the hand of a killer, a hand that had taken many, many lives. He had been prepared for a bully's grip, but instead it was disarmingly gentle.

"They call you Dom?" The Iceman's voice matched his handshake, soft and low, almost lilting.

"Yeah. Dom. I go by my middle name."

Kuklinski nodded as if he were thinking something over. "Call me Rich."

Dominick nodded. "Okay."

They walked into the Dunkin' Donuts together in silence. The place was dead. A young black girl in a beige gingham waitress uniform was rearranging doughnuts on the large metal trays that lined the back wall. A Hispanic kid in ripped jeans and high tops, cat scratches shaved into the scalp on the sides of his head, was devouring a huge honey-dip doughnut, sipping soda from a wax cup. The faint sound of easy-listening music drifted out from the back room.

Kuklinski nodded toward the seats at the far end of the counter, away from the waitress and the Hispanic kid. He wanted privacy. So would "Michael Dominick Provenzano."

The waitress came over as they sat down. "Can I help you?"

"Yeah. Two coffees," Dominick said. He looked at Kuklinski. "You wanna doughnut or anything?"

Kuklinski spoke to the waitress. "I'll have a cinnamon bun if you've got one."

The girl nodded, then turned to Dominick. "Anything for you, sir?"

Dominick thought about it for a second, but then shook his head no. Normally he would have ordered a plain doughnut or a cruller, something small, but seeing Kuklinski's girth changed his mind. Dominick tried to stay fit. He jogged every day he could and worked out regularly, but when he didn't watch himself, he could put on ten pounds overnight, it seemed, and undercover work was not conducive to healthy habits. Bad guys like Michael Dominick Provenzano tend to spend ninety percent of their time hanging out, drinking coffee, eating crap, talking shit.

Dominick watched Kuklinski sitting there, quietly waiting for his coffee. With that sculpted beard of his, he looked like an evil duke from some mythical kingdom calmly contemplating his next murderous plot. Dominick knew not to say what was on his mind just yet. It wasn't the way bad guys operated. They had to feel each other out first, circle each other like boxers in the first round. They had to talk shit first.

"So you keeping busy, Rich?"

Kuklinski nodded. "Yeah. I do what I can. How about you?"

"Yeah, I'm doing all right. Can always do better, though. I know I ain't gonna hit the lottery, so I gotta make it myself. You know what I mean?"

"Yup."

Kuklinski's newspaper was folded on the counter by his elbow. He seemed to be reading it, not really paying attention to Dominick. The waitress returned with two mugs of coffee and a cinnamon bun the size of a saucer. Kuklinski peeled the tops off two plastic containers of half-and-half and poured them into his coffee. Dominick stirred in one container and took a sip from his mug.

Kuklinski nodded toward the plate glass window behind them to the Shark. "How do you like the Lincoln?"

"It's nice. I used to have an Eldorado, but I like this one better. Better ride with the Lincoln."

Kuklinski bit into his cinnamon bun. "You're right. Lincoln's a nice car. Nice and roomy up front."

They talked cars for a while, comparing different models, wondering why really rich people were abandoning the Caddys and Lincolns for Mercedeses, reminiscing about good cars they'd had in the past. It was all very friendly, and it gave Dominick a chance to ease into his undercover role with his target, but they were just talking shit, still circling each other. Finally Dominick decided it was time to get down to business. He saw an opportunity to steer the conversation into it.

"You know, Rich, one car I could never get used to was the Corvette. The Stingray, you know what I mean? I always feel like I'm sitting on the floor in those damn things. I know Lenny's got one, and he says he loves it, but I dunno . . . It's not for me."

Kuklinski didn't say anything for a moment, just chewed and sipped his coffee. "Corvette's not a bad car."

Dominick knew from the state police reports that Kuklinski had driven Corvettes in the past, stolen vehicles. That was probably why he wasn't anxious to share his enthusiasm for that particular model. He wasn't sure about Dominick yet. Dominick had to keep talking and hope that he could find some common ground with Kuklinski, something that would gain a little bit of his trust and open the door for him. He decided to push a little farther.

"Yeah, that Lenny, he's something else, isn't he?"

"Yeah . . . He's something else." Kuklinski was distracted, staring down at his newspaper again.

Dominick knew that if he didn't connect with Kuklinski soon, he might as well pack in the whole thing. He had to make Kuklinski warm up to him, just a little bit, but now he felt stuck. He thought Kuklinski would respond to his mentioning Lenny DePrima. Kuklinski supposedly trusted DePrima.

Dominick took a sip of his coffee. He didn't want to keep bringing up DePrima's name. He was afraid that if he kept harping on DePrima, Kuklinski would think he was a nobody showing off the only real contact he had. Kuklinski wasn't interested in wannabes. If Dominick smelled like bullshit, Kuklinski would just walk away and have nothing to do with him, ever. Dominick needed to connect with this guy, but he had to be careful.

Just to keep the ball rolling, Dominick was about to bring up the New York Giants, who had beaten the Steelers in an exhibition game that Sunday, ask if Kuklinski was a fan, anything to jump-start the conversation. But then Kuklinski took off his sunglasses and looked Dominick in the eye. Dominick met his gaze. He couldn't come off as submissive in any way, or Kuklinski would pick up on it like a bloodhound. Dominick already intended to grab the check when the waitress brought it. It would be *his* treat.

"I hear you got some connections, Dom." Kuklinski was still staring at him.

"Yeah. I got a few connections." Dominick sipped his coffee, but his eyes never left Kuklinski's.

Kuklinski lowered his voice. "Can you get the white stuff?"

Dominick paused, sizing him up for effect. "We talking about the cheap white stuff or the expensive kind?" Cocaine or heroin?

"The cheaper one."

Dominick shrugged. "Maybe. How much you want?"

Kuklinski stuck out his bottom lip and tilted his head. "Ten. Maybe more later."

"Yeah, sure. I can do that."

"How much per?"

Dominick stroked his mustache and thought about it. "Thirty-one five." Thirty-one thousand five hundred dollars a kilo.

Kuklinski nodded and sipped his coffee as he thought about it. "Kinda steep, Dom. I know a guy, I think I can get it for between twenty-five and thirty."

"So get it from him and don't waste my time," Dominick snapped back. He wasn't about to dicker with Kuklinski because he didn't want Kuklinski to think he needed the sale. He had to establish his control over the situation, even if he had to risk turning Kuklinski off for good. This had always been Dominick's strict personal policy.

Kuklinski tore off a piece of his cinnamon bun and put it in his mouth. He seemed unperturbed by Dominick's attitude. "How about cyanide?" he asked.

"What?" Dominick's heart stopped. He wished to hell he were wearing a wire.

"Cyanide. Can you get any?"

"Whatta'you, funny? You need cyanide, go to a hardware store, get some rat poison. They got all the fucking cyanide you want."

Kuklinski shook his head. "Not that stuff. I need *pure* cyanide. Lab quality. The kind of stuff they make you sign for when you try to buy it."

"Whattaya need that for?"

"Something personal I gotta take care of."

Dominick shrugged as if it didn't make one bit of difference to him what Kuklinski wanted to do with pure cyanide, but inside, he couldn't believe Kuklinski had come right out and asked for the poison on their very first meeting. Kuklinski was a suspect in several cyanide poisonings. It was supposed to be one of his favorite methods of killing. Dominick never expected to get this lucky, not this fast. But immediately he was suspicious. Why was Kuklinski asking *him* for cyanide? They'd just met. And why couldn't Kuklinski get it for himself? From all indications he'd never had any trouble getting it before. Was he really that desperate for the poison? And who did he plan to use it on?

"So can you get it for me, Dom?"

"Yeah, sure. I know a guy. I'm pretty sure he can get it. How much you need?"

"Not much. You don't need a whole lot of that stuff."

"A little dab'll do ya, huh?"

"Yup." Kuklinski tore off another piece of his cinnamon bun. "Tell you what, Dom. You see if you can get me that stuff, and in the meantime, I'll take ten of the white stuff off your hands."

"At what price?"

"What you told me. Thirty-one five."

"I thought you could get it for twenty-five."

"Yeah, I could maybe, but that guy's a jerk-off. He's not that careful about his business. I don't like people who aren't careful. You know what I'm saying?"

"Absolutely. Guys like that you don't need. They're fucking liabilities."

"Exactly."

Dominick signaled to the waitress that he wanted a refill. "Listen, Rich. Maybe there's something you can help me with." He leaned closer to Kuklinski and lowered his voice. "I got a buyer who's looking for heavy steel. Not street stuff. Military grade. Machine guns, grenades, rocket launchers, that kind of stuff. Silencers, too. Small-caliber guns fitted with silencers."

"You're looking for hit kits."

"Right. Hit kits and heavy steel."

Kuklinski raised his eyebrows. "What's your buyer wanna do? Take over a country?"

Dominick glared at him. "Never mind about my buyer."

"Hey, don't get hot. I don't wanna know who your buyer is. I would never try to go around you and cut you out. I don't work that way."

"Good. So can you help me out here?" Dominick was both relieved and grateful that Kuklinski hadn't been turned off by his quick temper. Kuklinski's question was out of line, and he'd realized that after he'd said it. Dominick's response was totally appropriate.

"Just tell me this, Dom. Does your buyer want this merchandise delivered, or would he be willing to pick it up?"

"Gotta be delivered. To New York." Dominick already had a cover story prepared. He was buying for the Irish Republican Army, and his usual sources couldn't get him what his customer wanted in the quantity they needed. But he wasn't going to tell

Kuklinski that right away. At this point it was none of Kuklinski's business.

"Hmm . . ." Kuklinski stroked his beard. "Gotta be delivered to New York. That might make it a little hard."

"It won't be staying in New York. It's going somewhere else."

"But they can't pick it up? Say, in Delaware?"

Dominick shook his head. "They won't go for it. I know these people. It's gotta be delivered or there's no deal."

"They good customers?"

"The best. They pay top dollar, and they don't dick around. You get 'em what they want, and they pay on the line. No bullshit with these people."

"They sound like good customers."

"Like I said, the best. If you can get me the right kind of stuff—military stuff, I'm talking—you can make a lot of money off these people. We both can."

Kuklinski laughed. "Can't argue with that, brother."

"I can almost guarantee it. I'm not talking about small quantities here. This'll be a big order. Big." Dominick knew that the bait had to be enticing or Kuklinski wouldn't bite.

"Lemme just ask you this. These people from New York, your customers, they connected?"

Dominick shook his head. "I buy for the wiseguys now and then, too. But this is different. This has nothing to do with the families."

Kuklinski nodded, sucking his teeth. "I think I can get what you want. I'll have to make a few calls to see what's around. I'll get back to you."

"Okay, fine. But don't take too long. They don't like to wait around, these people. They find a better deal, forget about it, they're gone."

"Don't worry. I'll get back to you as soon as I know something. Just tell me how I can get in touch with you."

Dom pulled a pen out of his shirt pocket and wrote down a

phone number on a paper napkin. "Here. This is my beeper number. You put your number in the system, and I'll call you back in fifteen minutes."

"Great."

"Now like I said, you come up with the right merchandise and we could make a lot of do-re-mi with these people. Believe me."

"I believe you, Dom. But don't forget about those things I want."

"I won't forget. I got a good memory, Rich. Ten of the white stuff and the rat poison."

"*Pure.* I need it pure."

"I gotcha, Rich. Don't worry."

The waitress came over then, carrying a Pyrex pot of coffee. She refilled the mugs without asking.

"Thank you, sweetheart," Dominick said to her. "Hey, Rich, you want another bun? Go 'head, I'm buying."

A slow grin spread under Kuklinski's mustache as he looked at Dominick. "Sure. Why not?"

Though it has a population of eighteen thousand, Dumont is practically a quaint village by northern New Jersey standards and one of the more modest communities in generally expensive Bergen County. Dumont is a town of simple saltbox Cape Cods and center-hall Colonials on winding streets lined with mature maples and sycamores, the trees that shed their brown paper bark as well as their leaves. A bedroom community for New York City and Newark, Dumont is a poor cousin to its more elegant neighbors, towns like Cresskill, Demarest, Alpine, and stately Englewood Cliffs, which borders the Hudson River and is noted for its proud old mansions on expansive rolling lawns. The residents of Dumont are an even mix of blue collar and middle-management white collar. However, there was one resident of this middle-class suburb who did not fit the local demographics: Richard Kuklinski.

Kuklinski was preoccupied as he drove the blue Camaro through the center of town later that afternoon. His brow was furrowed as he sailed up Washington Avenue and past St. Michael's Catholic School, then took the next left, heading for Sunset Street. The houses he swept past were as solid and respectable as the town itself, but over the years additions and modern flourishes had sprung up here and there like mushrooms: skylights, brick walkways, expanded decks, sun-rooms, central air-conditioning units—items that reflected spurts in the various owners' personal finances. Turning onto Sunset Street, Kuklinski guided the blue Chevy into the driveway of number 169, a neat split-level with a cedar shake facade and a custom-made twenty-five-hundred-dollar carved mahogany door. He turned off the engine and sat there for a moment, chewing his bottom lip. He was sorting through the details, considering the possibilities, trying to figure out how Dominick Provenzano could fit into his plans.

The dog had started to bark as soon as the car pulled in. Lost in thought, Kuklinski blinked, finally noticing Shaba's yelping. The big black Newfoundland was tied up in the backyard, waiting for someone to walk him.

Kuklinski let himself in through the front door and climbed the short flight of steps that led to the living room. His son, Dwayne, was stretched out on the sofa, headphones over his ears, a yellow Walkman by his side, holding a book up over his face. Seventeen-year-old Dwayne was a good-looking kid with dark hair and a ruddy complexion. He was a smart kid, too. He liked to read, just like his mother. Barbara and Dwayne often read the same novels and discussed them late into the night at the kitchen table. But sometimes Kuklinski felt that his son was *too* smart, that the boy was smarter than he was. He had to admit to himself that at times he was even jealous of Dwayne's relationship with Barbara, particularly when they talked about the books they'd read. He had tried to read what they did, but books just never held his attention. It had taken him until he was sixteen to finish the eighth grade. The only thing he ever read was the newspaper.

He looked down at his son, lost in his own world. "Dwayne."

The boy didn't answer. The Walkman was cranked up so loud

Kuklinski could hear it on the other side of the room. Heavy metal. He couldn't wait for Dwayne's head banger phase to pass.

"Dwayne!" he repeated, raising his voice. *"Dwayne!"*

The boy finally heard his father and turned down the music, though he left the headphones on.

"Hey, Dad. What's up?"

"Do me a favor, will ya?"

"Sure. What?"

"Take the dog for a walk."

"I thought you always liked to—"

"I gotta make some phone calls. Go 'head before he does it in the yard."

"Okay." Dwayne sat up and threw the paperback he was reading down on the coffee table. *The Bourne Identity.*

Kuklinski glanced down at the book as he moved on to the kitchen. Something smelled good in there.

"Daddy." Twenty-one-year-old Merrick, his oldest child, got up from the kitchen table and threw her arms around her father. Tall and dark-haired like her brother, Merrick kissed his cheek, and he gave her a squeeze.

Twenty-year-old Christen, the middle child, was standing at the counter, watching. "Hi, Dad," she mumbled. Christen was fair and slender, like her mother. If only she smiled a little more.

"Since when did you guys learn to cook? Your mother thinks you two don't even know where the kitchen is."

Merrick laughed. "C'mon, Dad. We're not that bad."

Christen went back to shredding lettuce for the salad. She kept her head down.

He went over to give her a hug, too, but the response wasn't the same as with Merrick. Christen always held back with him, and there always seemed to be an awkward, uncomfortable undercurrent when they were together. Maybe it was him, or maybe it was the competition with Merrick, who'd always been more demonstrative, more outgoing, more "Daddy's girl."

He suddenly thought of his own brother and sister. He had two siblings, and now he had three kids, both families the same size. Kuklinski frowned, angry that he'd even think there was any comparison. There was *nothing* similar about his family then and his family now.

"What's the matter, Daddy?" Merrick asked.

"Nothing."

He was thinking about his kid brother, Joey. When he was a young man in his twenties, Joey had thrown a twelve-year-old girl and her little black dog off a roof. The dog survived. Joey was locked away in the nuthouse now, but Kuklinski was convinced that it was that awful upbringing in Jersey City that had ruined Joey's mind. That was why Kuklinski had vowed to himself a long time ago that he would provide only the best for his own kids. He would never in a million years let his children go through anything like what he had gone through growing up in the projects. Never. And the only way to ensure it was with money.

When he was a kid, poverty had made his mother so bitter it turned her into a cancer, he thought. She destroyed everything she touched, out of spite. Whenever her children looked to her for encouragement, her nasty comments cut them down and humiliated them instead. Life had dealt her a rotten hand, so she wanted to ruin the game for everyone else. Eventually cancer—the real thing—destroyed her.

But as bad as his mother was, he knew his father was far worse. At least she made an effort to keep her family together. His father just came and went as he pleased, usually drunk, and always ready to beat Richie, the eldest, just for the hell of it. The old man would disappear for a few years, then just about the time Kuklinski had finally forgotten about the bastard, he'd come drifting back in a drunken rage to cause a little more misery before he left again.

After many years of separation Kuklinski had gotten back in touch with his father. He'd thought maybe he could reconcile with the old man, that things could be different now that he was married and established and had a family of his own. But he was dead wrong. His father hadn't changed one bit. He was the same coldhearted bastard he'd always been, and he didn't give a shit about his son or his son's family. The old man was fine as long as his son was buying him drinks at a bar, but one day, when Kuklinski stopped by at his father's apartment to see how he was doing, the old man wouldn't even answer the door. He told his son to go away and leave him alone.

Standing alone in that dimly lit hallway, Kuklinski felt the burn of humiliation. It wasn't worth trying to do something good if this was what you got for it.

There was a time when Richard Kuklinski had been well on his way to falling into the same bitter poverty trap as his parents. When he was still a teenager, he'd gotten some woman in the projects pregnant and ended up having to marry her. She was twenty-six, and he was just a kid. They didn't even live together, but he ended up having two sons by her. He wasn't even twenty yet, and he saw himself turning into his old man.

Thank God he'd met Barbara. She turned his life around. She showed him that life wasn't all shit, that there was a better way. When Barbara's mother paid for his divorce from his first wife and he married Barbara, he swore he would never go back to the kind of life he'd had in the projects. Never.

Richard focused on his daughters, pleased with the way they had turned out. They were nothing like his mother or his first wife. They were fine young women with good taste and good looks and good educations. It was all thanks to Barbara. She'd taken care of all the child rearing.

"Where's your mother?" he asked the girls.

Merrick was assembling a lasagna, layering wide strips of curly-edged pasta, tomato sauce, slices of mozzarella cheese, and gobs of ricotta in a baking pan. "Mom's upstairs lying down. She's got a headache."

"Oh." He looked to Christen, but she was busy slicing a cucumber.

"Where's that boyfriend of yours, Christen? What's his name? Matt."

Christen shrugged but wouldn't look at him. "I dunno. He's home, I guess."

He looked at Merrick, grinned, and winked. "Oh, yeah? Once he smells that lasagna, he'll be over here like a shot."

Christen sighed. She didn't like her father's cracks about Matt. He made it obvious that he didn't like her boyfriend. Ever since that night he caught them making out on her bed and screamed at them for over an hour straight.

Merrick pursed her lips and tried not to laugh at her father's needling, for her sister's sake.

Richard reached around Christen, picked out a slice of bell pepper from the wooden salad bowl on the counter, and popped it into his mouth. "I'm gonna go check on your mother."

He went back through the living room, climbed a short flight of carpeted steps, and went to the master bedroom. The door was closed. He turned the knob without a sound and peeked in. Barbara was on her back in bed, one arm draped over her face. She was wearing designer jeans and a peach-colored knit top. The satin pillow under her head was the one he'd brought back from Los Angeles.

"Rich?" she moaned, and lifted her arm.

"You all right, babe?"

She nodded behind her arm. "It's just a headache." She raised one knee and curled her toes. At forty-six Barbara still had the kind of figure a fashion model could envy.

Kuklinski stepped into the room and sat on the edge of the bed. He felt her forehead. Her eyes looked more tired than usual.

"It's just a headache, Rich."

"You take any aspirin?"

"I just took some. I'll be fine by dinner. I just need a little quiet. That's all."

Kuklinski nodded to himself. She had said she was fine that time he went to Switzerland. He wasn't there thirty-six hours when he got a call from Merrick: "Mom's in the hospital. They don't know what's wrong." He got right back on a plane and rushed home to be with her.

He stood up from the bed. "You rest as long as you want. Okay? You can eat later." He started to go but then stopped and looked at the walls, narrowing his eyes and staring hard at them.

"This room needs another paint job," he said, more to himself than to his wife. "I can see the letters coming through."

Barbara looked up at him and sighed. "Don't start with that again, Rich. I keep telling you, it's your imagination."

"It's not my imagination. I can still see it."

"The painter used a special primer and three coats of paint to cover it. Believe me, you can't see it. It's your imagination."

He shook his head. He could still see it. The words he'd written on the walls in a moody rage one night when Barbara wouldn't listen to him, when that stupid telemarketing job was taking over her life, when she refused to quit after he told her she had to. Four-foot letters in black marker stretching across one wall and continuing onto the next, stopping abruptly at the wardrobe. LOVE HATE DEATH DEATH DEA—

Barbara closed her eyes and draped her arm over her face again. "Let me rest for a little while longer, Rich. I'll be down for dinner."

He didn't answer. He left the bedroom and went down the hall to the bathroom. Opening the medicine cabinet, he scanned the shelves. The green plastic Excedrin bottle was on the top shelf. He shook out two aspirin, popped them into his mouth, and chewed. He didn't have a headache, but he often took aspirin to prevent headaches. He had a feeling he was due.

He left the bathroom and headed for his office downstairs, passing the huge, gilt-framed oil painting of a vase full of flowers that hung in the foyer. He shut the office door behind him and glanced at his desk. The red light on the telephone answering machine was blinking. He switched on the desk lamp and saw that he had one message. He pressed the play button.

"*Rich, it's 'Tim.' I gotta talk to you. Today.*"

The hang-up was a curt bang. It had an attitude. "Tim" had an attitude, a bad attitude. "Tim" was the name John Sposato used on the phone just in case anyone was listening in. Sposato thought a lot of himself. He was under the mistaken impression that he was a somebody, that he mattered, that he could tell people what to do. He was wrong.

Kuklinski sat down at his desk. By rights John Sposato should have been dead by now, he thought as he reached over and picked up his attaché case from the floor, setting it on top of the desk. He opened it and took out his knife, a heavy-duty hunting knife with a curved six-inch blade. There were ten notches in the wooden handle, eight on one side, two on the other.

He left the knife in its leather sheath, held it in one hand, and slowly ran his thumbnail down the eight notches, one after the other. When he got to the bottom notch, he started again at the top.

Nobody got away with the kind of shit Sposato tried to pull. Not with Richard Kuklinski. That fat-ass slob had had the nerve to come to his house last month. *His house.* Came with two goddamn Puerto Ricans to collect money. *Came to his home.*

He had watched them from the upstairs window. Sposato sitting in his car like he was some kind of king while the spics came to the door and hassled Dwayne. They asked Dwayne where his father was, said they didn't believe him when Dwayne said his father wasn't home, said they wanted to come in and look for themselves. Kuklinski stood at the top of the stairs and listened to all this shit. He had a gun in his hand, and he was ready to shoot the two of them if they showed their faces inside the door. His home and his family were sacred, and anyone who messed with them was asking for trouble. Big trouble.

But Sposato didn't know how lucky he'd been that day. The spics didn't press their luck with Dwayne. They weren't stupid. They were probably afraid "Big Rich" was in there waiting for them.

Standing there, listening, he'd heard the two greaseballs telling Dwayne they'd be back later. He went to the window and saw them going back to their car. Kuklinski was ready to rush down and follow them in his car, run them off the road, shoot that bastard Sposato right through his fucking thick head. But a police car happened to pass by, and the cops stopped to see what these scumbags were doing in a neighborhood like this. Kuklinski stayed upstairs. If the cops hadn't shown up, Sposato and his two Puerto Ricans would be rotting together someplace right now. Sposato didn't know how lucky he'd been.

Later that day he had gotten Sposato on the phone and told him point-blank, "You do not come to my house. You do not talk to my family. You do not *look* at my family. Ever!" He threatened to go down to Sposato's place in south Jersey that very night to show Sposato he wasn't kidding.

That put the fear of God into Sposato for a little while because the fat slob knew Kuklinski would do it. But Sposato remained a problem. Sure, they'd been making money together, but Sposato seemed to feel that he was the senior partner from the way he'd been acting lately. He thought he could talk any way he wanted to Richard Kuklinski. He must have figured he had enough on Big Rich that he could throw his weight around. He was very wrong about that.

Sposato was going to die. There was no question about it. But not right away. Once again Sposato had gotten lucky.

As he ran his thumbnail down the notches in the wooden knife handle, it all started to jell in his mind.

He was going to be needing Sposato a little while longer because there was still money to be made with him, gun money. Dominick Provenzano had just given Sposato a new lease on life. Kuklinski's fingernail clicked down the notches as he thought this all out, considering all the angles.

Dominick wanted heavy steel, military weapons. Sposato had access to all kinds of weapons. If Dominick was on the up-and-up, he could make a nice profit brokering Sposato's merchandise to him.

But there was one thing Kuklinski had to take care of first, something that had been bothering him for a long time, clouding his thinking, making him crazy: Percy House and his woman, Barbara Deppner. Percy, the pointer. They *had* to be the ones who talked to those two cops, Kane and Volkman.

Percy House had been the "foreman" of a gang Kuklinski used to run. They mainly did burglaries and car thefts. But there were a few killings, too. Kuklinski ended up having to kill the two workers in the gang, Barbara Deppner's ex-husband, Danny, and her cousin Gary Smith. They had become weak and scared, and that made them liabilities. Percy House was stuck in jail at the time, so he couldn't keep them in line, and Kuklinski could not risk having Danny Deppner and Gary Smith out of his control—they knew too much.

Barbara Deppner hadn't exactly been an active member of the gang, but she always seemed to be around when things were going down and she had big ears. She and Percy had shacked up together with her eight kids when she was still married to Danny, and the word going around now was that the state had gotten to them. Kuklinski knew that the state police were very interested in him. And he was willing to bet that Percy and Barbara had spilled their guts to those two detectives—not completely, but just enough to keep their asses covered. Percy knew enough not to play all his aces. From what Kuklinski had heard, the state had even relocated the couple and given them new identities in exchange for their cooperation. But nobody hid from Richard Kuklinski. He had sources, he'd find them. And when he did, he'd have to get rid of them fast and quiet—no guns, no blood. That was why he needed cyanide. To take care of a couple of rats.

Kuklinski pressed his lips together and shook his head. Too bad he had gotten rid of "Mister Softee." At the time he didn't realize that you had to sign papers to buy pure cyanide and that it was sold only to companies that had a legitimate use for it. He couldn't risk trying to get it for himself, not now, not that way. The state cops would love to catch him buying cyanide. Somehow "Mister Softee" had never seemed to have any problem getting it. Kuklinski sucked his teeth and shook his head. If he'd only known.

He stared at the late-afternoon light coming through the blinds as he sorted it all out in his mind. The way he saw it he would first have to do the coke deal with Dominick Provenzano just to gain his trust; actually he didn't even need the stuff, but he wouldn't have any problem getting rid of it. Then once Dominick got him the cyanide, he'd do Percy and Barbara, get those two rats out of his life. Then he'd arrange a nice arms deal with Dominick, something big. He'd string Dominick along for a while, put the guy off a couple of times just to make him hungrier, then he would tell him he was having problems, that he was sorry but he was going to have to up the price a little. Maybe tell him he could get him something better to make the guy good and crazy. Finally he would tell Dominick to meet him someplace, Sposato's warehouse maybe. He'd tell him to bring cash. When Dominick showed up with the money, *boom!* One right in the back of the head. Stick his body in a steel drum, fill it with cement, then make it disappear. Nice and neat.

Kuklinski grinned at the thought of telling Sposato they'd be splitting a million in cash, maybe more, on the arms deal with Dominick. The grin grew into a toothy smile as he imagined Sposato's face as he held a gun in the fat bastard's face later on, after they'd gotten rid of Dominick's body, and he told Sposato he was taking *all* the money. It would almost be worth taking a picture just before he pulled the trigger.

Yes, yes. Sposato was going to die. No question about it. But not until Kuklinski took care of some business and made some money. Because that's what it was all about, really. Making money. It was only the green that counted.

Kuklinski clicked his thumbnail down the notches.

Percy House.

Barbara Deppner.

Dominick Provenzano.

John Sposato.

He let out a long sigh of satisfaction. He felt better now. He didn't think he was going to get that headache after all.

A short knock came from the other side of the door. "Daddy? Dinner's ready." It was Merrick.

"I'll be right there, honey."

He tossed the knife back into the attaché case, shut the lid, closed the latches, and set it on the floor beside the desk. He switched off the desk lamp and left his office.

The aroma of the baking lasagna filled the hallway. "Smells good," he called out as he headed for the kitchen.

He was hungry.

WEDNESDAY, SEPTEMBER 3, 1986—11:55 A.M.

The next day Richard Kuklinski sat at his desk and stared at the paper Dunkin' Donuts napkin in his hand. Dominick Provenzano's beeper number was written in ballpoint pen on the napkin. Kuklinski couldn't decide whether he should call him or not. He wanted to get things rolling with Dominick, but he didn't like going to people, coming right out and saying what he wanted. It made you seem desperate and put you in a weaker position. He preferred to have people come to him.

But he needed the cyanide. Percy House and Barbara Deppner were out there somewhere. They could get in a jam and start talking again. They would tell stories about him just to save themselves. They'd cut another deal with the state, agree to give up a bigger fish in exchange for dropped charges. They'd do it, no question. That's why Kuklinski needed the cyanide, and he shouldn't wait on this. Dominick said he could get it.

Kuklinski picked up the phone and punched out Dominick's number. He waited for the tone that gave him the go-ahead to enter his own phone number into the system. After it sounded, he hesitated for a second, then punched out his number. He hung up the phone and waited.

A half hour later the phone rang. He stared at it and let it ring a few times. He didn't want to seem anxious.

"Hello?"

"Hello. Rich?"

"Yeah."

"Dom."

"How ya doing?"

"Good, good. Yourself?"

"I'm okay."

"What's up?"

He glanced down at his briefcase on the floor. "Remember what we were talking about yesterday? The stuff we were talking about? The white stuff?"

"Yeah?" Dominick sounded cautious.

"Is it okay to talk?"

"Yeah, don't worry about it. I'm at a pay phone. How about you?"

"I'm at home."

"Oh." Dominick sounded cautious again, and suspicious.

"Listen, I was wondering. How much of that stuff could you get?"

"How much do you need?"

"A lot."

"How much is that, Rich? What're we talking about here?"

"Fifty."

"Sure, no problem." Dominick didn't hesitate. "Let's get together and we'll figure out the when and where."

"Yeah, okay. Soon as I know my buyer is serious, we'll get together."

"Whattaya mean, 'serious'? You never done business with this buyer before?" Dominick sounded upset.

"No, I've worked with the guy before. He knows I don't like no bullshit, so he's always been straight with me. When he knows for sure he can put the cash together, he'll call me. Then I'll call you."

"Oh."

"No sense our wasting our time for nothing, right? I like sure bets."

"Of course." Dominick still sounded suspicious.

"So you can get it?"

"I told you, no problem. My guy's good for it. All I need is two days' notice. Okay?" Dominick seemed very confident of his source.

"Soon as I know my buyer's good for the money, I'll call you."

"Great. I'll give my guy a call to make sure he's got stuff coming in. But don't worry. This guy's never run dry on me before."

"Good."

"Okay, Rich, you call me when you know something. I'll be talking to you—"

"How about that other stuff we talked about, Dom?" Kuklinski picked up the Dunkin' Donuts napkin.

"What stuff?"

"The other stuff."

"Oh, the stuff for the rats?"

"Yeah."

"I'm working on it. I got a call in to someone. I'm waiting to hear from him."

Kuklinski crumpled the napkin. "Okay. I just wanted to make sure you didn't forget."

Dominick laughed. "My friend, when it comes to business, I do not forget."

Kuklinski smiled into the phone. "That's what I like to hear."

"Okay, if you want to do this big order, you call me. Soon as I know about the other stuff, I'll call you. Can I usually get you at this number? Three-eight-five—?"

"Yeah. If I'm not here, the machine picks up."

"Okay then. I'll talk to you soon."

"Right. Take it easy, Dom."

Dominick hung up on his end. Kuklinski laid his receiver back on the cradle. He looked out the window at the backyard. *Bullshit*, he thought.

He picked up the phone and dialed the pay phone at "the store." It rang twice.

"Hello?"

"Is Lenny DePrima there?"

"Yeah, he's here. Who's this?"

"Tell him it's Rich."

"Who?"

"Just tell him it's Big Rich. He'll know."

"'Big Rich'? Okay."

He could hear the hubbub of "the store" coming through the line. Kuklinski picked up a pen, smoothed out the napkin, and drew a box around Dominick's phone number. There were very few people he trusted in the world. Lenny DePrima was one of them. Lenny had always played straight with him, no bullshit.

Someone finally came back to the phone. "Hello, Rich?"

"Yeah."

"Hey, how's it going?"

"I don't know yet."

"Huh? Whattaya mean, big guy?"

"This Dominick Provenzano—is he for real or what?"

"Sure, he's for real."

"How do you know?"

"Hey, Rich, if he wasn't for real, do you think I'd send him to you?"

"Yeah, but how do you *know* he's for real? What do you know about him?"

"I know he's connected."

"Yeah, right. Everybody's connected these days."

"No, for real. I heard that from someone else. I sold Dominick some stuff myself. He's always been good for it with me. I never had any problems with the guy."

"So you think he's for real."

"Hey, his cash is green, and he keeps his promises. That's about as real as he needs to be as far as I'm concerned."

"Yeah . . . I guess so." He underlined Dominick's phone number a few times. "As long as his cash is green, that's all that counts."

DePrima laughed. "You can say that again, brother."

"All right, I just wanted to make sure before I got into anything with him."

"He's okay, Rich. You don't have to worry about him."

"Tell me something. You hear anything about Buck lately." Buck was Percy House's nickname.

"Whatta'you, kidding? He knows better than to come around here, the bastard. I hope he's got cancer, the fuck."

"Nobody's seen him?"

"Nah. State's got him in protective custody. You know that. He won't be coming around here no more. Not after what he did."

Percy House had worn a wire for the police and got a kid in his own gang to admit on tape that he took part in a house robbery where a man was killed. The cops were dying to lock up somebody for that murder, and the kid was good enough. Thanks to Percy, he was serving a life sentence in Rahway now. Percy would rat on his own mother, Kuklinski felt. As for Barbara Deppner, she had helped Percy try to trap her own cousin Gary Smith into admitting to that murder, but Gary wouldn't talk about it. These two were inhuman. They'd turn in their own families. Richard Kuklinski knew he had to take care of them before they did any more damage.

"You still there, Rich?"

"Yeah, I'm here."

"Listen, don't worry about Dom. He's okay. And listen."

"What?"

"If you find Buck, you let me know. I know a lotta people around here who'd love to pay him a visit. You know what I mean?"

"I know. Take it easy, Lenny."

"Yeah, you, too, Rich."

He hung up the phone and swiveled his chair toward the window. Looking out through the venetian blinds, he could see the two small concrete lions on the patio. He was thinking about Gary Smith. Percy House and Barbara Deppner had to go to sleep the same way Gary had gone to sleep. Maybe not as messy as Gary had been, but he wanted them to go the same way. He ran the edge of his hand over the crumpled napkin on the desktop. That's why he needed the goddamn cyanide.

Thanksgiving 1982 had started out fine for Gary Smith. That morning while his wife, Veronica, prepared the turkey dinner in their kitchen in Highland Lakes, New Jersey, he and his six-year-old daughter, Melissa, cuddled on the couch in front of the TV to watch the Macy's Thanksgiving Day Parade. Gary got a big kick out of his daughter's excitement every time a new giant balloon creature filled the screen and she recognized the cartoon character.

Melissa was growing up, and Gary's feelings for her had changed. When she was younger, he'd pretty much taken her for granted. Veronica took care of the baby, and he worked—it was as simple as that. But Melissa wasn't a baby anymore. She was a kid, someone he could talk to and share things with. He was really beginning to enjoy being a father.

The house was warm with the smell of the roasting turkey by the time Percy House's wife, Connie, and her children arrived early in the afternoon. While Connie helped Veronica in the kitchen, the kids ran around the house, giggling and screaming, having a great time. Gary beamed as he watched little Melissa mixing in and playing with the bigger kids. She was having a ball.

Watching Melissa set Gary to thinking about his responsibilities again. For the past few months he'd been giving a lot of thought to this, and he'd pretty much made up his mind to quit Percy House's gang and go straight. He'd been with Percy a long time, but it wasn't like he was committed to being a crook for the rest of his life. He'd just sort of drifted into it about five years ago, when he couldn't find a job and he really needed money. Working for Percy, stealing cars and robbing stores, just scraping by—that was okay when Melissa was a baby and all she needed to keep her happy was a bag of cookies and Bugs Bunny on the TV set. But things had changed. Being a two-bit thief just didn't seem right anymore. It wouldn't be fair to Melissa if he kept on doing what he was doing. She needed a more stable life. That's why he wanted to go straight, and he intended to tell Percy that very day.

But when Percy showed up later that afternoon with Danny Deppner, the other worker in the gang, Gary's announcement did not get a warm reception. Percy scowled at him and just kept shaking his head. You don't understand, he kept saying. It's not that simple. You *can't* quit, Gary.

Danny sat on the couch, nodding like Howdy Doody, agreeing with everything Percy said. Danny didn't dare disagree with Percy. He was scared shitless of Percy. Percy beat him up regularly. At one point he'd made Danny live in his basement and would throw pizza crusts down to him as if he were a dog. Percy had said that Danny needed an "attitude adjustment." That was one way of putting it. Danny seemed to get a lot of "attitude adjustments" from Percy. Christ, Percy had even stolen Danny's wife. Just started shacking up with Barbara and took her for himself, and Danny didn't say boo. He didn't dare. Well, Gary wasn't Danny, and he didn't want to have to put up with any of that shit anymore. All he wanted was to go straight, period.

As the children ran around them, chasing each other through the living room, Gary tried to plead his case without begging. All he wanted to do was quit. Whatever they'd done together in the past was in the past. He'd never talk about it to anyone, never. He promised.

But Percy kept shaking his big ugly head, telling Gary he didn't understand, his face getting flushed, his growl getting louder. "You don't get it, Gary. You don't fucking get it, do you?"

"Whattaya mean, I don't get it?"

"You can't quit, Gary, and that's all there is to it. I'm not gonna let you out, and Richie sure as hell ain't gonna let you out either."

Gary's stomach sank. Richie Kuklinski. He'd been trying not to think about Richie. He'd hoped that maybe he'd only have to deal with Percy, the foreman of the gang, not Richie, the boss. Richie didn't come around all that much. He liked to keep his hands clean. That's why Gary thought he might be able to avoid a confrontation with him. Percy he could deal with. Percy was a bully, and he liked to use his fists, but Gary wasn't like Danny. He was a pretty big guy—six-two, 190 pounds—and he could stand up to Percy. Richie, on the other hand, was a real big son of a bitch, but that wasn't what made him scary. When Percy got mad at you, he stayed mad until he blew up and burned himself out. When Richie got mad, his temper might explode, but then all of a sudden it would pass and he'd be real calm as if nothing had ever happened. But Gary knew that Richie never forgot; he just waited.

By the time the women called everybody to the table, Gary didn't have much of an appetite, though Percy and Danny ate like there was no tomorrow. Gary felt like he'd spent the last two hours talking to a brick wall. Later, after pumpkin pie and coffee, Percy took Gary out onto the porch and picked up the discussion where they'd left it, trying to make Gary understand in his blunt way why he couldn't quit.

Richie was already upset with him, Percy explained. All this talk about going legit for his daughter's sake was getting on everybody's nerves. What was he, getting soft? What would he do if the cops leaned on him? Was he gonna be a real upstanding citizen and tell them about everything he'd done with the gang? Is that what going straight was all about? He had to get his head right about this. They weren't all gonna take a fall because Gary had decided he wanted to play *Father Knows Best* all of a sudden.

Gary tried to make Percy understand that he wasn't going to do that. He would never rat on anyone in a million years.

But Percy kept shaking his head, saying that the best thing he could do would be to just be a good boy and do what he was told because Richie already had it in for him and you never get to strike three with Richie.

Gary didn't even have to ask what Richie had against him. He knew. Billy Cudnyg's goddamn black Corvette.

Richie had a thing for new Corvettes. They'd stolen a bunch of them that year for him. Usually they got them right off the lot from car dealerships. Percy would go in during the day and make like he wanted to buy one. He'd ask the salesman to see the bill of sale to see what the dealer was paying for the car so that they could negotiate. Usually salesmen had no problem with that. Except that Percy wasn't interested in the price. He was interested in the eight-digit key number. Percy would stare at the sheet and memorize the number, then afterward he'd go to a locksmith and have a duplicate key made from that number. A couple of nights later either Danny or Gary would take the key, unlock the car, and drive it right off the lot, easy as that.

But Cudnyg's car was different. They didn't steal that one. Billy Cudnyg, one of the guys who hung out at "the store," owned it for real. Richie had figured he could make a profit on both ends with that one. He and Cudnyg would split the insurance money when Cudnyg reported the car stolen, then Richie would sell the car to a guy he dealt with up in Connecticut and get about a quarter of the book price for it. When Cudnyg started having second thoughts about doing this, Richie convinced him it would all work out fine. Besides, as he pointed out to Cudnyg, he already had duplicate keys to the car because he'd rented it from the man a couple of times, so he could go ahead and steal it anyway and cut Cudnyg out completely. Billy Cudnyg had no choice but to go along with the scam.

On December 21, 1981, the theft was staged at the Willowbrook Mall in Fairfield, New Jersey. The car ended up with Gary Smith, who was supposed to keep it hidden until Richie was ready to bring it up to Connecticut. Gary kept the car at his house for two weeks, but it was making him nervous, so he moved it around from place to place, wondering when the hell Richie would take it off his hands. By February he was running out of hiding places he could trust, so he left it with a woman he used to work for when he was a teenager. Unfortunately the police happened to spot the stolen car in her driveway. After checking the Vehicle Identification Number plate on the dashboard to confirm that it was indeed the stolen Corvette, they had it towed away.

The car was returned to Billy Cudnyg. Kuklinski was furious when he found out about it. That was strike one against Gary. Three weeks later the car had to be stolen a second time. This time Kuklinski traded it to a man from Bloomfield, New Jersey, for a vintage 1964 Corvette coupe.

Afterward everybody kept throwing it up to Gary, needling him about the black Corvette that had to be stolen twice, Richie warning him not to lose any more cars or else he'd be very sorry. Gary was getting sick of hearing this shit. It wasn't his fault. If he had thought the cops would've spotted the car in that lady's driveway, he would never have left it there, for chrissake. But they kept on his back about it, and that was when he started thinking that maybe he wasn't cut out to be a thief. Maybe he ought to start thinking about getting into another line of work where the bosses weren't like Percy and Richie.

For weeks after that Thanksgiving dinner, Gary mulled over his position in the gang. He really wanted out, but it looked like he was going to have to ease himself out gradually, maybe stay with them through the winter, then slack off, get a real job, start avoiding Percy, and maybe by spring they'd leave him alone.

But then on December 17, 1982, the shit hit the fan and everything got crazy.

Gary Smith, Danny Deppner, Percy House, Barbara Deppner, and several of her children were driving to her mother's house in West Milford. They were going there to drop the kids off for the day. As they approached the house, they noticed a police car parked off the road, backed up into the woods. Percy was immediately suspicious. It wasn't the kind of road where the police would post a speed trap. When they got to Barbara's mother's house, they saw that her car wasn't in the driveway. Percy ordered Gary and Danny to get out and go hide in the woods behind the house. He figured that if the cops were up to something, having the gang all together would give them a reason to haul them in.

Percy's instincts were right. When he and Barbara backed out of the driveway and drove up to a stop sign at the top of the hill, police cars came out of nowhere and surrounded their station wagon. As the police emerged from their vehicles with guns drawn, shouting for Percy and Barbara to show their hands and not move, the frightened children wailed in the backseat. Percy snapped at them and told them to shut up. This was all a lot of bullshit. He'd been through this before. These sons of bitches were just out to hassle him, he figured.

But Percy was wrong about that. Passaic County had a seventy-nine-count indictment against him for an assortment of offenses, including theft and forgery of motor vehicle registrations. The cops weren't just out to hassle him this time. Their intention was to put him and his gang away. They had arrest warrants for Gary and Danny, too.

As the police leaned Percy House over the hood of the station wagon to handcuff him while they read him his rights, he looked over at pregnant Barbara Deppner clutching her screaming baby.

He didn't have to say a word. His sad, baggy eyes said it all. She knew right away what he wanted her to do. Call Richie. She looked around at the faces of all the policemen. They were all focused on Percy. She nodded to him that she understood.

Later that day she caught up with her cousin Gary and her ex-husband, Danny, at Gary's house. Veronica, Gary's wife, was hysterical. Detective Pat Kane of the state police had been there earlier with a search warrant. He was looking for Gary. Danny and Gary were frantic. They were on foot, they didn't have much money, and they didn't want to get caught hanging around there, so Barbara drove them to the Sussex Motel in Vernon, where she rented a room and they all spent the night. She had already gotten in touch with Richie, right after Percy was arrested.

Barbara didn't have that much money herself, but Danny had just put down a security deposit on a house in Lake Hopatcong, so the next morning they drove there in the hope that Danny could get the deposit back. But the landlord wasn't around when they got there, and they didn't want to stick around. They all piled back into the station wagon and headed east on Route 80. Richard Kuklinski had instructed Barbara to take Gary and Danny to some place called Paul's Diner on Route 3 somewhere in Hudson County.

Forty-five minutes later they pulled into the parking lot of Paul's Diner. A white Cadillac with a blue top was parked at the far end of the lot all by itself. Richard Kuklinski was sitting behind the wheel. Barbara pulled the station wagon up alongside the Cadillac and rolled down her window. The Cadillac's power window glided down, and Kuklinski looked right through her, glaring at Danny and Gary.

"Follow me," he said.

"Where we going?" she asked.

He narrowed his eyes, and his stare bore into her. Her fingers were suddenly freezing. "Just follow me," he repeated. His window glided up, and the Cadillac's engine roared to life.

Barbara Deppner followed him to the Liberty Motel in North Bergen, where Kuklinski gave Danny some money and he rented a room under the name Jack Bush. Relieved to have the fugitives out of her car, Barbara headed straight back to her sister's place, where she'd left her children.

Percy, in the meantime, was stuck in the Passaic County jail, being pressed for the whereabouts of his associates Gary Smith and Danny Deppner. He repeatedly told the police that he didn't know where they were, but the cops kept hounding him. Actually Percy wanted to know where they were and what they were doing himself, particularly Gary. He didn't trust Gary anymore, hadn't trusted him since Thanksgiving. Gary still had it in his head that he could reform himself, and Percy feared that if the cops got to him, he'd want to cooperate just to show them what a real good citizen he was now. Gary would turn on them, sure as shit. He was a time bomb waiting to go off. Sitting in his cell, Percy got the sweats just thinking about it. He'd done time before, but he'd never gotten used to the feeling of being locked up. The thought of doing another long stretch was making him short of breath. He couldn't do it, he just couldn't. He'd go crazy. He needed to know where the hell Gary was, but the goddamn cops weren't letting him make any calls. For three days he waited, barely containing his panic until finally they let him have a visitor, Barbara Deppner.

Sitting across the table from Percy in a room with guards within earshot, Barbara told him not to worry because the big guy was baby-sitting the boys. Percy was still uneasy. He leaned forward, smiling sweetly for the guards' benefit, and growled in her face. "Tell Richie to send Gary to Florida."

A chill ran through Barbara Deppner's veins. She knew exactly what he meant. Send Gary to Florida. Send him away. Have him killed. Gary was her cousin, but Percy had been ranting and raving for months about how dangerous Gary had become to them. To her, too. She could be charged as an accomplice. She could go to jail, too. The thought terrified her. Who would watch all her kids?

And what would happen to the one she was carrying now? Would she have to deliver the baby in jail, then give it up immediately? No. She wasn't about to let that happen. Gary was her cousin, but Percy was right. Gary was dangerous.

The next day she drove down to the Liberty Motel, where Gary and Danny were hiding, to deliver Percy's message. Danny was in the room with Kuklinski when she arrived. Gary had gone out to get a soda.

She spoke quickly, fearing that Gary would walk in on them. "Percy says you should send Gary to Florida."

Kuklinski was sitting in the one armchair in the room, seemingly lost in thought. She started to repeat it, but he cut her off. "I heard what you said."

A few minutes later Gary returned with a couple of cans of Coke. She was startled to see his bruised face. He kept his eyes down, barely saying hello to her. Kuklinski explained to her that Gary had been a bad boy last night. First he had gotten caught shoplifting at the convenience store across the street, and the manager had almost called the cops on him. Then he'd hitchhiked home so he could see his wife and daughter. Danny whittled his index fingers at Gary, shame-shame. Then he balled his fist and nodded toward Kuklinski. "A little attitude adjustment," Danny whispered.

Richie was staring at Gary sitting on the bed.

Barbara's heart started to pound.

The next day, December 23, 1982, Kuklinski moved the fugitives again, to another motel in North Bergen, the York Motel, a two-story green stucco building perched on the edge of the rocky palisades on Route 3, five minutes from the Lincoln Tunnel. Again, Kuklinski gave Danny Deppner some cash and sent him into the office to rent a room. Under the blinking glare of multicolored Christmas lights strung around the plate glass window, Danny signed the register as Jack Bush and took the key to Room

31, a first-floor room that faced the narrow parking lot and a wall of gray jagged rock beyond.

At five o'clock that afternoon Barbara Deppner arrived at the York Motel at Richard Kuklinski's request. She had her baby daughter, Jennifer, with her. When Kuklinski had called her, he didn't say why he wanted her there, but she knew better than to question Big Richie. He was obviously unhappy with the whole situation, and she prayed he wouldn't take it out on her.

When she knocked on the door to Room 31, Danny answered. Through the doorway she could see Gary moping on the bed. Kuklinski wasn't there. Danny told her to go over to the coffee shop at the Holiday Inn down the hill. He'd meet her there in a little while.

Over an hour later Danny finally showed up. Sounding as desperate as Percy had sounded in jail, he told her "the plan." They were going to kill Gary tonight. They had to. He'd hitchhiked home again, and Richie was pissed as shit. Gary was gonna rat on them. He had to go. Richie was gonna bring them some hamburgers later. The one without the pickles would have poison on it. That was the one they would give to Gary.

Barbara clutched her baby so close the infant started to scream. She didn't want to hear about it. She didn't want to know. Then her ex-husband informed her that Richie wanted her to come back later that night with the car so they could dump Gary's body.

Barbara couldn't answer. Her throat ached. She started to shake her head, but Danny started shaking his.

"Better not say no," he warned her. "Richie'll get mad."

Danny was serious.

But even though she didn't say anything to Danny, she made up her mind on the spot. She wasn't coming back. She didn't want any part of this. As she drove out of the parking lot of the Holiday Inn, she was determined to go home and stay home. She loved Percy, and she felt sorry for Danny, but Gary was her cousin, for God's sake.

＊　＊　＊

Later that evening Richard Kuklinski returned to the York Motel with a bag of hamburgers and french fries. Gary and Danny were hungry. They didn't have any money, and they hadn't eaten all day. As Kuklinski handed out the burgers, he exchanged glances with Danny Deppner. Danny unwrapped his hamburger and lifted the bun. He checked to make sure his had pickles on it.

Gary unwrapped his and dug in. But as Kuklinski watched him devouring the food, he wondered why the hell the cyanide was taking so long.

Then it happened. Gary had eaten better than half of the hamburger when it finally started to work.

Gary Smith dropped the burger and fell back on the bed where he was sitting. His throat was on fire straight down to his stomach. The room was spinning, and he felt as if his face were going to explode.

He knew Richie was going to kill him. He'd known it all along, and now it was happening. In his last moments he pictured his daughter Melissa's room the way it was two nights before, when he'd hitchhiked home. He'd gone back there to say good-bye to her. She was sleeping, and he didn't have the heart to wake her up. His wife was in the doorway, whispering to him, begging him not to go back to the motel, that Richie would kill him.

"I know," he'd murmured, and he started to cry. The tears streamed down his face and spattered the sheet around Melissa's chin as he bent down to kiss her good-bye for the last time.

"I have to go back," he told his wife as he walked past her, heading for the front door. Richie had threatened him after he had hitchhiked home the first time. Richie had promised that if he tried to run away again, he'd find Melissa and he'd kill her. Richie hadn't yelled or screamed the way Percy did when he made threats. He said it nice and calm, just a plain statement of fact, a reality of life. There was no question in Gary's mind that Richie would do it. That's why he had to go back to the York Motel. For Melissa.

Blurry shapes loomed over Gary as he started to black out.

Danny and Richie were laughing at him. "Look at his eyes," Danny said. "Look at his eyes. They're all goofy."

They kept laughing at Gary as he choked and writhed on the bed. But then Richard Kuklinski stopped laughing. Gary wasn't dying fast enough. Maybe he hadn't eaten enough. Maybe there wasn't enough cyanide in his system.

He looked around the room for something they could use to finish Gary off. There were two lamps in the room, one on either side of the bed.

Danny saw the lamps, too. He wasn't laughing now. This wasn't the way it was supposed to go down. Gary was supposed to die fast. Instead, he was choking, making too much goddamn noise. Someone was gonna hear him. Why the hell wasn't he dead yet? He'd eaten the damn hamburger.

Danny unplugged one of the lamps, stepped on the cord, and jerked it out of the base. Wrapping the ends of the cord around his hands, he went to the bed, put one knee on the mattress, and hovered over Gary. His heart was pounding as he looped the cord around Gary's neck and yanked Gary back. Gary put up no resistance. Danny held him tight, jerking him back and up as if he were riding a wild horse. He pulled so hard, the cord snapped. Gary flopped back on the bed. Danny quickly took the longest piece of cord and wrapped it around Gary's neck again, continuing to strangle him even though he wasn't moving anymore. When his hands started to cramp, he finally let got.

Danny looked at Kuklinski, panting for breath. "Is he dead, Rich? Or should I do some more? What do you think?"

Four days later, on December 27, 1982, the guests in Room 31 called the motel office to complain that there was an awful stink in their room. They said it was coming from the bed.

The bed in Room 31 was a simple wooden frame built to support a mattress and box spring. The space under the box spring was hollow and completely enclosed. As the manager walked out into the cold without a coat to go see what the problem was, all he could think was that somebody must have left some food or something under the bed and forgotten about it. One of the goddamn maids probably.

But the stink in Room 31 was unlike any rotting food he'd ever smelled. He got his fingers under the box spring and mattress and lifted them off the frame. The stench made his eyes water. Then he saw the face, and he dropped the mattress. He ran back out into the cold and went to the office to call the police.

The first two officers on the scene held handkerchiefs to their faces as they shined a flashlight into the space under the mattress. When they called in their report of the body found under the bed, they identified the deceased as "an overweight black male."

Sealed in the enclosed space under that bed in an overheated room over the Christmas weekend, Gary Smith's body had decomposed rapidly. He was so bloated, the buttons were popping on his plaid flannel shirt. His tongue was so swollen, it protruded from blubbery lips. His eyes were dull and milky. His skin was charcoal black.

FRIDAY, SEPTEMBER 5, 1986

Special Agent Dominick Polifrone checked his watch as he strode down the hallway at the offices of the state Organized Crime and Racketeering Bureau in Fairfield. It was almost 7:00 P.M. Now that he'd finally made contact with Kuklinski, Operation Iceman was in full swing. The special task force targeting Kuklinski had basically amounted to a lot of promises, theory, and intention until three days ago. Now it was time to get down to business.

The door to the conference room where they were scheduled to meet was open. Dominick glanced around the long table as he walked into the room. He recognized the three men in plainclothes, but he didn't know the man in uniform. Dominick could see from the uniform that he was a captain in the state police, and he appeared to be in his mid-fifties.

"Gentlemen," Dominick said, "how goes it?"

"Hey, Dom, how's it going?"

"Che se dice, Dominick?"

"How ya doing, Dom?"

Investigators Paul Smith and Ron Donahue of the state's Organized Crime and Racketeering Bureau and their boss, Deputy Chief Robert T. Buccino, got up to shake his hand. The captain stood up, waiting for an introduction.

"Dominick, this is Captain Brealy," Buccino said.

"Nice to meet you, Captain." Dominick shook his hand.

Captain Brealy smiled and nodded. "I've heard a lot about you, Agent Polifrone. I hear that you've lived up to your reputation this week."

Dominick's brows furrowed. "Excuse me, Captain?"

"You've met the Iceman at long last. We're all very happy to be making some progress on this thing finally."

Dominick was ready to take this the wrong way, but he let it pass. "Yes, Captain," he said with a smile, "I'm very happy, too."

"So, Dom, did you see our friend today?" Paul Smith nodded at an eight-by-ten surveillance photo taped to the wall that showed Richard Kuklinski getting into his car. With his smooth unlined face, big mischievous smile, and thick hair, Paul Smith looked like a kid compared with the others. He was in his mid-thirties, but he could easily pass for someone ten years younger. "I know you went for coffee with him, Dom. I hope you didn't let him buy you a hamburger."

Ron Donahue snorted up a laugh. Ronny was the crusty grand old man of the Organized Crime and Racketeering Bureau, an old-fashioned Irish cop who didn't take any guff and sure as hell knew how to dish it out. Though he rarely talked about himself, anyone who was anyone in law enforcement in the state of New Jersey seemed to have a good Ron Donahue story. Wiseguys throughout the state despised him, and Mafia defendants routinely booed and jeered at him in open court whenever he showed his face. He was that good.

Deputy Chief Buccino rolled his eyes and chuckled. Unless you knew him, it was hard to believe that Bobby Buccino had spent most of his career with the spit-and-polish state police, retiring as a lieutenant. With his round face, ready smile, and easygoing manner, he looked like everybody's favorite uncle—except to those who'd seen him in action.

As Dominick took a seat at the end of the table, he squinted and pointed a menacing finger at the young investigator. "Smith, I should've killed you when I had the chance."

The men howled with laughter, except for Captain Brealy, who just looked confused and a little put off by their private joke.

"You see, Captain," Dominick explained, "two years ago I was working an undercover down in Monmouth County, posing as a bad guy, same as I'm doing now with Kuklinski. Well, there was this accountant down there who approached me about doing a hit for him. The guy was under investigation for the murder of his partner. He asked me if I could get rid of this investigator from the state who was on his tail. An investigator named Paul Smith." He scowled at Paul and shook his head. "I could've done it and gotten *paid* for it. What was I thinking?"

Paul Smith pressed his fingers to his eyes he was laughing so hard. Captain Brealy still looked puzzled.

A big man in a dark blue suit breezed into the room then and hung his jacket over the back of the seat next to Dominick. "Sorry I'm late, gentlemen." Deputy Attorney General Robert J. Carroll of the Division of Criminal Justice was built like a pro football player, and in fact, he had played tackle for Wake Forest. Once a street investigator for the Essex County Prosecutor's Office, he had worked his way through Seton Hall University law school at night. The attorney general of New Jersey, W. Cary Edwards, considered Bob Carroll the state's top investigative attorney. When the Kuklinski file had landed on the desk of the director of the Division of Criminal Justice, Robert T. Winter, he reviewed the case and, recognizing its importance, passed it on to Carroll for evaluation. After spending the weekend with the file, Carroll came up with several investigative possibilities, and within a month the Operation Iceman task force was formed with Bob Carroll as the man in charge.

The deputy attorney general loosened his tie and sat down. "So what have I missed?"

"Nothing. I just got here," Dominick said. "Kuklinski called me again on the beeper this morning. That's the second time in three days. He wanted to know if my source came through with the cyanide yet. I told him cyanide was a hot item right now because of the Lipton soup thing down in Camden, but I told him to hang tight, I'd get it for him."

Earlier that week, purely by coincidence, a New Jersey man had died of cyanide poisoning. Traces of the poison were found in the Lipton instant chicken noodle soup he had eaten for lunch. The story had been all over the papers, and the timing was perfect for Dominick. It gave him a good excuse for not being able to get Kuklinski the cyanide he wanted right away. But Dominick knew he wouldn't be able to put the guy off indefinitely.

Bob Carroll pulled a yellow legal pad out of his briefcase and started to take notes. "Did you discuss anything else?"

"I told him I would also get him the coke he wanted, but I was all tied up right now getting guns and shit for my big customer. He told me he was gonna be talking to his source today to see if he could get me the kind of arms I need. He promised to get back to me. I asked him if I could get in touch with him at the number he beeped me with. He said I could use that number, but that I should be careful what I say when I call him."

Dominick looked from Bob Carroll to Bobby Buccino. "Now what have you decided about the cyanide? If I keep making excuses, he'll think I'm a bullshitter and that'll be the end of that. He'll disappear. I've gotta give him something."

Buccino's smile flipped over, and he shook his head. "Can't give him the real thing. No way. He'll use it."

"Yeah, but you can't give him fake stuff either," Paul Smith pointed out. "He's used it before. He knows what cyanide's like. He may know it's bogus the minute he sees it."

Ron Donahue gave Paul Smith a sour look. "What the hell's

wrong with you, Paulie? You can't give Kuklinski the real stuff. What if he tries to use it on Dominick?"

"Yeah, but if we give him a fake and he finds out, we'll lose him," Smith said. "Then again, if we give him nothing, we may still lose him."

Captain Brealy extended two fingers in order to be recognized. "May I suggest something? We have several qualified undercover people in the state police. Let's introduce one of our people to Kuklinski, say, as Dominick's cyanide contact. It would ease some of the pressure of having to make excuses to the man, and it would give us the security of having two men. . . ."

Dominick tuned the captain out. He had been afraid of this. Cooperation between law enforcement agencies was almost unheard of, and Operation Iceman was a very unusual three-way marriage, two state agencies with a federal agent by himself out on the line. But Dominick had a feeling something like this would happen sooner or later. Someone would decide that he needed "help" with the undercover end.

"Frankly, Captain," Dominick said, "introducing a new man to Kuklinski wouldn't be a very good idea at this point. I just met the guy. We know he's very cautious. If I try to introduce somebody new to him now, he'll back off. We'll lose him."

Captain Brealy raised one eyebrow. "You don't know that for sure. You say Kuklinski is desperate for cyanide. If he's that desperate, I think he'll deal with a new person."

Dominick bit his tongue before he said something he'd regret. "Captain, with all due respect, I've been doing undercover work for a very long time. I know what it's like out there and I know how bad guys think. Kuklinski may be desperate for cyanide, but he's not stupid. The man has been an active killer for at least six years. No matter how badly he needs the poison, self-preservation is his highest priority. If he gets suspicious because all of a sudden there are too many new faces in his life, I'll lose him, and I won't get him back. I guarantee it."

The captain leaned forward on his elbow and fixed Dominick with a stare like a bald eagle. "You seem awfully confident of your instincts." He shifted his gaze to the deputy attorney general. "It seems awfully foolhardy to hinge an entire operation on one man's gut feelings."

Bob Carroll started to explain why Dominick had been specially recruited for this job, how his unique undercover abilities had been invaluable in the arrests and convictions of dozens of Mafia members over the years.

But Dominick was only half listening. Obviously Captain Brealy did not believe that Dominick Polifrone was any different from any other undercover agent. He had to be convinced that Dominick actually was unique. Dominick stared the captain in the eye and became "Michael Dominick Provenzano."

"Excuse me, excuse me," he said, interrupting Bob Carroll. "With all due respect, sir, I think there's something you don't understand here. Richie Kuklinski is a mother*fucker*, a cocksucking mother*fucker*. He kills people the way the rest of us go take a shit. He just does it, doesn't even think about it. It's his right. That's how he thinks. If he wants something bad enough, he'll fuck you, he'll fuck me, he'll fuck anybody he has to to get it. He also thinks a lot of himself. He thinks he's hot shit. So if he doesn't *respect* you, he won't bother with you. And to get Richie Kuklinski's respect, you gotta be a mother*fucker* just like him. No, worse."

Captain Brealy was sitting back in his seat, stunned. All cops curse to one extent or another in order to assert themselves, but Dominick Polifrone was the master of the ballistic "fuck." Normally he didn't like to curse, but when he had to, he could use the word like a weapon. When he cursed, you felt as if you'd been whacked in the chest with a lead pipe.

The room fell silent. Bob Carroll was tapping his pen against his lips. Paul Smith was struggling to contain his grin. The captain coughed into his fist. He looked as if he were about to respond to Dominick when someone's beeper suddenly went off.

"It's mine," Dominick said, pulling the small device out of the pocket of his leather jacket. He looked at the phone number on the LCD readout. "It's Richie," he said. "The home number."

"There's a phone right there," Captain Brealy said, nodding to the sideboard behind Dominick. "Call him."

Dominick shook his head. "Let him wait."

The captain's eyes shot open. "Let him wait? You'll lose him, for God's sake. Call him back."

"No. I'm not gonna suck up to him. He has to come to me."

Captain Brealy frowned and looked to Bob Carroll. "Is *this* how your office plans to run this investigation?"

The deputy attorney general tucked in his chin and blew out his cheeks. He looked sideways at Dominick. "Maybe you could—"

Dominick held up his hand and cut him off. "Lemme tell you something, Captain. The name of this game is control. If I go running to him every time he calls, he's gonna think I'm bullshit. And once he thinks that, he's not gonna want anything to do with me. That's why he's got to come to *me*. *I've* gotta call the shots. Not him. *I* have to maintain control over *him*, not the other way around."

Captain Brealy focused on Bob Carroll. "Who's running this investigation, Mr. Carroll? I wasn't aware that ATF was running the show."

"This is a joint effort, Captain. Alcohol, Tobacco, and Firearms is *participating*, not supervising."

"It doesn't seem that way to me."

Bob Carroll sat back in his chair and said nothing for a moment. His face was placid but determined, the defensive tackle waiting for the snap. "I have every confidence in Agent Polifrone's abilities, Captain. I plan to rely on his expertise as far as the undercover phase of this investigation goes."

Captain Brealy didn't back down. "Well, I'm beginning to question the federal agent's judgment. I'm going to have to call my headquarters in Trenton and see what they decide."

"You can call anywhere you want, Captain, but this decision will be made in this room. And it's already been made," Carroll said.

Brealy glared at the deputy attorney general as he pointed at the beeper in Dominick's hand. "The target has made contact. I believe we should respond."

Dominick tossed the beeper down onto the table and looked at Brealy. "I do plan to respond, Captain. But not now. Richie's gonna wait until *I'm* ready to talk to him."

Captain Brealy frowned at Dominick, then shot an angry glance at every man in the room. His chest was heaving. He was pissed.

Dominick sat back and crossed his arms over his chest. He wondered how long this happy marriage would last.

It was twenty after midnight when Dominick finally got home that night, and everyone was in bed. He was too wound up to go to sleep, so he poured himself three fingers of scotch, lit a cigar, and went out on the deck. He sat down in his favorite redwood chair and stared into the woods beyond his backyard. The Polifrones lived in northern Bergen County, about five miles from Kuklinski's home in Dumont.

At nine-thirty Dominick had returned Kuklinski's call from the Organized Crime Bureau offices in Fairfield. Kuklinski said he wanted to get together to discuss the arms deal. He wanted to meet tomorrow at the Vince Lombardi Service Area off the New Jersey Turnpike in Ridgefield. Dominick told him he couldn't make it, he was busy. Kuklinski told Dominick he'd bring his source, who would tell him just what kind of weapons he could get. Dominick repeated that he was too busy right now. He told Kuklinski to call him over the weekend.

Dominick drew on his cigar. Kuklinski was baiting the hook, offering to introduce him to his gun source. Dominick knew better than to bite at that one. Why would Kuklinski link him up with his source? Dominick could do an end run around the middleman and cut a deal directly with the source, leaving Richie out in the cold.

Kuklinski was smarter than that. What he was really doing was trying to lure Dominick out. But why? And why at the Lombardi Service Area?

At the meeting of the task force earlier that evening they hadn't decided what to do about Richie's request for cyanide. All they could agree on was that they would not give him the real thing. Whether Dominick would give him a fake substance or continue to stall him indefinitely was left unsettled. And that had left Dominick unsettled.

At one time Kuklinski had his own source for cyanide, so it was possible that he could go back to that source. Dominick kept thinking about the Vince Lombardi Service Area, having coffee with Kuklinski at the Roy Rogers there, Richie sneaking cyanide in his coffee. . . .

Okay, if they went for coffee, he wouldn't let Kuklinski get the food, never. He'd watch Richie and the food from the moment it left the fast-food counter.

But logically Kuklinski had no reason to kill him. There was no profit motive, no money to be made. Why kill Michael Dominick Provenzano, a guy with Mafia connections? Kuklinski knew better than to screw with a connected guy.

Unless he knew that Dominick wasn't connected. Unless he knew that Dominick was really a cop. What if Kuklinski's old buddy Lenny DePrima from "the store" had warned him? What if DePrima was playing both sides of the fence?

Dominick took a long sip of scotch and considered that possibility. If a wiseguy ever found out you were an undercover cop, you'd get the beating of your life, but he wouldn't kill you, not on purpose. It was mob policy. But Richard Kuklinski might not show the same kind of restraint.

Dominick tried not to think about what the Iceman might do to him if he ever found out who he really was. Maybe he'd freeze him like that guy from Pennsylvania. Maybe worse. Maybe a lot worse. Maybe he'd cut him up and dispose of the parts. They'd never find his body. Maybe put him in a junk car and let the crusher pack it down to the size of a steamer trunk. Maybe—

"Dominick?"

He jumped, spilling his drink. He looked up to see his wife, Ellen, silhouetted in the floodlights. She was in her robe, her dark hair tousled.

"Why don't you come to bed, Dom? It's late."

Dominick's eyes were wide open. His heart was pounding. "Yeah . . . I will. Soon as I finish my cigar."

Ellen nodded and went back inside.

Dominick drew on his cigar and stared into the dark woods. His heart was still pounding.

Early in the afternoon of July 1, 1981, Louis L. Masgay left his home in Forty Fort, Pennsylvania, twenty miles south of Scranton, and headed for Little Ferry, New Jersey. Masgay, who was fifty years old, owned and operated Leisure City, a discount variety store, in nearby Plymouth, Pennsylvania. Before he left, he told his wife that he was going to New Jersey to meet a supplier who had agreed to sell him a large quantity of blank videotapes at a very good discount. To make this purchase, he was going to use all his savings in addition to a forty-five-thousand-dollar loan he had obtained from a local bank, the First National Bank of Wyoming. He was taking the money in cash, nearly a hundred thousand dollars, which he had stashed in a concealed compartment in the driver's side door of his black 1980 Ford Carry Van. The "supplier" he was going to meet was Richard Kuklinski.

As he backed out of his driveway that afternoon, Louis Masgay was anxious and a little apprehensive. He'd already traveled to New Jersey five times in the past month to meet Kuklinski and conclude this deal, but Kuklinski had stood him up each time. There was always a problem. Each time Masgay would come home, his van empty, and

Richie would call a few days later to apologize and tell him that his connection had screwed him up again but that he had another connection who could get him more tapes, only this guy's price was a little bit higher than the last guy so Masgay would have to bring a little more cash next time. Masgay had wanted to tell Richie to go to hell, forget about it, but even with the increase, Kuklinski's price was still very good. Too good to pass up really. He knew he could move those tapes at his store and make a nice profit. But this was going to be Richie's last chance. If Kuklinski stood him up this time, he *would* tell him to go to hell.

Masgay's son, Lou Junior, worked for his father and was already on his way to pick up a load in New York that day. Since they were going to be in the same area, they agreed to meet at the Golden Star Diner in Little Ferry, New Jersey, where Louis Masgay always ate when he was picking up merchandise in the northern part of that state. Lou Junior did meet his father at the diner where they had coffee together. He asked his father if he wanted any help loading the videotapes. Masgay assured his son that he wouldn't need any help and told him to head on home so he wouldn't miss his regular bowling night.

But Louis Masgay did not return home that night, and his wife started to worry. This was unusual for him. He always let her know if he was going to be staying away overnight so she'd know where he'd be. By midnight Mrs. Masgay had called the Forty Fort police and filed a missing persons report with Detective Henry Winters. Detective Winters asked Mrs. Masgay and her son to try to remember as many details as they could, what Mr. Masgay had said before he left, where he was going, whom he was going to see, how he appeared at the diner in New Jersey, what his mood was—anything they could think of. The next morning Detective Winters contacted the Bergen County Sheriff's Department in New Jersey and notified them that Louis Masgay was last seen in their jurisdiction.

Several days later Detective Winters learned that Louis Masgay's black 1980 Ford Carry Van had been found abandoned on Route 17 North in Rochelle Park, Bergen County, New Jersey. It was found on a narrow stretch of the highway where there is no shoulder, and the van was blocking the right lane of traffic. The cab was locked, and the police had to break in to move it. They found that the primary gas tank was empty, but the secondary tank was full, leading them to suspect that whoever was driving the van did not know how to engage the reserve tank. A hidden compartment in the driver's side door was also discovered, but it was empty.

Detective Winters pursued the case for more than two years with little satisfaction. At times he felt that the authorities in New Jersey just weren't very interested in pursuing the case of Louis Masgay. Except for the Masgay family and Detective Winters, no one seemed to care about the missing man.

Then, in September 1983, a body was found in a wooded area off Causeland Mountain Road in Orangetown, New York, three miles north of the New Jersey border. The body was taken to the Office of the Rockland County Medical Examiner, where the chief ME, Dr. Frederick Zugibe, performed the autopsy.

The body had been carefully trussed with tape and then wrapped in fifteen to twenty plastic garbage bags, a task that must have taken some time and effort, Dr. Zugibe noted. One arm was taped to the body, but the other had apparently come loose during the wrapping. This hand was less protected than the other, and it had dried out. In effect, the hand was mummified.

As the final layer of plastic was removed, Dr. Zugibe saw that decomposition had begun and that the flesh was greasy. The color of the man's skin was putty beige. There was a single bullet wound in the back of the head. The contorted, openmouthed expression on the face was similar to that of the famous woodcut by Edvard Munch entitled *The Shriek*.

When he opened up the body, Dr. Zugibe noticed something very peculiar. The organs were fresh. Decomposition had started from the outside, which is the reverse of the normal process. Checking the heart muscle, he discovered ice crystal artifacts, which supported his immediate suspicion that the body had been frozen, perhaps by a killer whose intention was to disguise the time of death. Had the murderer let the body thaw out completely before he dumped it, the time of death might have been completely disguised and Dr. Zugibe probably would have concluded that this was a recent killing. The problem was the killer had been too meticulous with his wrapping. The layers of plastic had insulated the body and kept it cold longer than he expected.

By soaking the mummified hand in water and glycerine, Dr. Zugibe was able to rehydrate the fingers and take prints. The fingerprints identified the body as that of Louis L. Masgay.

When Detective Winters arrived at the Rockland County ME's Office to inspect Louis Masgay's body, he discovered something very odd among his personal effects: his clothes. They were the same clothes Masgay's wife and son had said he was wearing on the day he disappeared, two years and two months before. Louis Masgay had apparently been murdered the day he left his home with a hundred thousand dollars in cash, and his body had been kept frozen all that time. Frozen solid.

Detective Winters could only shake his head in disbelief. What the hell kind of monster could kill a man, then keep him in a freezer for two years? It was beyond comprehension. He stared down at the clothes in their plastic evidence bags and just shook his head.

He asked a lab tech who happened to be passing by if there was a phone he could use. He figured he'd better tell the Bergen County Sheriff's Department about this. Maybe those guys down in Jersey would sit up and pay some attention now. Maybe they'd go have another little talk with this guy Masgay was supposed to have been going to see to buy videotapes that day, Mr. Richard Kuklinski.

THURSDAY, SEPTEMBER 25, 1986—10:30 A.M.

John Sposato ran his fingers through his greasy, shoulder-length hair and looked at his watch again. "Why isn't he calling back, Rich? We gonna wait here all day?"

Richard Kuklinski looked up at the sky. He was leaning against the fender of his white Cadillac in a supermarket parking lot in Millville, New Jersey, sipping coffee from a styrofoam cup. A flock of honking Canada geese flew overhead in a V formation. He didn't answer until the geese had passed and couldn't be heard anymore. "Don't worry. He'll call."

Sposato started pacing in front of the phone booth. He'd already shredded his coffee cup, and the pieces were all over the ground. "I'm gonna get something to eat," Sposato suddenly said, and he started toward the supermarket. "I'll be right back."

Kuklinski caught his eye, and Sposato froze. He didn't have to say a thing.

"This is nuts, Rich. The guy is bullshit. He ain't calling back."

Kuklinski muttered behind his coffee cup. "Dominick is not bullshit."

"Then why ain't he calling?"

"He must be tied up."

"Tied up with what? This is bullshit. The guy's yanking your chain, Rich."

Kuklinski just stared at him. Sposato blinked and had to look away.

"He's not bullshit, John. You know 'the store'? Dominick walked in there one day with two hundred grand in cash. Lenny DePrima saw it. Dominick is for real."

"Okay, so he's for real. But he ain't calling us back, so what's the point?"

"It's not worth waiting a few more minutes for a half million bucks?"

"C'mon, Rich—"

"No, John, you c'mon. The guy wants all kinds of guns and shit. Last time I talked to him he told me he's buying for some broad in New York who's with the Irish Republican Army. They want big stuff, a big order. I've already told you all this, John. You don't listen."

"No, Rich, that's not true. I do listen. I do."

"Then you don't listen the right way. You only hear what you wanna hear. That's your whole problem."

John Sposato shook his head, but he wouldn't look Kuklinski in the eye. "That's not true, Rich."

Kuklinski grinned behind his coffee cup. He knew Sposato was thinking about what had happened after he'd made the mistake of going to his house with the two Puerto Ricans that time. He knew not to cross Richard Kuklinski again.

"You really think he'll come up with that much cash, Rich?"

Kuklinski shrugged. "We won't find out unless we try."

"Yeah, but—"

Kuklinski closed his eyes and shook his head, and Sposato stopped talking. "Listen to me, John. Do what I tell you, and this'll work out nice for the both of us. When Dominick calls, I'll give him to you. I'll tell him your name is Tim. Okay? That's all he needs to know. You tell him about all the guns you can get for him. Don't tell him you can get him everything he wants because then he'll start to think *you're* bullshit. Make it sound real, but keep him interested. Give him all that NATO jazz, you know what I mean?"

"Yeah, yeah. I know what you mean."

"We'll get him a sample of something, something small, anything, just something to show him we're for real. Then we set up the big deal, tell him to bring cash. We'll do it down in Delaware, at the warehouse. When Dom's not looking, we shoot him in the head, take his money, and then dump him. The more we get, the more we split. Simple as that."

"Yeah, but—"

"Believe me. Just keep it simple, and it'll all work out. I've done it before."

"Yeah, I know. You told me. . . . Okay. We'll see what happens."

Sposato was nodding, looking at the ground. He was finally coming around. Kuklinski could tell. He'd seen it happen before with plenty of other guys, and it always amazed him when it did. People believe what they want to believe. It's human nature. Sposato really wanted to believe that Kuklinski was letting him in on his plan to rip off Dominick Provenzano. It was amazing how stupid people get when it comes to money.

"You know, Rich, I was thinking—"

The pay phone started to ring, and Sposato jumped.

Kuklinski grinned as he got off the car and went to the booth. "There he is. You ready, John? You know what to say?"

"Yeah, yeah, go 'head. Answer it."

"Take it easy. I got it." Kuklinski reached into the booth and answered the phone. "Hello. Dom?"

"Rich?"

"Yeah. How ya doin'?"

"All right. How about yourself?"

"I'm okay."

"Where are you? Down south?"

"Yeah, I'm in south Jersey. Listen, I have a fella here with me who will tell you all about the product they have here, okay?"

"Okay."

"His name is Tim."

"Tim?"

"Right. And I told him your name is Dom. All right?"

"Okay, fine."

"Hold on."

Kuklinski stepped out of the booth and handed the phone to Sposato. Kuklinski went back to the Cadillac and leaned on the fender, crossing his arms over his chest and listening to "Tim" make his pitch.

"Twenty-millimeter? Yeah, sure, I got some. I got a million two hundred rounds, twelve lengths. I got four hundred thousand rounds, fourteen lengths. That's hermetically sealed, electric primers. NATO stuff . . . You need C-4?" Sposato glanced out at Kuklinski. "No, I don't have any right now."

Kuklinski nodded to him. He was doing okay.

"Machine guns? Maybe. Someone's making me an offer right now, but it'll be a couple of weeks before I can check this stuff out, so I don't want to make you any promises until I know the merchandise is good. . . ."

Kuklinski looked up at the sky and watched a cloud passing in front of the sun as he listened to Sposato telling Dom about all kinds of military arms he had access to, telling him how he did business, telling him that he required a 30 percent deposit on all deals, telling him that yes, he could also get him small handguns fitted with the "quiet things," silencers. Sposato had a good line of shit. He looked like a pig, but if you didn't have to see him, he could sound very knowledgeable, almost like a Harvard grad. He was a clever guy, no doubt about that. But not quite clever enough for Richard Kuklinski.

Just like everybody else in the world, John Sposato was greedy, and his greed was going to be his downfall. Kuklinski knew that in his mind Sposato already had the money spent that they were going to take from Dominick. But that's just the way some people are. Money makes them stupid.

Richard Kuklinski shaded his eyes as the sun started to beam through the wispy ends of the passing cloud. When the time came, and he put a couple of slugs into Dominick's head, Sposato would be jumping out of his skin, his eyes bugging out, thinking about all that money they were taking. But Kuklinski couldn't wait to see Sposato's fat face when he turned the gun on him and put a few slugs into *his* head. Two birds with one stone. Dump the two of them and the whole kitty would be his. Could be as much as five hundred grand. Not too bad. It would be the biggest score he'd ever pulled off by himself. Not bad at all.

"Hey, Rich. Rich." Sposato had his hand over the mouthpiece. "He wants to talk to you."

Kuklinski took the phone and exchanged places with Sposato in the booth. "Hi. Dom?"

"Hey, Rich, I told Tim what I needed. Now tell me the truth. Is this guy gonna deliver? I don't wanna hear a lotta promises, then get a lotta excuses down the line. You know what I'm saying?"

"You don't have to worry, Dom. If he says he can get you something, he'll get it. If he can't, he'll be straight with you."

"All right. I don't wanna end up looking bad on this. My IRA girl, she looks like a schoolteacher, but she can be a real ball-buster. You disappoint her once, that's it, no second chances. She'll find somebody else. And I'm telling you, she's one customer I do not want to lose. You understand me?"

"I hear you, Dom. I hear you."

"Now I understand that Tim's got all his heavy stuff in the Mediterranean, so it's gonna take some time to get us some samples. But let's keep my girl happy, okay? Get me some silencers so I can show her something. Just something I can show. I'll pay you for it—don't worry about that. But just get me something."

"Did Tim tell you he had silencers available?"

"Yeah."

"Here?"

"Yes."

"Then don't worry about it. We'll get you something as soon as we can."

"Okay, but don't make me wait. I'm telling you. We can both make a lotta money off this broad. Let's not screw it up. Okay?"

"I hear you. Don't worry."

"Okay, Rich, let's stay in touch—"

"Say, Dom, you didn't get any word on that stuff I was looking for. You know what I'm talking about?"

"Yeah, I know. I talked to my people, but they're all nervous about this Lipton soup thing."

"Why? That was a couple of weeks ago."

"They heard that there's a lot of federal people going around asking questions about all that shit. Now I know they got a chemist who gets that stuff for them, but like I said, they're all nervous. I got stuff like that from these people before for other customers of mine, so I'm pretty sure they can get it. They just wanna wait till this Lipton soup thing cools down before they'll give it to me. In the meantime, I'll get you the other stuff, the—you're on a pay phone, right?"

"Yeah, aren't you?"

"Yeah, of course. Now the coke I can get you, but the other stuff, the cyanide, you gotta be careful because, you know, I don't know how you fucking want to use it. But that's your business, Rich. I'm not asking."

"Well, it won't be a problem of exposure. I don't intend to resell it to anybody. I'm intending to use it myself."

"Yeah? Well, don't *you* take it."

Kuklinski laughed. "No, no, I don't intend to. I just have a few problems I want to dispose of. I have some rats I want to get rid of."

"Yeah? Why not use a fucking piece of iron to get rid of these fucking people? Why fuck around with cyanide?"

"Why be messy, Dom? You do it nice and clean with cyanide."

"Lemme ask you something then. You do the same thing I do once in a while. But I always use steel. You know what I'm saying?"

"Yeah, I understand what you're saying."

"So what I'm asking is, would you be willing to do a—you know—a contract with me?"

"Dominick, if the price is right, I'll talk to anybody."

"Yeah?"

"Sure."

"And you mean to tell me your way is nice and clean, and nothing fucking shows up?"

"Well, it may show, my friend, but it's quiet, it's not messy, it's not as noisy—"

"Yeah, but how the fuck do you put it together, you know what I'm saying?"

"Well, there's always a way. There's a will, there's a way, my friend."

Dominick laughed. "All right, listen, we'll have to talk about this sometime. It sounds interesting."

"There're even spray mists around."

"Yeah?"

"Sure. You put that stuff in a mist, you spray it in somebody's face, and they go to sleep."

"Fast? How long does it take?"

Kuklinski snapped his fingers. "About that fast."

"No shit. I thought—you mean, you don't have to put it in the guy's drink, something like that?"

"Not necessary. That will work, too, but it's very detectable that way."

"Yeah?"

"You make it up as a mist. As soon as they inhale it, they've already had enough."

"Just one squirt?"

"That's all it takes."

"Well, shit, if it's that easy, Rich, there are definitely a couple of things we could get involved with, without any fucking problems. You know, as I said, contracts."

"Can do it either way. If a guy wants it done with lead, then it could be lead. If the guy wants to prove a point and he wants steel, it could be done with steel. I'm not averse to guns, I'm not averse to knives, I'm not averse to, you know, whatever."

"As long as he's dead, that's the bottom line, Rich."

"Well, that's the thing, isn't it? If that's what they want."

"Your way sounds like a fucking James Bond movie, but if it works, then—"

"Dominick, I've done it all ways, whatever you've known or heard. There aren't too many things I haven't tried. I'll try whatever sounds workable. Some guys want it done messy and they want it as proof of the pudding. They want it shown. So I'll do it that way."

"But your way, what you were telling me, with the cyanide—there's no problem with that?"

"I don't have a problem. I'm not saying it's not detectable. I'm just saying it's quiet and it's fast."

"In other words, you've done this before. You *know* there's no problem?"

"Well, nobody's going to give you proof of anything like that, my friend—"

"I'm not saying proof. I'm just asking if it's really been done."

"It's been done."

"This sounds interesting. We gotta fucking go for coffee, break bread over this thing. It sounds good."

"Well, Dom, you know what they say. There's more than one way to skin something."

"I hear ya, I hear ya."

"It all depends on how determined you are to get it done."

They both laughed.

"As long as it gets done. Right, Rich?"

"As long as the guy who's paying you gets it done the way he wants. It's the finished product that they're interested in. And I haven't had any complaints because as you can see, I'm still around. If I had any complaints, I'm sure I wouldn't be here."

"I hear you, brother. I hear you. But getting back to the other stuff with Tim, what should we do? You wanna beep me or should I call you?"

"Why don't you call me this weekend? But just in case I'm not at that other number, lemme give you my beeper number."

"You got a beeper now, Rich?"

"Yeah. This number is for me and Tim. We both use it. Okay?"

"I understand."

"Okay, the number is 1-800-402. . . ." Kuklinski gave Dominick the number, and Dominick repeated it back to him. "Now like I said, one of us will be carrying the beeper, either me or Tim."

"Okay."

Kuklinski looked out at Sposato, who was waiting by the car like a puppy desperate for a little attention. "Tim and I will work together on this. We work together pretty much on a lot of things."

Sposato was grinning. If he had a tail, he would've been wagging it.

"All right, take care of yourself, Dom. Bye-bye."

Sposato practically lunged as soon as Kuklinski hung up the phone. "He went for it, Rich? He really bought all that stuff I told him?"

Kuklinski stepped out of the booth and nodded. "Yup."

"How much is he gonna buy, Rich? How much money will he bring?"

Kuklinski stared up at the sky. The sun was bright and warm on his face. "Don't know yet. Dom's gotta talk to his buyer. You know that."

"Yeah, I know. I just thought he would've told you something. . . . You know what I mean?"

Kuklinski didn't answer. He took out his dark glasses and put them on so he could face the sun and soak up the warmth. The hook was in. Sposato had dollar signs in his eyes. He was ready to do anything to make this deal happen. Same thing with Dominick. He was eager to make this buy. Maybe not as eager as Sposato, but he'd get there. They all do. It never fails. They all want the easy buck, and they all get stupid. Just like the pharmacist.

He adjusted his glasses and soaked up the warm Indian summer sunshine. It felt nice. It was gonna be a nice day.

The pharmacist had thought of himself as a player, but he wasn't. His name was Paul L. Hoffman, from Cliffside Park, New Jersey, and in 1982 he was fifty-one years old. He used to show up at "the store" now and then, looking for a deal on anything he could move in his drugstore, Farmacia San Jose in Union City. He bought a lot of hot perfume, especially Charlie, which was a popular item with his Hispanic customers.

The regulars at "the store" thought Hoffman was a pest, a bullshitter who tried to convince everyone that he was a big deal, a player, but he never brought in any merchandise to sell, he only bought. They tolerated him, though, because he always paid cash up front.

One day when he showed up at "the store," Lenny DePrima pulled him aside and asked him if he knew anything about some little white pills called Tagamet. Hoffman explained that Tagamet was a prescription drug for ulcers. It was *the* ulcer medication; everybody who had ulcers took it. Tagamet was probably the most prescribed drug in America, Hoffman said. He asked why DePrima wanted to know. The fence said that he'd gotten one of those big plastic jars of it, a couple of thousand pills, and some guy bought it off him right away, treated it like it was gold. When Hoffman found out how much DePrima had sold it for, his jaw dropped. It was a third of the price he had to pay for Tagamet legitimately. He begged DePrima to get him some, as much as he could get.

DePrima knew that the jar of Tagamet was just a one-time deal, something that just happened to come in with a bigger load. He didn't have a connection who could get him more, but he didn't tell Hoffman that. He figured he'd bust the pesky pharmacist's balls a little, string him along and make him crazy. But it turned out that DePrima's balls were the ones that were getting busted because Hoffman wouldn't leave him alone about the Tagamet. He called every day, twice a day, stopped by just to remind DePrima that he was still interested and that he had cash on the barrelhead.

One day when Hoffman showed up at "the store," Richard Kuklinski happened to be there. Disgusted with the pain-in-the-ass pharmacist, DePrima pointed across the room to Kuklinski and told Hoffman to go ask him about the Tagamet, hoping to get rid of him. He figured anyone with half a brain wouldn't bother the guy they called the one-man army.

But DePrima was wrong. Hoffman went right over to Kuklinski. But he didn't ask him outright. He tried to be clever about it. Knowing that Kuklinski sold pornography, Hoffman told him that he could get porno into Israel and suggested that they might go into a deal together. He bought five 8mm reels from Kuklinski to prove that he was serious. Kuklinski played along with him just to make the sale. He knew how DePrima felt about the guy. But neither one of them wanted to tell Hoffman to go take a hike because he always did have cash. Kuklinski gave Hoffman a phone number where he could be reached, figuring he might be able to sell anything to a character like this.

But Kuklinski hadn't counted on Hoffman's persistence. Over the next couple of months he called Kuklinski sixty-two times, always wanting the same thing: "The Tagamet, Rich. Did you get it yet?" Kuklinski stopped returning his calls.

Then early on the morning of April 29, 1982, Hoffman called Kuklinski at home, and Kuklinski happened to pick up the phone. Hoffman told him he had to meet him right away. He sounded both desperate and testy. He said he was serious about this, that he wanted to get some Tagamet right away. He told Kuklinski to meet him at a diner on Bergen Boulevard in Cliffside Park. Hoffman said he'd be bringing cash, twenty-five thousand dollars.

Kuklinski didn't like Hoffman's attitude, but he held his tongue, remembering that the pharmacist always paid cash. But was the guy really stupid enough to carry twenty-five grand to a meeting where he wasn't even sure there'd be any merchandise to buy? Hoffman was a real piece of work, more nerve than brain. He just might.

Kuklinski couldn't believe it. The guy was practically begging for it.

He met Hoffman at the diner and told him it was all set up. His connection would be delivering some Tagamet to his garage in North Bergen. He told Hoffman to follow him in his car.

But as Kuklinski sat in his car, watching Hoffman go to his car in the rearview mirror, he started to have doubts. Who did this guy think he was kidding? He had a beat-up station wagon from the year one. He didn't have any cash, not that much, not twenty-five grand.

But then again Kuklinski did know of a few guys with money who lived like paupers. So maybe Hoffman was telling the truth; maybe he did have the money. It was possible.

As soon as Hoffman got his old heap started, Kuklinski pulled out of the parking lot and headed for his garage on Newkirk Avenue near Seventieth Street in North Bergen, about two miles from the diner.

The garage was one of five that were tucked away behind a two-story building in an overpopulated, mixed commercial-residential area. A steep, narrow driveway led down to a muddy courtyard that was too small for a car to make the sharp turn into Kuklinski's garage without a lot of maneuvering. Kuklinski unlocked his garage and lifted the green overhead door. He pulled his car in, then let Hoffman back his old station wagon in. Hoffman turned off his engine, and Kuklinski walked up to his window and told him to get comfortable. It would take the guy with the Tagamet at least two hours to get here. He went over and closed the garage door then. He'd already made up his mind that he was going to kill the pharmacist.

Hoffman got out of his car and started yammering again. Talk, talk, talk—all this guy ever did was talk. He talked about his kids, his wife, his drugstore, his customers, anything and everything. He wanted to hear about Kuklinski's family, and he kept asking questions about them. Kuklinski didn't say much. His family was none of anybody's business. He leaned against the trunk of his own car, his foot propped up on the bumper, watching the pharmacist go on and on like some kind of crazy mynah bird. Kuklinski just nodded and smiled, not even listening to what he said, thinking instead about the .25-caliber pistol in the pocket of his jacket. He'd just picked it up yesterday, hadn't even fired it yet.

But as Hoffman kept talking, Kuklinski changed his mind again. This guy really was bullshit. He didn't have any money. No way. And if he didn't have any money, what good was killing him? Kuklinski figured he might have to beat the shit out of the guy to teach him a lesson, but why bother killing the little bastard?

But the pharmacist's nonstop yakking got faster and more agitated then. Hoffman was getting huffy. He *needed* that Tagamet, he said, and he didn't understand why it was taking so long. After they'd been there for about an hour, he asked if Richie had a phone in the garage. He had to call one of his employees to tell him to open up the drugstore because he was going to be late today.

Kuklinski shrugged and told him he didn't have a phone here.

Hoffman said he'd have to go find one. Kuklinski felt the weight of the gun in his pocket as he watched Hoffman lift the garage door and let himself out to go find a pay phone. Here's his chance to save himself a lot of pain and grief, Kuklinski thought. If he's smart, he won't come back.

But twenty minutes later Hoffman did come back, and he was all worked up now. He couldn't find anyone to open up the drugstore, and now he was losing money sitting here, waiting. If he waited around much longer, the money he'd make on the hot Tagamet might not make up for the lost income from having the store closed. The guy was in a real state, telling Kuklinski that he didn't want to wait around forever, that he wasn't shitting around, that he was serious about this. He went to the back of his station wagon, pulled out his car keys, and opened the gate. He threw back the carpeting over the spare tire well. Wedged in around the spare were packets of dollar bills, tens and twenties bound with rubber bands. It looked like a lot of money.

Kuklinski moved closer and stared down at all the cash. Son of a bitch, he thought. The guy did have it.

"See, Rich? I got it," Hoffman said, almost pleading. "You didn't think I had it, did you? Well, I do have it. Now where's the merchandise?"

Kuklinski pulled the gun out of his pocket and stuck it under the pharmacist's chin. "There is no merchandise."

He pulled the trigger, and Hoffman's head flew back with the impact of the first shot. But when Kuklinski pulled the trigger again to finish him off, the goddamn thing jammed. Hoffman was on his knees, clutching his throat. He was gurgling, blood pouring out of his mouth. But he wasn't dead. Kuklinski grabbed the tire iron from the spare tire well and smashed him over the head. The pharmacist scrambled to his feet and tried to run, but Kuklinski hit him again and again. Hoffman collapsed to the floor, flat on his face. Kuklinski stood over him with the tire iron in his hand, watching the blood pool around his head, then branch off like a snake slowly feeling its way along the oily floor to the drain in the middle of the garage.

Richard Kuklinski waited and watched the still body to make sure Paul Hoffman was really dead before he started to remove the packets of money from the spare tire well. He did a quick count. There was only about twenty thousand. Hoffman had said he had twenty-five. Kuklinski smirked and shook his head as he put the money in a plastic bag and locked it in the trunk of his own car. He then went to the back of the garage where he had a fifty-five-gallon steel drum. He rolled it on its rim to Hoffman's body, filling the enclosed space with a noise that sounded like a gathering thunderstorm. He turned it on its side and shoved Hoffman's body in. After setting it upright, he put the lid on but didn't seal it.

He took the keys out of the tailgate of Hoffman's station wagon and drove the car down the hill to Route 440 to a Rickel Home Center in Jersey City. He bought five bags of Sakrete instant concrete and returned to the garage.

He removed the lid from the drum and dumped the instant concrete over Hoffman's body, turning away so he wouldn't have to breathe in the powdery mixture. He shook the drum after each bag so that it would all sift down. After the fifth bag of Sakrete, he uncoiled the garden hose that was attached to a spigot near the front of the garage and filled the drum with water. When it started to overflow, he turned the spray to the floor and washed all the blood and excess concrete down the drain. He took his time washing the blood off the tire iron, then wiped it down with a rag before he threw it back into the tire well of Hoffman's station wagon. He re-coiled the hose, then checked the drum to make sure no part of the body was sticking through the surface. He wanted it to look like nothing but solid concrete after it hardened. Satisfied that the pharmacist was totally submerged, he put the lid back on, sealed it, and left it there.

A month later Kuklinski decided it was time to get rid of the drum. He'd read some stories in the local papers about police efforts to find the missing pharmacist, but that didn't concern him. The damn barrel was just getting in the way. He rented a van and rolled the heavy drum into the back. Then, after dark, he headed down the hill to Routes 1 and 9. The hill was steep, and the barrel shifted as he took a corner, smashing into the sidewall of the van. Kuklinski slowed down and looked over his shoulder. One of the windows had shattered. He turned around in his seat and stepped on the accelerator. Good thing he had taken the insurance, he thought.

He drove north on 1 and 9, then west on Route 46, stopping at a motel in Little Ferry that was next to a little hot dog joint he liked called Harry's Corner. He pulled the van up alongside the motel and rolled the heavy barrel out the back, letting it drop to the pavement. He rolled it up against the wall so it would be out of the way, turned it upright, and left it there.

A few days later he stopped by Harry's Corner and ordered two hot dogs with mustard and chili. He sat on a stool at the counter that ran along the window overlooking the driveway between Harry's and the motel. The drum was still there, right where he'd left it.

Every week he managed to stop by Harry's Corner for a couple of hot dogs, and he always sat at that counter, staring at the fifty-five-gallon drum as he ate. Then one day he came in and noticed that it was gone. Someone from the motel must have gotten sick of having it there and decided to have it hauled away and dumped somewhere. He just assumed the body was never discovered or else he would have heard about it at Harry's. It would have been big news if a body in a steel drum full of concrete had been found next door.

Richard Kuklinski bit into his first hot dog. Staring at the spot where the drum had been, he chewed and wiped chili from the

ends of his mustache. He took a second bite. It was a good thing
they hadn't found Hoffman, he thought. Harry made a pretty good
hot dog. If they'd found the body, he'd have to stop coming here
for a while.

THURSDAY, SEPTEMBER 25, 1986—1:00 P.M.

Dominick Polifrone still couldn't believe it. He was grinning as he drove the Shark through the intersection of Bloomfield Avenue and Route 23, passing a White Castle hamburger joint on the corner. The cassette, a copy of the recording he'd made of the telephone conversation he'd had with Richard Kuklinski and "Tim" that morning, was in his pocket. He was coming from the Bureau of Alcohol, Tobacco, and Firearms offices in Newark, where he'd returned Kuklinski's call on a phone rigged to a tape recorder. The Operation Iceman task force had been hastily summoned for a meeting, and he was heading for the Organized Crime Bureau offices in Fairfield.

Dominick couldn't wait to see Bobby Carroll's face when he heard what was on this tape. The deputy attorney general was gonna get up and do a dance on the table. Kuklinski had actually admitted to killing with cyanide. It was *on tape*. And that business about putting it in a spray mist—Jesus! How could a jury *not* convict this guy when they heard that? Carroll was gonna think it was his birthday.

A traffic light turned red up ahead, and Dominick pulled to a stop. There was a small shopping center with a Newberry's on the right and a Chinese restaurant called the Great Wall of China on the left. Suddenly Dominick's beeper went off. He pulled the device out of his pocket and glanced at the number on the LCD readout just as the light turned green. Area code 609-327. . . . It was the same number in south Jersey that Kuklinski had called from that morning. The car behind him honked its horn, telling him to go.

Dominick gave it some gas and drove on, wondering what he should do. His policy was to make Kuklinski wait, to maintain his control over the situation, but he had a feeling that might not be the best thing to do right now. He'd asked Kuklinski to find military arms for him; he'd told him it would be a big order, up to a half million dollars' worth. Even Michael Dominick Provenzano wouldn't play it cool for a deal that big. It wouldn't make sense, and Kuklinski could get suspicious. If Kuklinski was as paranoid as most bad guys were, he might think Dominick always took his time getting back to him because he needed time to set up recording equipment. Kuklinski might start to think that he was working with the cops or that he even was a cop. Dominick decided it might be smart to return this call right away. He spotted a phone booth outside a diner up ahead on the left, turned on his signal, and pulled into the lot.

In the phone booth he read the number off his beeper and punched it out. It rang twice before it was picked up.

"Hello?" It was Kuklinski.

"Hello, Rich? It's me."

"Hey, Dom. How's it going?"

"Good. What's up?"

"You at a pay phone?"

"Yeah, we can talk."

"Okay, listen. We made some calls, and Tim's getting a sample for you."

"Oh, yeah? What's he getting?"

"A hit kit."

"What caliber?"

"It'll be a twenty-two, already fitted with a screw-on silencer."

"What's the price?"

"Eleven hundred dollars for this one. You place a bigger order, we'll see what we can do."

"That's eleven hundred for the set, right?"

"Right."

"Okay, that sounds good to me. I'll give the girl a call and see if she's interested."

"Okay. And if she is, we can get together so you can look the piece over. Gotta check the merchandise out before you buy it, right?" Kuklinski was chuckling.

"Of course. Whattaya think?" Dominick laughed with him.

"You know the Vince Lombardi exit off the turnpike up north?"

"Yeah?"

"We can meet there."

"Okay . . . that sounds possible." Dominick was still wondering why he wanted to meet there.

"When do you want to get together then?"

"Well, lemme talk to my girl first. She may not want this kind of stuff."

"Whattaya mean, Dom?" Kuklinski's good humor faded. "I thought you told Tim you were looking for hit kits?"

Dominick turned on the attitude. "I did, Rich. But you know how broads are. They ever give you a fucking reason for changing their minds?"

"No, but—"

"Is there a problem with holding on to the piece until I can talk to her?"

"No, that's not it—"

"Then lemme find her so I can make sure this is what everybody wants. That okay with you?" Dominick was on the border between aggressive and belligerent. He was stalling Kuklinski, but he couldn't make it sound like he was stalling.

"All right, I tell you what, Dom. I'll beep you in a couple of days, and we'll take it from there."

"Beautiful."

"You're sure your girl wants this stuff? I mean, the whole order, the big one."

Dominick laughed. "She wants it. Believe me, she wants it. But I'll be honest with you, Rich. For the first deal she's gonna bust balls 'cause that's the way these people are. But once they trust you, she'll be buying so much fucking shit you're gonna change your name to Sears. You know what I'm saying?"

"I hear you." Kuklinski laughed, but it sounded forced.

"Okay, you beep me over the weekend, and we'll set up a date. I'm ninety-nine percent sure she'll want these pieces, but I wanna make sure. Okay?"

"Okay. I'll be talking to you."

"Take it easy."

Dominick hung up and stared blankly at traffic whizzing by on Route 23. He wondered what Kuklinski was thinking. Did he think Dominick was stalling him? And why did he want to meet at the Vince Lombardi Service Area? Why there? It was a busy place, good for getting lost in the crowd, but a lot of bad stuff went down there. Where exactly at Lombardi would he suggest they meet? In the men's room? No way. Too hard to place backups in a bathroom. Besides, it was an enclosed space. What if he had a little nasal spray bottle full of cyanide?

Dominick headed back to his car. He knew he was going to have to meet Kuklinski again sometime, and it looked like he might have to go along with Richie's meeting place of choice, the Lombardi Service Area. The problem was, how would they control the situation there?

He turned the key in the ignition and started the engine. As he pulled back out into traffic, he wondered how quickly he could react if he was sprayed in the face. Would he stand a chance if he held his breath? Maybe he'd better find out some more about this stuff. His eyes stung just thinking about it.

THURSDAY, OCTOBER 2, 1986—2:45 P.M.

The Vince Lombardi Service Area off the New Jersey Turnpike in Ridgefield, New Jersey, is always busy. It's the last rest stop before the highway becomes I-95 again and crosses the George Washington Bridge, going into New York City. Coming the other way, it's the first rest stop you can see from the road after leaving New York, an oasis for travelers who've been keeping their knees together waiting for a bathroom, choosing not to risk the ominous exits along I-95 as it winds through Harlem and the Bronx, where dingy tenements and monolithic housing projects loom and the stripped remains of abandoned cars litter the shoulders like big-game carcasses after the vultures were through with them.

The main building at the Vince Lombardi Service Area has two fast-food restaurants—a Roy Rogers and a Bob's Big Boy—as well as several smaller concessions. Outside there's a Shell gas station and two large parking lots—one for cars, the other for trailer trucks. If you look west from the parking lot, you can see vehicles crossing an elevated section of the turnpike, the loud diesel engines roaring through the sky. To the east is the Manhattan skyline. Fields of seven-foot-high grasses and cattails in the

ANTHONY BRUNO

swampy wetlands surround the service area, which is bordered by a ribbon of access road. It takes about three and a half minutes to drive around this access road and circle both parking lots if you drive a little faster than the speed limit, as practically everyone does. On this cool, cloudy Thursday in October, Deputy Attorney General Bob Carroll and Investigator Paul Smith knew exactly how long it took. They'd been doing it for the past forty minutes.

Paul Smith was driving the silver gray sedan; Bob Carroll was in the passenger seat. In their suits and ties they could easily be mistaken for a Mutt and Jeff pair of traveling salesmen, Smith being the junior trainee even though he was actually only two years younger than Carroll.

Investigator Ron Donahue was crouched on the floor of an otherwise unoccupied state police car parked at the curb near the entrance to the Roy Rogers. Two other investigators—a man and a woman—were "making eyes at each other" in another unmarked car in the lot near the bank of telephone booths. They were all watching Dominick Polifrone, who was sitting on a picnic table on the grass near the phone booths, his foot propped up on the seat. They were all waiting for Richard Kuklinski.

Paul Smith sighed and drummed his fingers on the steering wheel. "So where the hell is he?"

Bob Carroll's eyes swept the parking lots like a constant lighthouse beacon. "For all we know, Richie could already be here."

Smith shook his head in disgust. "I wouldn't be surprised."

They both knew how Kuklinski could be. He was the most cautious criminal they'd ever come across. He'd come to meetings early and just stand around, surveying the scene; then he'd stay late afterward, doing the same. Once, when the state police were following him in an unmarked car on the Garden State Parkway, he just pulled over to the side of the road and sat there for an hour, waiting and watching. They could never figure out how he knew they were following him. He was either superparanoid or supernatural.

As Paul Smith drove by the rows of gas pumps at the Shell station one more time, the AID radio receiver in the attaché case on the seat between him and Bob Carroll hummed and crackled with background noise. Dominick was wearing a concealed Kel transmitter as well as a Nagra tape recorder. Ron Donahue and the "couple" had similar receivers. They were all listening to the same thing, the rustle and squeak of Dominick's leather jacket whenever he moved. In other words, they were listening to nothing.

"I can just hear Ronny now," Smith commented with a wry laugh. "Curled up under the dash like that for all this time—he's gonna let Dominick know about it. You can bet on that."

Bob Carroll grinned at the thought of Ron Donahue chewing out Dominick for his sore back, but his eyes never stopped scanning.

Suddenly the receiver broadcast the sound of a beeper. Looking back over the seat, Carroll could see Dominick standing up and going over to the bank of phone booths.

Dominick's voice came through the receiver. *"It's him. The home number."*

Smith and Carroll listened intently to the AID receiver as they glided around the access road. Dominick was calling Kuklinski back.

"Hey, Rich, it's me. Where the fuck are you? I been waiting here for a half hour already. . . . Then why didn't you call sooner? . . . Oh . . . All right, but don't make me wait too long. I got people to meet, you know what I mean? . . . Okay, I'll see you in a little bit."

The receiver picked up the sound of Dominick banging the phone as he hung up.

"So what'd he say, Dom?" Paul Smith asked even though he knew Dominick couldn't hear him.

"He says he got tied up with a bunch of phone calls. He said he's coming now." The disgust and mistrust in his voice reflected the rest of the team's feelings.

Smith and Carroll continued to circle the access road on their mobile surveillance, driving and waiting. They had to wait another thirty-five minutes before the blue Chevy Camaro finally came down the exit ramp off the turnpike. They watched it heading for the bank of phone booths, Paul Smith maintaining a steady speed.

The slam of a car door came through the receiver, then Kulinski's voice.

"I got stuck on the phone with this guy. I finally looked at my watch and said, 'Holy Christ, I got someone waiting for me. Lemme hit this guy's beeper before he scrams.' That's when I called you. It takes me a half an hour to get here."

"I thought something happened to you."

Kuklinski's voice was a little fainter than Dominick's because he was farther from the mike, but the transmission was still loud and clear, which pleased Bob Carroll. A cassette tape recorder in the attaché case was recording the transmission just in case Dominick's Nagra malfunctioned.

As Paul Smith drove around the bend and started back toward the bank of phone booths, Bob Carroll frowned. He could hear Kuklinski's voice, but he couldn't see him. All he could see was Dominick, who looked like he was talking to the booth on the end. But as Smith drove closer and the perspective shifted, Carroll could see that Kuklinski was standing in the doorway of the booth, filling it completely. He was dressed entirely in black. With Dom looking up at him like that, he appeared to be enormous. Bob Carroll suddenly recalled the *Mighty Joe Young* movies they used to show on the *Million Dollar Movie* on Channel 9 when he was a kid. The only difference was the gorilla in the movie was friendly.

"So whattaya wanna do?" Dominick said.

"I got the thing in the trunk." Kuklinski headed back to his car. Dominick followed him.

As Dominick and Kuklinski passed between two parked cars, a shivering, emaciated dog came out of nowhere and was nearly hit by a passing pickup truck.

"Look at that poor little dog," Dominick said with genuine sympathy in his voice.

Paul Smith nearly jumped out of his seat. "What the hell is wrong with him? He's supposed to be a bad guy. He's not supposed to give a shit about poor little dogs." He gestured at the windshield. "What the hell is wrong with you, Dominick?"

Bob Carroll shushed him.

Kuklinski opened the trunk of his car. *"This is a twenty-two long-barrel military capacity with a screw-off front. You screw the suppressor on."*

"Right. This is everything?"

"Everything's here."

"Okay. Now I'm gonna bring this back to the girl. She'll show it to her people."

"All right."

"Now you said you can do the quantity with these. I don't want to be embarrassed with these people, so if you can't do it, tell me now. That's all I'm saying. Otherwise, if you make an agreement with them and then you disappoint them, you can kiss your sweet ass good-bye."

"How many do they want?"

"Hey, I'm talking big bucks. They may start out with a couple hundred thousand in the beginning. I don't know."

"My guy tells me that right now they got ten thousand suppressors and the equipment to go with them. So hey, that's a pretty good order."

"Lemme take a look at this thing." The sound of rustling paper came through the receiver.

"Here you go," Kuklinski said.

"Just don't use it on me, you fuck you." They both laughed.

"Here. You take it. I don't wanna touch it. I already wiped it down, but I'll show you what we got here. This here, this piece screws off. And this screws on."

Bob Carroll and Paul Smith looked at each other. Kuklinski was showing Dominick how to put the silencer on. Bob Carroll's face was tight. Selling Dominick the gun was good—they could indict

Kuklinski on that—but to get a murder indictment, Dominick would have to draw Kuklinski out, get him to talk, get him to say something incriminating, get him to talk about cyanide again. If they could get more of that on tape, Bob Carroll knew he could get a conviction in court.

"*Now, Rich, what about the explosives and stuff for these people?*"

"*My guy says he can get that.*"

"*Grenades, fragmentation, all that shit. That's what they want.*"

Dominick and Kuklinski got into a discussion about grenades and other military explosives and how it was always best to deal with one connection at a time when you were buying weapons like this. Paul Smith drove around the bend again and approached the phone booths. They could see Dominick and Kuklinski standing by the open trunk of the blue Camaro. Bob Carroll glanced down at the turning reels of the cassette in the attaché case.

"*Listen, Rich. Remember you were telling me about how you use cyanide?*"

"*Yeah?*"

"*I got this fucking rich Jewish kid I been supplying with a lot of coke. He wants me to get him two kilos now, which I can do, but the kid's a real fucking pain in my balls, you know? So what I'm asking is, you think it's possible we can dope up the coke with cyanide?*"

"*Definitely.*"

"*What I was figuring we can make a quick score. Do the kid and go halfsies on the bread he brings for the two keys.*"

"*Does he always come alone?*"

"*Yeah, he always comes alone.*"

"*And he brings cash?*"

"*The kid's rich from his old man. He's rolling in it. Money's not the problem. He's the problem. I can't stand the little fuck anymore.*"

Silence. Kuklinski was thinking about it.

Bob Carroll bit his bottom lip.

"*All right. Just tell me when.*"

The deputy attorney general's face lit up. He could see the words typed up on an indictment: conspiracy to commit murder.

As Paul Smith drove past the blue Camaro, Kuklinski changed the subject. *"Dom, you understand that the price for these pieces goes up after this one, right? It's eleven for this one, but it'll be fifteen a piece, even in quantity."*

"Without the nose?"

"No, with the nose. The same as you got here, except it'll be fifteen hundred, not eleven."

"What caliber?"

"I didn't even ask. Probably twenty-two."

"Hey, what the fuck do I care? It's the Irish broad's money, not mine. I don't give a fuck. Personally I could give two shits about their cause over there. I'm gonna give you your price today. Whatever it is tomorrow is her problem."

"Whatever. I'm just telling you, Dom. And as for that other guy, that sounds very interesting. Fuck it, I'll hit a Jew in a minute. Who the fuck cares?"

"Yeah."

"Not only that, you say we can make a nice buck off this."

"That's what I'm telling you, Rich. You know what we can do? I don't know if you wanna do this, but I can bring the kid here someday. I'll meet him here for coffee, and you can come and take a look at him if you want."

"No problem. Tell him you'll meet him over by the phones, and I'll park over there so I can see what he looks like."

"Good, good. Only thing is, Rich, I don't want him whacked. His old man's got money up the ass. He'll hire private investigators and all kinds of shit. That's why it's gotta look like an OD. You know what I'm saying?"

"No problem. I can do it, but you gotta get me the cyanide. I'll make it up and hit him in the face with it. I can make the—you know. Then just one hit, and that's it. He goes to sleep."

"Or we put it in the coke. I don't give a shit really, just as long as he's gone and it looks like an overdose."

"My friend, there's more than one way to do it. You don't want him shot, we can do it another way. There's millions of ways."

"An OD, that's what I want."

"Well, we can give him some pure shit and make him really OD."

"Whatever. I gotta run now, but we'll talk about this some more later. All right, big guy?"

"You got it. See you later."

Paul Smith slowed the car down as he came back around. Kuklinski was closing the trunk of his car. He had a paper bag in his hand. Dominick was walking away holding a small gym bag. Dominick had the hit kit, and Kuklinski had eleven one-hundred-dollar bills provided by the state of New Jersey.

Smith looked over at Bob Carroll. "So what're we gonna do about this 'rich Jewish kid' business?" Since they had heard Kuklinski making anti-Semitic remarks on previous surveillances, the Operation Iceman task force had been toying with the idea of luring Kuklinski with a Jewish "victim."

Carroll was fiddling with the tape recorder. "I was thinking we could play it out a little more, see how far we can go with it."

Paul Smith glanced at him again as he drove. "You thinking about introducing somebody or you just gonna let Dominick talk it up?"

"No, I thought we might introduce somebody. Not right off, but maybe down the line."

Smith pulled the car over to the side and looked at Bob Carroll again. "Who were you thinking of?"

Carroll frowned, raised his eyebrows, and shrugged as if he hadn't given it much thought. "Actually I was thinking about you."

Paul Smith rolled his eyes toward the deputy attorney general and exhaled a weary laugh. "I figured." Through the windshield he could see Kuklinski's blue Camaro heading for the entrance ramp to the turnpike.

WEDNESDAY, OCTOBER 8, 1986—11:45 A.M.

Richard Kuklinski used his last triangle of toast to wipe up the egg yolk from his otherwise empty plate. From his booth at the diner he could see a strip mall on the other side of the road. He looked at his watch. He'd beeped Dominick a while ago and given him the pay phone number here at the diner. He wished Dominick would call him back before the place got crowded for lunch so they could talk with a little privacy.

He chewed and sipped coffee, staring out at the sunny fall day. The leaves hadn't started to turn yet down here in south Jersey, but it wouldn't be long. The days were getting crisper, and it was beginning to feel like fall.

The pay phone by the cash register started to ring. Kuklinski sipped his coffee, waiting for one of the waitresses to get it. The old blonde with the tinted glasses answered it.

"Hello? . . . Who? . . . Hold on a minute." The waitress looked around the diner. When she spotted the big bald man with the gray beard sitting by himself, she went over to him. "Sir, are you waiting for a call from a Dominick?" she asked Kuklinski.

"Yes, I am." Kuklinski got out of the booth.

"Can I get you anything else, sir?"

He looked over his shoulder at his empty coffee cup. "Yeah, sure. How about a refill?" He continued toward the phone and made sure no one was nearby before he picked up the receiver.

"How ya doing?"

"Rich?"

"Yeah, how's it going?"

"All right. Who was that who answered the phone?"

"That was the waitress here at the restaurant."

"So what're you doing?"

"Not much. I called to see if anything is happening with your girl."

"As a matter of fact, everything's fine with her."

"Yeah?"

"They're very pleased with what I showed them."

"Yeah?"

"So it looks like good business, you know what I'm saying?"

"Good. And how did you make out with the rich kid? Is he gonna do that thing with you?"

"Yeah, we're gonna do that. You know . . ."

Kuklinski grinned. "Well, whenever you're ready, give me a beep."

"Yeah, all right. How long you gonna be down there in south Jersey?"

"Don't worry about it. It'll take me two and a half hours to get up there, my friend. That's all."

Dominick laughed. "I hear you. There's no rush on this thing, though, you know what I'm saying? The kid bounces around, goes away with his family sometimes, disappears for a while—"

"He who hesitates is lost, my friend."

"You're right about that, Rich."

"Gotta strike while the iron is hot."

"I hear you, I hear you. I'll let you know when the time is right."

"Okay. And how about the other thing with the girl?"

"Don't worry. I'll be in touch as soon as I hear from her."

"Okay. You know how to find me."

"Right. I'll be in touch."

"Take care now."

"Bye."

Kuklinski hung up and went back to his booth. The saucer was on top of his coffee cup. The waitress had poured him a fresh cup and covered it to keep it warm. He shook out two packets of sugar, ripped the tops, and poured them into the cup. He was thinking about the rich Jewish kid. Dominick had said the kid wanted two kilos of coke. The price would be sixty-five thousand. The kid would bring cash. They'd kill him, take his dough, and split it. That would give him another thirty-two five on top of whatever he and Sposato ripped off from Dominick with the bogus arms deal.

Kuklinski brought the coffee cup to his lips and sipped as he looked out the window. He who hesitates is lost, he thought. He who hesitates . . .

There was one time when he had hesitated, and he ended up regretting it. Back in the early seventies a guy who owed him money was telling people that he didn't intend to pay up. Richard Kuklinski wasn't about to let it get around that he sat back and allowed people to stiff him, so he paid the deadbeat an unexpected visit late one night at his office in midtown Manhattan. The man was very surprised to see him. He was more surprised to see Kuklinski's .38. Kuklinski told him he'd done wrong, and there was no making up for it now. The man just fell apart.

"Please, Rich, no. Please don't do this. Please, God, don't let this happen to me. *Please!* God, please make him listen. Please, God."

Kuklinski stood over the deadbeat as he fell to his knees. The man couldn't walk he was so upset, crying and pleading, praying to God for mercy, promising God he'd do anything if He just helped him this one time.

Kuklinski sneered down at him. "I tell you what," he said. "If you believe so much in your fucking God, I'll give you a half hour to pray to Him. We'll see if He can do something for you. Okay?" He leaned on the desk and made himself comfortable, then looked at his watch and told the guy the clock was ticking.

That was a mistake.

The guy started to blubber something awful, crying and wailing and begging. It was pathetic. It was degrading. The guy couldn't even get up he was such a mess. He tried to drag himself across the floor like some kind of cripple who'd lost his wheelchair. Eventually the guy shit his pants, literally. It was disgusting. Kuklinski never thought anyone could be this desperate. After a while he couldn't take it anymore, so he just shot him and got it over with. He hauled the body down in the service elevator and threw him in a Dumpster. He never heard another word about the guy after that, but that one still haunted him. He shouldn't have hesitated. He should've just shot him right away and kept it simple. Doing it that way, making the guy beg like that—it wasn't worthy of Richard Kuklinski. It made him feel small, and he knew he was better than that. He learned a good lesson from that one, though: He who hesitates is lost.

"More coffee, sir?" The waitress was hovering over the table, ready with the coffeepot.

"No, thanks," he said. "Just the check."

"Yes, sir." She scurried back behind the counter to tally up his check.

He drained his cup and waited.

SATURDAY, OCTOBER 25, 1986

Ellen Polifrone was genuinely happy. Dominick could tell. His wife never complained when he was on assignment, but he knew it never thrilled her. He watched her from the dining-room table as she pulled a roast out of the oven. She was happy because tonight was a real occasion. Her husband was home for dinner for a change.

Operation Iceman was turning out to be the longest undercover assignment Dominick had ever been on, nineteen months now, but Ellen knew very little about it. She had no idea who Richard Kuklinski was, and that was the way she wanted it. If she knew the details of her husband's work, she'd go out of her mind worrying about him. As it was, whenever one of his cases broke and she read about it in the newspaper, she'd nearly have a fit. She would never sit by a window in a restaurant with Dominick anymore because she was afraid some Mafia assassin would try to get back at Dominick for something he'd done to the mob.

Dominick watched her spear the steaming roast and put it on a serving platter. He'd known Ellen since high school, and he often said she was the one who kept him sane, but right now he was tempted to break their long-time understanding and tell her what was going on with the Kuklinski investigation. The strain was getting to him, and he really wanted to unload some of what he was feeling.

Ellen looked at him over her shoulder as she carved the roast. "Call the kids, Dom. Everything's ready."

Dominick stayed in his seat, clutching the glass of scotch in front of him. "Keri! Drew! Matt! Dinner's ready. C'mon, let's go."

Ellen rolled her eyes, but she didn't say anything. She knew her husband had a lot on his mind. Whenever Dominick took a glass of scotch out onto the deck, lit up a cigar, and stared out at the trees, she knew something was bothering him, something about work. Lately it seemed like he was going out there a lot more than usual.

"Hey!" Dominick suddenly erupted. "I said dinner's ready. Get up here or forget about eating."

"I'm coming, I'm coming," Drew yelled up from the den. Drew, their second child and the older boy, was eleven years old, and his fresh mouth occasionally got him into trouble, especially with his father.

Thirteen-year-old Keri, the oldest, wandered into the kitchen and asked her mother if there was anything she could do.

Matt, the youngest, tripped into the dining room wearing a red satin cape, a matching cap with red horns that tied under his chin, and a pair of horn-rim glasses with a rubber nose and a black feather mustache. Halloween was still a week away, but the seven-year-old was so excited he tried on his costume every day and dreamed out loud about all the candy he'd get trick-or-treating. He sat down at the table and waited for his father to notice him.

Dominick noticed, but the smile for his son was forced. The red satin horns on Matt's head reminded him of one of the names they had for Richard Kuklinski at "the store": the devil himself.

Keri started putting out plates and silverware, and Ellen brought out the food, but Dominick wasn't paying attention. He was thinking about *him* again. That's all he could think about these days, *him*, the devil himself. Kuklinski's face was the last thing he saw when he closed his eyes at night and the first thing he saw when he opened them in the morning. He was afraid that they were losing him now.

A week after he'd returned Kuklinski's call at the diner in south Jersey, Dominick beeped Kuklinski, but it was Tim, Kuklinski's arms supplier, who returned the call. He told Tim that he needed to talk to Richie about the IRA deal, and Tim said he'd give Richie the message. Later that day Kuklinski called him, and they discussed the possibility of getting five to ten more hit kits like the one Dominick had already bought. But Kuklinski seemed hesitant, insisting that his people wouldn't sell these guns "piecemeal." He was clearly looking for a bigger order, playing hard to get. Dominick didn't accommodate him. This was what the girl wanted for now, he told Kuklinski, that's all. He was sticking to his policy of not conceding anything to Kuklinski.

But now he was beginning to have second thoughts about his strategy. Eleven days had gone by with no word from Kuklinski. Then today, while he was raking leaves in the front yard, his beeper went off. He pulled it out of the waistband of his sweat pants and saw right away that it was Kuklinski's home number.

When he returned the call, Dominick could tell from Kuklinski's voice that things had definitely changed. The Iceman was cool and noncommittal. Dominick reminded him that the "rich kid" rip-off was still on the table if Kuklinski was interested, and he suggested that they get together to discuss it. Kuklinski didn't say he wasn't interested, but he didn't seem all that enthused about it. The conversation was short, but Dominick felt like he was pulling teeth the whole time, trying to jump-start the guy. Kuklinski promised to give him a call on Monday, but Dominick didn't think he would. He was afraid that the Iceman had lost interest in him.

Of course, in hindsight it made sense. Almost two months had gone by since they'd met, and the only money Kuklinski had made on this relationship was the eleven hundred Dominick had paid him for the one gun and silencer, which he probably had to split with Tim. This was small potatoes for Kuklinski. He probably thought he was wasting his time with Dominick.

Dominick stroked his mustache. He should have put in a bigger order when he talked to him two weeks ago. Five to ten guns was nothing. He should have realized that. Same thing with the "rich kid" scheme. He should have been more definite about it. He should have given Kuklinski a tidbit he could taste to make him really hungry. Kuklinski probably thought he was a small-timer who was stalling him because he couldn't come through with what he'd promised. Kuklinski thought he was bullshit.

"Dominick? . . . Dominick?"

"Huh?"

Ellen gestured with her head. "Dinner's ready."

Dominick looked down and suddenly realized there was a full plate in front of him—roast beef, string beans, baked potato, and a salad. Keri was in her seat, and Ellen was standing over Matt, cutting his meat for him. Drew's place was empty.

Dominick's brows furrowed. "Where's Drew?"

Keri shrugged.

Dominick exploded. "Drew, if you don't get in here right now, you can forget about—"

"I'm right here, Dad. You don't have to yell." Drew raced in through the kitchen and jumped into his chair. He was wearing his catcher's mitt.

Dominick pointed at the mitt. "Get rid of that thing. You don't bring that to the table. What's wrong with you?"

Drew gave him an exasperated look and took off the mitt. He was about to pitch it into the living room when Ellen stopped him and saved him from his father's temper. "Just put it under your chair, Drew."

Ellen sat down, and everyone dug in. Dominick sliced his roast beef and absently took a bite.

Kuklinski thought he was bullshit. He knew it.

Dominick took another bite. He didn't even know what he was eating, he was so preoccupied.

"Is it good?" Ellen asked.

"Huh?"

"The meat. Is it overdone?"

"Oh . . . no. It's good. . . . It's very good. . . ."

He was watching Matt in his devil costume buttering a roll. That reminded Dominick of something he always said to Kuklinski. "We gotta break bread over this, Rich. We gotta break bread." He speared another piece of roast beef and shoved it in his mouth. But *when* were they gonna break bread? he wondered. When? There was no reason for Kuklinski to meet him, no incentive, no big bucks, no big score, nothing. They were stalling Kuklinski, and the bastard knew it.

Dominick chewed and chewed, thinking about Kuklinski, and finally he realized that the roast beef didn't have much taste.

"Hey, Matt," he said to the seven-year-old, "pass the fucking salt, will ya?"

The little boy's jaw dropped.

"Daddy!"

"Dominick!" Ellen scowled at him.

Drew thought it was hilarious. "Oooo! What you said, Dad."

Dominick clenched his teeth and felt his face turning red. He was just about to scream at Drew when he caught himself. He turned to Matt and tenderly pushed the devil's horns off his head. "I'm sorry, Matt. I didn't mean that."

The little boy looked up at his father, his shocked expression slowly fading. "It's okay, Dad." He looked at his mother. "We understand."

Dominick rubbed his face and let out a long sigh. "Sorry."

Later that evening, while Ellen and the kids were downstairs in the den watching TV, Dominick was pacing around the house, searching for something to do with himself. He had tried watching television with them, but he couldn't concentrate on any of the programs. He thought about going out for a jog, but it was raining too hard. He wanted to go down to the gym, put on the gloves, and work on the heavy bag for a while, but this was the first Saturday night he'd been home in months. He couldn't leave now. His best friend, Alan Grieco, was out for the evening. He'd already tried calling him. So Dominick sat at the kitchen table, staring at the phone, debating about whether or not he should call. His eye kept going back to the bottle of Chivas on the counter. Either he was going to make the call or have another drink and brood. He snapped up the phone and punched out the number.

It rang five times before she answered. "Hello?"

"Hey, how are things in Glocca Morra?"

"Dominick!" The woman on the other end had a distinctly New York accent. She sounded both incredulous and scolding. "It's Saturday night, Dominick. Get a life, will ya?"

"I'm trying, Margie, I'm trying."

Margaret Moore was assistant special agent in charge of the ATF office in Philadelphia. She had started her career with the New York City Police Department, working in undercover narcotics, but in 1976, after two and a half years on the job, she had been laid off. She was then hired by the Bureau of Alcohol, Tobacco, and Fire-arms, where she was teamed with a brash special agent who was as Italian as she was Irish. Together they formed an act that was unique in undercover law enforcement: Dominick would pose as a connected guy in the market for guns; Margaret, with her blue eyes and strawberry blond hair, would be the "IRA girl," his good customer who needed the guns. They were a very effective duo. Whenever they would go to meet a bad guy with guns to sell, Margaret would go off into a corner by herself and Dominick would do all the negotiating, going back and forth between the buyer and seller. In their biggest case together they recovered three thousand silencers from a mob gunrunner. Even though they weren't partners anymore, they stayed in touch. But ever since

Operation Iceman had started to heat up, it seemed like he'd been calling her every other night.

"So what's he done now, Dom?" Margaret Moore knew all about Richard Kuklinski.

"Nothing. That's the whole problem. I think we're losing him."

"You think he's on to you?"

"Nah, I don't think that's it."

"You sure?"

"No, he doesn't know who I am."

"Well, don't be a jerk. If he starts getting hinky on you, back out. Protect yourself first."

"Don't worry, Margie. It's okay. He doesn't know."

"Hey, I know you. You'll tough it out no matter what. Don't be stupid. Remember, you don't have me around anymore to keep you in line."

Dominick laughed. "Don't make me curse, Margie." The muscles in his forehead were relaxed all of a sudden.

"So, Dom, you want me to put in a petition to let me help you out with this guy? You introduce me as the IRA girl and we'll wrap this thing up quick, just like we used to."

They both laughed, but they both knew it was more complicated than that. Kuklinski wasn't some street punk with a few guns to sell, and this wasn't the same kind of buy-bust situation that they had been used to. This was a homicide investigation. Dominick had been on this case a year and a half now, and it didn't look like they were going to wrap it up soon because the state of New Jersey had first dibs on Kuklinski for murder. Selling illegal firearms was just a side dish at this feast. Dominick knew that his old partner would jump in to help him in a minute if she could, but Margaret Moore was a supervisor now, and supervisors were officially prohibited from returning to street duty.

"You getting good cooperation from the state?" she asked. She sounded like a protective mother.

"Oh, yeah, these guys are great. No complaint there. The guys from the Attorney General's Office are top drawer."

"So why isn't this thing moving? What's the problem?"

"We gotta get Kuklinski for the murders. I gotta get him to talk more on tape. Bobby Carroll's running this show, and he says we keep going until we get enough on tape to nail Kuklinski in court for good."

"Yeah, but, Dom, doesn't he understand that Kuklinski is gonna fly the coop if you jerk him around too long?"

"He understands that."

"Does he understand that it's your life hanging out there on the line with this ape? Does he understand that?"

"Yes, Margie, he understands that." Dominick was touched by the ferocity of her concern for him.

"Look, Dominick, I shouldn't have to tell you this, but I'm gonna say it anyway. Nobody understands what it's like being out there by yourself on an undercover. No matter what these guys tell you to do, you do what you *have* to do. It's *your* life that's on the line, not theirs."

Dominick stared out the sliding glass doors at the teeming rain in the floodlights out on the deck. "I know, Margie. Believe me. I know."

WEDNESDAY, OCTOBER 29, 1986—1:50 P.M.

At the Vince Lombardi Service Area, Dominick Polifrone stood just inside the glass doors at Roy Rogers, his hands in the pockets of his black leather jacket, holding his gun in the right pocket. The Nagra tape recorder concealed on his body was running. Three investigators from the state's Organized Crime and Racketeering Bureau were at different booths in the fast-food restaurant, blending in. One of the three was Ron Donahue, who was hunched over a paper cup of tea, drinking it slowly and making it last. A fourth investigator was sitting in a stall in the men's room, just in case. They were waiting for Richard Kuklinski.

Dominick had waited all day Monday for Kuklinski's promised phone call, but it never came. Tuesday had passed, and there was still no word from him. Dominick was discouraged. He'd thought about calling Kuklinski himself, but he didn't like that idea. The way Kuklinski had sounded the last time they talked, it was as if they'd never met. At this point, if Dominick called him, in effect they'd be starting all over again, clean slate, except Dominick would be in the weaker position because he'd be the one doing the pursuing. That, he didn't want.

He'd decided to wait it out a little longer and see what would happen.

Then, that morning, Kuklinski finally beeped him, but when they'd talked, he was still cool and evasive. He was making excuses, telling Dominick that he'd lost his number and that's why he hadn't called sooner. Dominick said he wanted to meet him so they could discuss a few things, but Kuklinski tried to put him off, saying that he didn't have the time because he was leaving for south Jersey in a little while. Dominick insisted, and Kuklinski finally agreed to meet him at the Vince Lombardi Service Area.

Dominick scanned the parking lot through the glass doors, then looked at his watch. He knew he was going to have to make the sales pitch of his life. Not hard sell, though. That would just send Kuklinski back into the bushes. No, he was going to have to be very subtle but also totally up front. He was going to have to appeal to the only thing that apparently turned the Iceman on: money.

The restaurant was visible in the reflection of the glass doors. Outside, it was cold and blustery. Dominick didn't like the idea of meeting Kuklinski inside, but given the weather, he didn't have much choice. For one thing, there were too many people inside. What if something happened and he had to pull his gun? Then there was the bathroom problem. What if Kuklinski wanted to go talk in the men's room? It was an enclosed space. What if Kuklinski was on to Dominick and he'd decided to get rid of him with his cyanide spray? The man stationed in the toilet wouldn't be much help in that case. That's why Dominick had already decided that he would try to head off any suggestion that they go into the bathroom by saying he hadn't had lunch yet and he was starved. Of course, the thought of eating with Kuklinski wasn't very comforting either. All Dominick could think of was Gary Smith's last hamburger. He was definitely going to make sure that he ordered the food and that it didn't leave his sight. He was glad Ron Donahue was sitting there. Ronnie would watch for something like that, and Ronnie wouldn't hesitate if he saw Kuklinski trying to pull something.

At two o'clock on the nose Kuklinski arrived, this time in a different car, a red Oldsmobile Cutlass Calais. Dominick watched the big man cross the parking lot. He was wearing his gray leather bomber jacket and pressed jeans with a sharp crease down the leg. He was also wearing the dark glasses again. A bad sign. The members of the task force had agreed that these were his "mother-fucker glasses." Whenever he wore them, that was usually the attitude he had.

Kuklinski pushed through the glass doors. "Hey, Dom. What's new?"

Dominick shook his hand. "You're getting smaller and smaller, my friend. Whatta'you, on a diet?"

Kuklinski laughed, but Dominick could tell that it was forced. "You want coffee? I haven't had lunch. C'mon, let's have something."

"Not for me. You go ahead."

They headed for the counter and stood in line together so Dominick could get something to eat.

"Those things I wanted, Rich. The five or ten? You know what I'm talking about? Can you get them for me?"

Kuklinski shrugged. "They're down there if you want 'em. You go get 'em yourself, though. They're in Delaware." He kept his glasses on.

"And you know that he's got ten?"

"Ten, twenty, thirty, whatever you want. But I don't wanna transport them. If you want 'em, you go get 'em."

Kuklinski was wearing his attitude like a fur coat. Dominick knew it was time to start his pitch.

"Tim explained to you that these pieces aren't for the girl, didn't he? This is a favor I'm doing for a wiseguy in New York. Small change. This isn't the big one. That's what I gotta talk to you about."

Dominick got to the head of the line, and Kuklinski waited for him to order. Behind the counter a pimply kid in a paper hat punched out Dominick's selections on the cash register, then went to fetch his order.

"My people are ready to buy. They said they don't need samples. All they want is a list of what you can get." Dominick lowered his voice. "I know they got at least five hundred grand to spend on ammo alone."

Kuklinski didn't answer. He was looking down at Dominick's plastic tray as the kid behind the counter filled it: a carton of milk, a Coke, large fries, and a cheeseburger. As Dominick paid, Kuklinski went to find an empty booth at the far end of the room by the windows. Dominick carried his tray over to him, passing Ron Donahue sipping his tea. They didn't look at each other.

At the table Dominick unwrapped his cheeseburger and took a bite. He wasn't going to put it down until it was finished. Kuklinski sat there with his fingers linked on the tabletop, a stone face behind the dark glasses.

"My people are looking for grenades, machine guns, all that kind of shit. You know what I mean? We're ready to put in our order."

Kuklinski sucked on his teeth. "Yeah, I keep hearing about this big order, but my guy wants to know when. It's getting embarrassing for me."

"I'm giving you the order now. If Tim can handle it, we're buying. Just get me a list of what he's got."

"Okay. I'll get you one." The big man sucked his teeth. "What's your girl gonna do over there? Start a war? I wanna know so I can move outta the way a little bit." Kuklinski was smiling. It seemed genuine.

"Rich, I don't give a fuck what she's gonna do with it. As long as her cash is green, that's all I care about."

"That's all I care about, too. I just want to get you two guys together and let you do your thing. I'm gonna step aside and stay out of it. All I want is my commission when it's all over."

"Of course." Dominick stuck a straw in his soda and took a drink. "But right now I need those ten pieces. Tell me the truth now, can I get 'em right away? I promised this guy I would try."

"You willing to go down to Delaware to get 'em?"

"No problem. I'll pick 'em up. Wherever they are."

Kuklinski took off his glasses. "Tim's got 'em. They're down there. If you'll pick 'em up, there's no problem."

"Good. You make the arrangements and get back to me, tell me when and where. Okay?"

Kuklinski nodded. "Will do."

Dominick stuffed a few french fries into his mouth.

"So what happened with your little Jewish friend?"

Dominick took a drink of soda and swallowed. "I wanted to talk to you about that. The kid says he may want to do two or maybe three keys now. Is it still possible to do what we talked about, you know, with the cyanide shit?"

"Dom, if you can get me a little bit of cyanide, I could take this kid out easy. Just walk up to him, spray it in his face, and he'll never see the next fucking minute."

"Guaranteed?"

"My friend, I've done it already. The kid will never know what hit him. Once it gets into his system, he's done for. He's gone."

"What about his car and stuff? What do we do with it?"

Kuklinski shrugged. "What do you want to do with it? All I'm interested in is taking his money. Just leave him. Don't touch nothing. You wanna move him, move him. But I don't see it as a problem. Just leave him where he is. He'll look like he's sleeping."

"That's what I want. Whack him without any fucking problems. Then we got his cash, plus the coke I bring to the meet."

"See that old guy sitting over there." Kuklinski pointed with his glasses.

Dominick turned around in his seat. He was pointing at Ronnie Donahue. Dominick's hand went to his lap, ready to go for the gun in his pocket. "Yeah. What about him?"

"I could walk by and—pssst—give him a little swish in the face, and I could walk right outta here and no one would even realize what happened to the guy. Except when someone asks him to get up and move. That's when they'd realize he wasn't with us anymore."

Dominick relaxed and reached for his soda. "You know, I get offers for these kind of jobs in the city sometimes. Would you be willing to teach me how to use this stuff on somebody? What's the best effect?"

"The best way is to hit 'im right in the nose with a spray so he inhales it. Once he inhales it, he's done. There ain't nothing he can do about it. Only thing is, you gotta be careful you're not downwind, 'cause if *you* inhale it, *you're* gone."

Dominick nodded. "Yeah. That makes sense."

"My friend, I've done it on a busy street where they thought the guy had a heart attack. I walked right up to him, made like I was sneezing into my handkerchief to protect myself, and sprayed him in the face. He tripped and fell, and everyone thought he had a heart attack. Later on they found out that that wasn't what killed him. I've done it on the busiest street in the world. People all over the place."

Dominick smiled and shook his head in amazement. He was trying to imagine what Bob Carroll's face was going to look like when he heard this. This was pure gold.

"And the beautiful part is, when they find out it's not an accident after all, they're not gonna know what happened. Once they do the autopsy, they're gonna know he sniffed something, but they'll never figure out that he sniffed cyanide. Nobody sniffs fucking cyanide."

"Right. Of course not."

"If you gotta do a job, Dom, that's the way to do it. Nice and neat. No mess."

"You're right. Nice and neat . . . nice and neat."

Dominick looked down at the last bite of cheeseburger in his hand and the french fries spread out on the plastic tray, and he suddenly remembered the photos of Danny Deppner's body. He wondered if that one had been "nice and neat," too.

In the last days of 1982 Danny Deppner kept having the same nightmare: that Gary Smith wasn't dead.

Deppner had watched Gary Smith eat the cyanide-laced hamburger that Richard Kuklinski had brought to the York Motel. He had seen Gary's eyes "go goofy" as he fell back on the bed and clutched his throat. He was the one who had taken the lamp cord and finished the job, strangling Smith until he stopped struggling. He had rolled Smith's lifeless body off the bed and helped Kuklinski get him into the bed frame, covering him with the box spring and mattress. But lying in bed, staring at the cracked ceiling in another motel room, Danny Deppner began to wonder: Could Gary still be alive?

On Christmas Eve, in Room 55 at the Skyview Motel in Fort Lee, Danny was jittery. He was stuck there, afraid to move, afraid to leave the room. Richard Kuklinski had paid for the room but again left him with no money. Danny kept the TV on to keep him company, but there was only a lot of dopey Christmas stuff on, cartoons and crap. He left it on, though, because the silence of the night made him nervous. He dozed off on the bed with his clothes on and the television going. That's when he had the nightmare for the first time.

Gary hadn't died. He was under that bed, but he wasn't dead. He was reaching out, trying to get out from under the mattress and box spring. He was struggling and moaning. Danny was lying on that bed, sleeping, tossing and turning, having the nightmare. Beneath him, Gary was on his back, reaching up. Danny wanted to escape, but he couldn't move. Suddenly Gary's rotting hands emerged from the mattress on either side of Danny's face—

Danny Deppner's eyes shot open, and he bolted off the bed. He stared at the mattress, looking for Gary's hands. He was drenched in sweat.

On Christmas Day, not knowing who to turn to, Danny called his ex-wife, Barbara, and asked her to come down for a while. Terrified herself, knowing what she knew about Gary Smith's murder, she told him she didn't think that was such a good idea. He begged her, but she refused. He was getting low on cigarettes, he told her, he had no money, and he needed a drink bad. An alcoholic who'd been trying to reform, Danny had started drinking again. His ex-wife kept saying no, she couldn't come down and be with him. She was too scared.

Danny Deppner spent the day alone in Room 55, fighting the urge for a drink and a cigarette, flipping channels on the TV, avoiding that bed.

That night he dozed off on the armchair and had the nightmare again. He didn't get much sleep.

The next day Barbara Deppner changed her mind and went to the motel to be with Danny, but he wasn't there. Afraid that he might be dead, too, she called the only other place she thought he could be, "the store." She asked if Danny or Big Rich had been around, but no one had seen either of them lately.

Later that day she returned to the motel and found Danny in his room. He said he'd gone out for a long walk, anything not to be cooped up in that room. She could see that he was a mess. He couldn't stop talking about how he and Kuklinski had killed her cousin Gary, begging her to listen to all the gory details. But she didn't want to hear about it. She had her own problems. Percy House was still in jail, and she had all those kids to take care of by herself. Anyway, the whole thing about what they'd done to Gary made her sick. But Danny had to tell somebody. If he didn't let it out, he'd go crazy, he said. She tried to get him to change the subject, but he wouldn't. He wanted her to go to Gary's house that night and ask Veronica Smith if her husband had returned home. Barbara thought her ex-husband had finally snapped, but Danny insisted that she do it. He had to know if Gary was really dead.

As she tried to reason with him, the phone suddenly rang, and they both froze. Danny picked it up. It was Kuklinski. He wanted them to meet him right now at the Fort Lee Diner, a five-minute drive from the motel. They were both too scared to disobey.

Kuklinski wasn't there when they arrived, so they waited in the parking lot. It wasn't long before the white Cadillac with the blue top pulled into the lot. Kuklinski motioned for them to get into his car, but Barbara shook her head. She was terrified of him.

Richard Kuklinski didn't like people saying no to him. He jumped out of the car, enraged, and snatched Barbara Deppner by the wrist. Where the hell did she get off calling "the store" and asking about him? he wanted to know.

Danny tried to defend her, but he knew better than to challenge Big Rich.

But then, as suddenly as he had erupted, Kuklinski calmed down and suggested they go into the diner and have something to eat so they could talk. Danny was suspicious. Why was he being so nice all of a sudden?

Inside, over coffee, Kuklinski explained his problem with this whole situation. He couldn't go on carrying Danny indefinitely, paying for motel rooms and bringing him food every day. Danny had to start pulling his own weight because he just couldn't afford it. He suggested that Barbara take Danny to a liquor store so he could hold it up.

After they left the dinner and Kuklinski departed, Danny told his ex-wife that he knew of a convenience store up in Sussex County that would be easy to knock off, the Ding Dong Dairy Store in Hardystown. Forget it, she told him. Her uncle worked there now. She didn't want him getting hurt. Danny pleaded with her, promising that he wouldn't hurt anyone, but she stuck to her guns. She dropped him off back at the motel and headed home. She wasn't going to help him rob stores. She already had more trouble than she needed.

On December 31, 1982, Richard Kuklinski moved Danny Deppner to the Turnpike Motel on Route 46 in Ridgefield, where Danny registered under the name Bill Bradly. His room was paid for each day just before checkout time. One of the maids at the motel remembered "Mr. Bradly," a tall man with dark, woolly hair and a thick mustache. He had tired eyes and drawn face. "Mr. Bradly" would never let her clean his room, just took the clean sheets and towels at the door and said he'd take care of it himself. She also remembered the white Cadillac with the blue top that came every day just before checkout time and parked in front of "Mr. Bradly's" room.

Danny was sleeping a little better now, but every once in a while he'd wake up in the middle of the night with that nightmare, Gary trying to grab him through the bed.

On Saturday, February 5, 1983, forty-four days after Gary Smith's death, Richard Kuklinski moved Danny Deppner once again, this time to an apartment in a residential section of suburban Bergenfield, New Jersey. The studio apartment belonged to a young man named Rich Patterson who was dating one of Kuklinski's daughters at the time. Patterson was away for the weekend, and Kuklinski had his own set of keys. Apartment 1 at 51 Fairview Avenue, Bergenfield, was the last place Danny Deppner ever had that nightmare.

* * *

On Sunday, May 14, 1983, a man was riding his bicycle along Clinton Road in Milford Township, New Jersey. It was a warm spring day, and the early-morning sun was sparkling off the waters of the Clinton Reservoir. The air was fresh, and the woods were alive with new growth. There was seldom very much traffic on this road, especially on Sunday mornings, and there wasn't a house for miles. It was beautiful.

As the man rode along the reservoir, something caught his attention to his left. An unusually large black bird was perched high in a tree. The man pulled his bike to the side of the road and stared up at the bird. It was a turkey buzzard, the biggest one he'd ever seen. He figured it must be looming over a carcass, probably a dead deer left behind by hunters. He got off his bike and went into the woods to investigate. Under the buzzard's tree he found something wrapped in green plastic garbage bags. One end of the large bundle was ripped, most likely by the scavenger bird. As he stepped closer, his stomach lurched. Part of a human head was peeking through the tear in the bag.

The bicyclist ran back to the road and marked the spot where he'd entered the woods with a fallen branch. He intended to ride down to the nearest house and call the police, but a car happened to come by, and he flagged it down. He told the driver to call the police, there was a body in the woods.

The police arrived within the hour and summoned Dr. Geetha Natarajan, the acting chief medical examiner of Passaic County. She examined the body at the scene but left it in the garbage bags. After photographs were taken, the body was carefully lifted off the ground and put in a body bag. Samples of the dead leaves underneath the body were taken. They would help Dr. Natarajan determine when the body had been left there. The body was then taken to the State Medical Examiner's Office in Newark, where she would perform the autopsy.

At the ME's office, Dr. Natarajan's first task was to remove the plastic bags, taking note of how many were used and how expertly the victim's limbs had been bound with paper tape. Then came the one job she detested most: dealing with the bugs. She took samples of all the insects and larvae she found present on the body, mainly carrion beetles and blowflies. The number of insect generations on the body would help determine how long it had been left in the woods. Identifying the types of insect would also be helpful since different species thrive at different times of the year. When Dr. Natarajan was certain that she had samples of all the species present, she hosed the rest of the swarm down the drain and ground them in the garbage disposal, glad to be rid of them.

Laying the body on a stainless steel worktable, Dr. Natarajan then began the autopsy. The victim was a male, six feet one and a half inches, 173 pounds. The man's face was almost totally skeletonized, and there was only partial flesh on the limbs, but the torso was very well preserved. Spring had come late that year, so the cold had kept him relatively fresh, and fortunately the buzzard had not had that many meals off this carcass.

She removed the clothing—a white V-neck T-shirt with extensive brown-red staining, a pair of blue jeans, a black leather belt, blue socks—and took note of the absence of shoes or a coat. There were no gunshot or stab wounds, but she did find hemorrhaging on the neck just above the Adam's apple and on the whites of the eyes. A pinkish flush was apparent on the skin around the shoulder and chest on one side. This kind of discoloration, called pink lividity, can indicate several things, most commonly carbon monoxide poisoning.

When Dr. Natarajan got to the stomach contents, she found more than two pounds of undigested food: beef, beans, potatoes, carrots, and beer. It was a large meal but not unusually so for a man this size. There was no sign of gastric emptying—the food hadn't moved on from the stomach through the digestive tract—which meant that the man was killed soon after he had finished his meal, perhaps during the meal. She examined the food itself and noticed that the beans had been burned. The meal was probably home-cooked, she believed, because a restaurant couldn't get away with serving burned food. The man must have been very hungry to eat it.

In the pocket of the man's jeans she found a black wallet that contained no money or identification. She did find five wet slips of paper in the wallet, which turned out to be motel receipts. There were also three photographs that had stuck together. She soaked them and carefully separated them, laying them on paper towels to dry. They were pictures of children, two boys and a girl. Dr. Natarajan bagged them and sent them up to the Passaic County prosecutor.

When he received the photos, the prosecutor laid them on his desk and stared at them. There was something familiar about those kids, but he couldn't place them. The pictures sat there for two days, haunting him, the little faces staring out at him, like three pathetic little orphans. Then it dawned on him. He did know those kids. They'd been in the Passaic County Prosecutor's Office with their mother and her lowlife boyfriend/common-law husband, whatever the hell he was, Percy House. Those were Barbara Deppner's kids. He picked up the phone and called the ME's office to tell Dr. Natarajan he had a good hunch who her body was. It was the father of those three kids, Daniel Everett Deppner.

Barbara Kuklinski didn't know what to think as her husband held the door for her and she walked into the
carpeted lobby of the restaurant. Richard was wearing his
dark glasses, even though it was evening, and he'd been
wearing them all day around the house, which always
made her uneasy, but now he was dressed to the nines in
his dark blue suit, a white shirt, and a maroon tie. This
was their favorite French restaurant, the place they always went to when they had something to celebrate.
He'd specifically asked her to wear the dove gray Christian Dior suit he'd bought her a few months ago. As they
went up to the maître d's station together, out of the
corner of her eye Barbara saw him take off the glasses and
put them in his pocket. He smiled at the maître d' as he
gave him their name. She couldn't figure it out. Richard
seemed to be in a good mood, but the dark glasses made
her suspicious. Was this really the good Richard, or was it
a new incarnation of the bad Richard?

The maître d' nodded to Richard and raised his finger
as if to say "just one moment." He turned and stepped
into the dining room, waving his hand at the pianist until
he caught the woman's eye. He nodded once to her, and

she stopped what she was playing and started a new song. Barbara recognized it immediately, Kenny Rogers's "Lady." When the record had first become popular, Richard declared it "her song," and whenever he was in a very good mood, he'd call ahead to the restaurant and make sure it was played for their arrival.

"Thank you, Richard," she said as the maître d' led them to their table.

He raised his eyebrows and smiled. "I haven't done that in a while."

"It's very sweet of you."

"Who else have I got to be sweet to?"

She smiled and squeezed his hand. But she was still suspicious.

As soon as they were seated, a waiter came and asked if they'd care for drinks. Richard wasn't much of a drinker, but he did like wine with his meals. The waiter fetched the wine list for him, but Barbara already knew what he'd order, a good Montrachet, their favorite red wine. The ones Richard ordered were never less than a hundred dollars a bottle.

The waiter returned with the bottle of Montrachet and showed Richard the label. He nodded his approval, and the waiter uncorked the wine, placing the cork in front of Richard, then poured a little into his glass. Richard took a sip, looked down, and considered it for a moment, then told the waiter it was very good. The waiter filled Barbara's glass first, then Richard's, then left to let them study the menu.

Barbara forced herself not to look at Richard over the top of her menu. She wasn't convinced that this was really the good Richard, and she knew from experience that anything could set the bad one off, though she was usually safe in public. Most times he saved his temper for behind closed doors. But not always.

There was the time she'd talked back to him at the house. He didn't sit on his temper that time. The explosion was immediate.

Barbara's father had been scheduled to undergo surgery that morning in Florida, and she was anxious to hear how he was. She and Richard weren't even dressed yet when the call came from her father's wife, and Barbara took it in their bedroom. She was understandably relieved when she heard that the surgery had been a success and her father would be fine. As she hung up the phone, Richard was just coming out of the bathroom in his underwear.

"So is the bastard dead?" he asked with a smirk.

She stared at him, stung by the senseless cruelty of his remark. "That wasn't necessary," she snapped back.

His face froze, and his eyes narrowed. Then she saw that look that always terrified her. His eyelids fluttered, and the eyeballs rolled back for a split second the same way a shark's does just before it's going to bite.

Panic filled Barbara's chest. She was already backing toward the door when he lunged.

"You do not talk back to me," he yelled. "Do you understand that? You do not talk back to *me.*"

She broke free from his grasp and ran down the steps into the living room, then down the flight of stairs to the front hallway, like a deer being chased by a grizzly bear. Though she was in her slippers and bathrobe, she didn't hesitate to throw the front door open and run out into the snow. Outside she'd be safe, she figured. He never showed his temper in public. She stood on the sidewalk, out of breath, clutching the robe close around her neck, wondering how long she'd have to wait before he calmed down and she could go back in.

But then the sound of the electric garage doors startled her. As the doors rose, an engine roared to life, and she saw the tailpipe of the red Calais spewing out exhaust on the cold air. The car screeched out of the garage in reverse. Richard was behind the wheel in his T-shirt. He bellowed out the open window, "You do not talk back to *me.*"

Barbara could see that he was out of his mind with rage.

She started to run. The sound of spinning tires was right behind her. He drove up onto the sidewalk, determined to run her down.

She ran for the next door neighbor's yard, slipping on the snow, heading for the big tree in the backyard. It was the only thing she could imagine that would protect her from the impact of the car.

She slipped once more before she reached the tree, falling on it, scrambling behind it, clutching it close, breathing so hard her chest hurt.

When she finally dared to peer around the tree, Barbara saw that the car was at an angle on the snow-covered front lawn. The engine was idling, and Richard was behind the wheel, but it wasn't moving. He wasn't pursuing her anymore. She took a closer look and saw that Richard was punching himself in the head, again and again, hitting himself hard with a closed fist. It was what he did when he was frustrated and couldn't vent his rage any other way. If he couldn't hit anyone else, he'd hit himself.

Reliving that horrible winter day, Barbara could feel her heart beat faster as she stared blankly at the menu in her hands. She refocused and started to read the selections quickly, afraid that Richard would know what she was thinking.

"Do you know what you're going to order, Rich?" she asked, looking over the top of her menu.

"Hmm?" Richard wasn't looking at his menu. He was staring at something at the back of the restaurant.

Barbara turned around and saw two couples seated at a leather banquette. One of the men was gesturing with his arms, telling a story that was making the others howl with laughter. The man was heavyset with a fleshy, oblong face and thin dark hair combed straight back. His jeweled cuff links glittered as he motioned with his hands. The women were considerably younger than the men, and one of them looked like a high-class call girl. The two men looked like hoods.

The corners of Richard's mouth drooped as he stared at the man telling the story. His eyes were narrow.

Barbara couldn't understand why this man was upsetting her husband. Her heart started to pound.

Richard Kuklinski touched his forehead where the scar was.

Barbara glanced quickly over her shoulder, but she didn't see any resemblance between this man and anyone she'd ever met. She shook her head, confused and anxious that their evening would be ruined after all, fearful that he would erupt right here in the middle of the restaurant.

He kept staring at the man. Suddenly Richard's eyes shot back at her. "That guy sort of reminds me of Roy."

Barbara swallowed hard and looked down at her menu, praying to God that this wouldn't set him off.

Roy DeMeo had a very bad temper, the kind of temper that flared fast and hot and came when you least expected it. A soldier in New York's Gambino crime family, DeMeo was subject to dramatic mood swings. He'd give you the shirt off his back one minute and cut your throat the next if you hurt his feelings.

Richard Kuklinski had seen for himself how evil DeMeo's temper could be one summer day in the late seventies, when DeMeo chartered a fishing boat out of Sheepshead Bay, Brooklyn, to take a few of his associates out for a pleasure cruise. They'd brought beer and wine, Italian bread and provolone cheese, sandwiches made with all kinds of Italian delicacies. Roy was a jolly host that day, regaling his men with jokes and stories as he encouraged them to eat, eat. It was a bright, sunny day, and the cool breeze was a relief from the sweltering heat of the city. The boat went out several miles, taking them to good fishing waters. The mood on board was pretty raucous by the time the captain cut his engines and moved to the stern, where he started to chum the waters with cut-up chunks of fish and fish blood in order to attract game fish. Chumming often attracts sharks, too, and

Kuklinski noticed several fins starting to circle the bloody water around the back of the boat. The men joked about the sharks and threw beer cans at them. Roy DeMeo had just finished making a toast to everyone's health and long life, his beer can held aloft, when out of the blue his face suddenly changed and he glared at one of his guests.

"You know, you got one motherfucking big mouth, pal."

The man was stunned. Everyone was. "Roy," he said, "I don't know what you're—"

"You know what the fuck I'm talking about."

DeMeo reached into the beer cooler, pulled out a pistol, and shot the man in the head, just like that. The man collapsed to the deck, and DeMeo put another bullet into his back. DeMeo then ordered his other guests to throw the bastard overboard to the sharks. No one dared object. The agitated sharks lunged for the body before it even hit the water. Their violent thrashing as they tore the body apart gave the mobster a grim satisfaction that only he understood completely.

Richard Kuklinski would never forget the twisted, sadistic look on DeMeo's face that day on the boat. It was a look he came to know very well.

DeMeo's crew hung out at a bar called the Gemini Lounge, on Flatlands Avenue in the Canarsie section of Brooklyn. Roy's cousin Joseph Guglielmo lived in the apartment behind the bar. His nickname was Dracula. One night Kuklinski had gone to the Gemini Lounge to see DeMeo, and Roy invited him to stay for dinner at his cousin's place. Kuklinski accepted the invitation and followed DeMeo through the back hallway into the apartment, where several young men were seated at the kitchen table. They were all members of DeMeo's crew. DeMeo preferred young guys; he felt they were hungrier and more willing to carry out his orders, no matter how gruesome.

Kuklinski took a seat at the table just as DeMeo's cousin Dracula was pouring out the big pasta pot into a colander in the sink. Steam plumed up around Dracula's head like a mushroom cloud. One of the young guys poured wine for everyone, and a big steaming bowl was brought to the table—angel hair and sausage. Kuklinski dug in. Wiseguys knew good food, and this was excellent. He was halfway through his meal, reaching for the bowl of grated Parmesan cheese, when all of a sudden DeMeo stood up and pointed a .22 fixed with a silencer at the kid across the table from him.

The kid dropped his fork. His eyes bugged out. "Roy! Roy! What—?"

"Shut up!"

The shots sounded like balloons popping. The kid's chair toppled over backward, and he crashed to the floor, dead.

DeMeo sat back down and returned to his meal, twirling pasta on his fork. One of the other crew members got up to move the body. "Leave him," DeMeo barked with his mouth full. "Finish eating," he ordered. "Everybody eat."

They all ate.

When DeMeo finally gave them the okay, his men did what they did best: They made the body "disappear." They took the kid's corpse into the bathroom and threw him in the tub, where they drained his blood, then proceeded to cut him up and wrap the pieces in small sealed packages. The packages were distributed to a number of Dumpsters around the city. DeMeo's crew had honed this chore down to an efficient assembly-line process. They'd done it many times before. As the boys went to work, DeMeo and Kuklinski sat down to espresso and biscotti and talked business.

In the mid-sixties Barbara Kuklinski's uncle had worked at a film lab in Manhattan, Deluxe Films, and through him Richard Kuklinski had gotten a job there. At the lab Kuklinski discovered that there was money to be made selling bootleg copies of popular films, particularly the Disney cartoon features. Kuklinski had access to 8mm loops, master copies from which legitimate copies were made. But he soon found that on the black market there were lesser-known celluloid heroines who were far more lucrative than Snow White and Cinderella, played by actresses with names like Holly Bangkok, Ginger Sweet, and Amber Licke.

Bootleg copies of legitimate films could only be sold piecemeal; selling more than five reels to a single customer was considered a big order. But porno movies, Kuklinski discovered, sold by the dozens to adult bookstores and mail-order outlets. Kuklinski saw that there were big profits to be made in porn. All he needed was a little venture capital. But this wasn't the kind of loan he could go to a bank for. The only alternative for financing illegal enterprises is a loan shark, and Kuklinski knew someone who knew someone who knew a loan shark who was an associate in the Gambino crime family.

Kuklinski was lent sixty-five thousand dollars, seed money to start mass-producing porno films. Kuklinski had no problem using the lab's equipment after hours to make the films; the problem he hadn't anticipated, though, was distribution. Selling porn wasn't like selling Mickey Mouse and Donald Duck out of the trunk of his car. He was sending his product across the country, and payments weren't always prompt. He had expenses to meet in order to keep his production up, so he just figured he'd put off the loan shark for a little while until those late payments came in. When he got paid, the shylock would get paid.

But Kuklinski had figured wrong. Back in the sixties he still had a lot to learn about dealing with the Mafia. To them, a due date is a due date. There are no extensions, and they rarely cut you any slack, especially when money is involved.

When Kuklinski fell behind in his weekly payments and then started disregarding the warnings, the loan shark sent someone over to see him, someone who specialized in "attitude adjustments."

Late one night Kuklinski was by himself in the basement of the film labs, waiting for the elevator. He'd been running the loop machine all night, making copies, and he was dead tired. All he wanted was to get home and go to bed. But when the elevator arrived, he was surprised to see three men inside. They walked out with their hands in their pockets, forming a circle around him. He had no idea who these men were, but they knew him. They hustled him into a bathroom and locked the door.

The biggest of the three stood right in his face. "So where the fuck is the money, Polack? Huh? C'mon, get it up."

"Who the f—"

The man on his right side, the one with the dark, evil eyes, kicked Kuklinski's knee out, and he fell to the cement floor. Then he was hit with something hard across the back of his head. Kuklinski linked his fingers behind his head and covered up. His ears were ringing.

"It must be true what they say about you Polacks," the big guy said. "Too fucking stupid to know what's good for them. Now I'm gonna ask you again: Where's the money, Polack?"

Kuklinski kept blinking, but his eyes wouldn't focus. "I—I don't—"

"No more fucking around, Polack. Get the money. Now."

The third guy booted him in the side and broke a rib. Kuklinski sucked in his breath and held it to stem the pain, but it didn't help much.

"So what's it gonna be, Polack? You gonna pay or what?"

"I—"

Evil Eyes kicked him in the kidneys. Kuklinski threw his head back and squeezed his eyes shut.

"No more fucking excuses, Polack. *We want the fucking money.*"

Kuklinski could hardly breathe. "This week," he grunted. "I'll get it."

"When?"

"Friday . . . I'll pay up on Friday."

"How much?"

Kuklinski couldn't catch his breath. He couldn't get enough air. "What I owe . . . up-to-date . . . everything."

"What the hell's wrong with you, you dumb fuck? You think this is forgive and forget? No fucking way. The whole note. You pay the whole fucking note by Friday or you're dead. You hear me, Polack?"

Kuklinski's vision cleared a little. He saw three guns pointed down at him. He started to nod. "All right . . . by Friday . . . the whole thing." Anything to get rid of them.

"Okay, by Friday. Now you're not gonna forget again, are you?"

Kuklinski winced and shook his head.

"Yeah, well, I'd like to believe you, but you Polacks aren't too smart. You people forget things. I'm gonna give you something so you don't forget. Okay?" The big man raised his gun hand and bashed Kuklinski over the forehead with his pistol.

Kuklinski fell back on his haunches and clutched his head. Blood streamed into his eyes. The three men had a good laugh as they filed out of the bathroom. The big man called back to him from the doorway, "Now don't you forget, Polack."

Kuklinski later found out that the big man was Roy DeMeo. The other two were goons from DeMeo's crew. That was Richard Kuklinski's first encounter with the man who eventually became his rabbi in crime.

Kuklinski came up with the money, and he let his anger simmer quietly inside him. But he soon found that dealing with the mob would be an occupational hazard he'd just have to live with if he intended to stay in the porno business, and as time passed, he came to learn how the Mafia operated. The beating DeMeo had given him was business, nothing personal, and since he'd come up with the money on time, all was forgiven. So much so that Kuklinski ended up becoming partners with the man who gave him the deep scar in his forehead, which he vowed to himself he would *never* forgive or forget.

By the mid-seventies Kuklinski and DeMeo had an office at 225

Lafayette Street in lower Manhattan, just around the corner from the film labs. By then DeMeo had become a major player in the pornography business, operating a network of bookstores and sex clubs around the country, including the infamous Plato's Retreat II in Brick Township, New Jersey. Kuklinski supervised a small staff of people who viewed, selected, and mass-produced porno films, while DeMeo took care of distribution through his bookstores.

During this period DeMeo came to appreciate the "Polack's" other abilities. Kuklinski was intimidating in size and demeanor, and he wasn't afraid to do whatever was necessary, be it with his fists or with a gun. Eventually DeMeo started subcontracting "little jobs" to Kuklinski, collecting from deadbeat loan shark customers who had fallen behind in their payments. But there was one problem: Kuklinski's temper. Kuklinski, who had already killed out of anger several times by this point in his life, had a hard time walking the line between physical intimidation and mortal violence, and a dead deadbeat isn't any good to anyone.

"Polack," DeMeo said to him one day, "you just don't have the temperament for this kind of work. A leg breaker needs to have a little restraint. But don't worry about it. I got some jobs you'd be perfect for." So under DeMeo's tutelage Richard Kuklinski learned how to kill for profit and became a hit man for the mob.

Their association was a very profitable one. At the time the minimum price for a professional hit was forty thousand dollars, but it didn't take long before Kuklinski's reputation brought his price up to twice that figure. Still, despite their success together, Kuklinski was never totally at ease around DeMeo. By the early eighties the mobster's mood swings had become more sudden and irrational. DeMeo wanted to be respected as a traditional "man of honor," but in fact, he was a loose cannon, and his erratic ways kept him from rising in the Gambino hierarchy. He was tolerated only because he brought in a lot of money for the family. But the crew he had assembled was not the typical band of proven earners. Instead he had put together a pack of obedient Doberman pinschers for himself. When Roy DeMeo said, "Kill," they killed. No hesitation. And though Richard Kuklinski did a lot of "jobs" for DeMeo and earned a lot of money for the mobster, he was not an official member of DeMeo's crew. To DeMeo he would always be "the Polack," which meant an outsider.

One night in Dracula's apartment behind the Gemini Lounge, Kuklinski was having coffee with DeMeo and a few of his crew members, discussing Corvettes. DeMeo wanted Kuklinski to get as many as he could. There was a big demand for them in the Middle East, where he'd been shipping stolen luxury cars and selling them for a nice profit. Kuklinski said he had a few guys in north Jersey who could steal brand-new Corvettes right off the lot. Kuklinski was in the middle of assuring DeMeo that he could get him whatever car he wanted when he suddenly realized that everybody had moved to the other side of the room behind Roy, and they were all smiling these weird little smiles. DeMeo was holding an Uzi machine pistol fitted with a silencer. It was leveled at Kuklinski.

"Hey, Polack, how would you like me to pull the trigger?"

Kuklinski had no idea what he'd done to deserve this, but by this time in his life he'd been in DeMeo's position many times. He knew the rush you felt holding a gun on someone, the adrenaline high of total control over another human being. Sitting there in Dracula's House of Horrors, where they cut and packaged people like Italian sausage, Kuklinski did the only thing he thought he could do: take the joy out of it for Roy.

He looked DeMeo straight in the eye. "It's up to you, Roy. I have no control over the situation. Do what you want." He made it sound as if he didn't care one way or the other.

DeMeo's grin collapsed. He sneered and glared, then lowered the Uzi and tossed it on the table. He forced a laugh and looked around the room at all his men. "The Polack's got some pair of balls on him," he announced.

The crew laughed with their leader and made like it was all a big joke.

But Richard Kuklinski knew better. He'd ruined it for Roy. He'd stolen the moment. There was no thrill in killing someone who didn't care.

Dracula poured more coffee, and the men returned to their seats. DeMeo shook his finger at Kuklinski and warned him with a twisted grin: "One of these days, Polack, one of these days. Either I'm gonna kill you or you're gonna kill me. Believe it."

Kuklinski shrugged as he spooned sugar into his coffee. "Whatever you say, Roy."

On January 10, 1983, Roy DeMeo missed an appointment with his uncle. He also missed a birthday party for one of his children that evening, which worried his family. It wasn't like Roy to miss a family event like that. A week and a half later his maroon Cadillac was discovered in the parking lot of a boat club in Brooklyn. When the police opened the trunk—four weeks after Gary Smith's bloated body was found under the bed at the York Motel in New Jersey—they found Roy DeMeo's body, frozen stiff from the winter cold. He'd been shot five times, encrusted wounds behind both ears. A chandelier was draped over his body. Law enforcement authorities are still trying to decipher the possible symbolism of this gesture.

Years later Richard Kuklinski indicated that he killed Roy DeMeo, but he refused to comment on the significance of the chandelier. When asked whether or not he felt the rush of total control as he pulled the trigger, he remained silent.

TWENTY-ONE

FRIDAY, OCTOBER 31, 1986—10:10ᴀᴍ

"So where the hell is he, Dom?" Investigator Paul Smith was sitting on a picnic table on the brown grass by the telephone booths at the Vince Lombardi Service Area, smiling and nodding as if he were saying something else. He could see his breath it was so chilly.

Dominick Polifrone was sitting next to him, smiling and gesturing. "How the fuck do I know? Just keep smiling."

Dominick scanned the parking lot without making it obvious. It was a raw, cloudy day, and motorists were rushing from their cars to get in out of the cold. He'd talked to Kuklinski yesterday and told him that he was going to be meeting the "rich Jewish kid" here at ten o'clock. He said he was going to be giving the kid a sample of the cocaine he wanted to buy. Dominick had suggested to Kuklinski that he come by to "eyeball" the kid so he'd know who he was supposed to kill when the time came. Kuklinski had agreed to come and take a look. He'd said he'd meet Dom after the kid left, inside by the men's room.

"I'm freezing my ass off out here, Dom." Paul Smith

was still smiling. "He'd better fucking show up. I did a lot of research getting ready for this."

Dominick's eyes narrowed. "What research?"

"I asked Ronnie Donahue how I should play the rich kid, how I should act to be believable."

"Oh, yeah? What'd he say?"

"He told me to act like a mutt."

"Oh . . . you mean he told you to 'act natural.' "

Smith pursed his lips and glared at Dominick. "That's *exactly* what he said. How'd you know that?"

"He told me."

They started laughing for real. Neither of them looked directly at the green sedan parked thirty feet away where Investigator Ron Donahue was sitting behind the wheel, pretending to be reading a newspaper. Donahue had an earplug in his ear that kept him in contact with the three other backups planted around the service area. A large wax paper soft drink cup sat on the dashboard in front of him. As soon as he heard that Kuklinski was spotted, he'd move the cup off the dashboard so Dominick and Paul would know the big guy was on his way.

"Don't make me laugh, Smith. I'm not supposed to like you that much."

"Why not? I'm the rich Jewish kid. I'm your best customer. I'm gonna buy two goddamn keys off you. I might even buy three. But I gotta tell you, Dom, your price isn't that great. So don't get wise."

Dominick gave him an evil look. "Smith, I should've killed you when I had the chance."

Paul Smith had to pinch his nose to keep from bursting out loud.

"Hey, Dom, don't you think it looks a little strange that two guys are hanging around out here in the cold, laughing like a couple of nuts? Maybe we'd better just do it in case Richie is out there somewhere in a different car looking at us."

Dominick scanned the lot. "Yeah, maybe you're right." He reached into the pocket of his leather jacket and pulled out an envelope. Inside was a plastic Baggie containing an ounce of powdered sugar, the rich kid's "coke" sample. He handed it to Paul Smith.

Smith peeked into the envelope and put it in his pocket. "Oh, thank you, sir, thank you."

"You know, Paul, I wouldn't be surprised if Richie sent someone else to come take a look."

Smith rolled his eyes. "Get outta here."

"No, think about it. I wouldn't put it past the son of a bitch."

"Get out. Who would he send?"

"Maybe his buddy Tim, the guy from south Jersey."

"Why would he do that? If he brought somebody else into this, he'd have to give him a piece of the pie."

"Hey, I'm not a psychiatrist. I don't know how his mind works. All I know is that any mutt who'd kill with fucking cyanide is liable to do anything."

"Hmm . . . maybe." Paul Smith wasn't smiling anymore.

Dominick glanced over at Ron Donahue's car. The cup was still on the dashboard.

"Do you really think he'd send Tim?" Smith asked.

Dominick shrugged. "Why not? We don't know what he looks like. He'd be perfect. He could be out there right now taking pictures of us."

"Pictures! Shit, I never thought of that. What if Richie gets a picture of me? He could follow me to the mall or something. He could follow me home! What if he decides to do you a favor and kill me on his own?"

"Calm down, Smith. Richie doesn't give it away. He'll wait for the big score."

"Yeah . . . I guess." Paul Smith didn't sound convinced.

The soft drink cup hadn't moved.

"You know, Dom, I hate to say this, but I think Richie's getting hinky."

"No, he's not."

"Dom, he told you he'd be here just to take a look. I don't think he'd send someone else. There's no risk in just looking. He should be here. He's definitely getting hinky, Dom. He is."

Dominick didn't answer. The same thing had crossed his mind, but he didn't want to believe it. He'd seen bad guys suddenly get suspicious and start acting strange before. It was pretty common actually. But that wasn't the case with Kuklinski. He knew it; he could feel it with this guy. Kuklinski was cautious, *very* cautious, but he wasn't hinky. At least not yet.

"We'd better wrap this up in case he is looking," Dominick finally said. "No sense hanging around."

"Right."

Dominick flashed his million-dollar smile and extended his hand to the "rich kid." "Well, my friend, it's been nice. I hope to be doing business with you soon. Next time I'll bring my big friend with the nasal spray. He'll give you a nice little nose job."

"Wonderful, wonderful. I can't wait." Paul shook Dominick's hand and flashed his wise-ass grin. He started to turn away. "I'll catch you back in Fairfield, Dom."

"Yup."

"Bye-bye now."

"So long."

They split up and walked back to their cars. As Dominick moved past Ron Donahue's green sedan, he saw the paper cup on the dashboard. He hammered his fist against the driver's door out of frustration as he passed.

Ron Donahue didn't flinch. He just turned the page of his newspaper.

EARLY NOVEMBER 1986

At the Organized Crime and Racketeering Bureau offices in Fairfield, the members of the Operation Iceman task force kept a bottle of Johnnie Walker Black. A photograph of Richard Kuklinski's face had been taped over the label. When meetings ran late and tempers got short, they'd bring out the bottle and everyone would have a shot to soothe the tension. Tonight the bottle was running low.

Deputy Attorney General Bob Carroll leaned back in his chair and linked his fingers behind his head. "So. What do we do now?"

Dominick Polifrone rubbed his eyes. They'd been asking variations of the same question all night, and it didn't seem like anyone liked his answer because they kept going over and over the same territory. Dominick hadn't heard from Kuklinski since the day before he had given the "rich Jewish kid" the "coke" sample at the Lombardi Service Area two weeks ago. His beeper had gotten so quiet he'd actually checked the batteries, thinking maybe they were dead. But that wasn't the problem. Kuklinski just wasn't calling. He seemed to have lost interest in "Dominick Provenzano" and dropped him like a hot potato.

T
W
E
N
T
Y
-
T
W
O

Sitting around the conference-room table, Bob Carroll, Paul Smith, Ron Donahue, and Deputy Chief Bobby Buccino had been casting around all night for new ways to get Kuklinski back on track, but Dominick thought they were starting to panic. They apparently didn't think much of his advice: Just leave the guy alone for now. If the guy really was hinky, he reasoned, then they've lost him, and Michael Dominick Provenzano didn't stand a chance anymore. But if Kuklinski wasn't suspicious, then he was just doing his usual thing, disappearing for a while to make his mark a little crazy. That's what Dominick thought was going on.

Deputy Chief Buccino stared down into his plastic cup. "I understand why you didn't want to call him before, Dominick. You had to establish your control over the relationship. But why don't you want to call him now? What've you got to lose?"

Dominick sighed. He was too tired to get mad. "Look, Pat Kane of the state police compiled six years' worth of information on Kuklinski. Whatta we do, just forget about all that? This is how Kuklinski operates. He gets you interested in a deal, then he pulls back and disappears to make you so hungry you'll do anything to get what you want. We *know* this. I'm telling you. This is nothing unusual for him."

Paul Smith leaned forward on the table. "But, Dominick, look at it from Richie's point of view. He hasn't made any money off you. Eleven hundred on the hit kit—big deal. You've been talking about this big arms deal with him, about the five to ten hit kits you need for the mob guys, about ripping off the rich kid, but so far he's seen zilch. Maybe he's saying to himself, 'This Dominick guy is bullshit. He talks a good game, but it's always wait and see with him. To hell with him.' Maybe it's time to throw him a bone, call him up and set up something definite."

"That's what you and I tried to do at Lombardi, Paul, but he didn't show."

"Yeah, but he hasn't made any real money off you yet, Dom—"

"Did he make any money off Paul Hoffman before he killed

him? How about Louis Masgay? I don't think money is the issue here. It's control. He's pulling back to make me hungry. So I've gotta do the same thing to make him even *hungrier*. Otherwise, if I go to him, we have to start playing the game by his rules, doing what he says. And that puts me at a disadvantage. Don't you see that?"

"But, Dom—"

"And would *you* want to be at a disadvantage with this mother-*fucker?*" The ballistic "fuck" quieted the objections.

Ron Donahue, who hadn't said much until now, broke the silence. "Dom's right. Fuck 'im. Let 'im stew."

Eyebrows went up. Ron Donahue usually didn't say much, but with a reputation like his, he didn't have to. He was known for getting results. His vote of confidence in Dominick meant a lot.

"Why do you think Dominick's right?" Bob Carroll ventured.

Donahue poured himself a little more scotch. "He just told you, for chrissake." Enough said.

Bob Carroll agreed with Dominick's reasoning, but he still wasn't comfortable with the idea of letting Kuklinski be. As head of the task force he was the one who had to answer for what they did or didn't do. He would have a hard time explaining to his superiors that they had officially decided to do nothing. He looked at Dominick. "Hypothetically, what if he kills again while we're sitting here, playing it cool?"

"You tell me. How the hell're we supposed to know what's going on in that crazy head of his? You wanna take him down right now on the federal charges with the hit kit, just tell me and we'll do it. But I thought the murders took precedence. This task force was formed to nail him on the murders. If you think we have enough to get an indictment, beautiful. Let's arrest him and wrap it up. Okay?" Dominick knew they didn't have enough evidence to get a conviction yet.

"Look," Dominick continued, "Kuklinski's been telling me things. He told me about the cyanide, how he's used it to kill. He's told me about arms deals he's done. He's told me a lot of things. He's been treating me like an equal. We're two bad guys of equal stature. Now if I go running to him, begging him to come kill the rich kid with me, what's that gonna do to my position? All of a sudden, in his eyes, I won't be an equal anymore. I'm gonna be just some mook who can't pull off a rip-off by himself. I'm gonna *need* him, and then we won't be equals anymore. Would you confide in someone you considered beneath you?"

Bob Carroll puckered his lips and reluctantly nodded. "Okay. I see your point. For now we'll wait. But if we wait another week, another *two* weeks and you still don't hear from him, then what? We're gonna have to do something."

Bobby Buccino spoke up. "If it comes to that, we'll figure some other way to smoke him out. It doesn't have to be Dominick. It can be someone else. Maybe we can send Kane and Volkman back to the house to talk to him."

Bob Carroll nodded in thought. "Okay. But start thinking about it. Just in case."

"Fine."

"There's just one thing that bothers me—"

A beeper went off. Everyone froze. They were looking at Dominick.

He pulled his beeper out of his belt and shook his head. "Not mine."

Paul Smith pulled his out and looked at the LCD readout. "Relax. It's my wife."

"Go call her," Bobby Buccino said. "Maybe it's an emergency."

Paul Smith rubbed his temples and wrinkled his face. "I just remembered. I told her I'd be home for dinner tonight. I *promised* her. Shit. I totally forgot."

It was five of ten. Paul Smith was gonna catch hell for this. The men around the table could all sympathize.

Paul Smith propped his head on his chin and looked at Bob Carroll. "So what were you saying, Bob?"

"I was just wondering, what if Kuklinski does have another source for cyanide? He could be out there plotting God-knows-what against God-knows-who."

Dominick had already considered the possibility. "You can never be sure of anything with this guy. He did seem pretty desperate to get the cyanide from me, but who knows?"

"That's right," Bobby Buccino said. "After all, he did have that other guy who used to get it for him. What's his name? The ice-cream man."

"Yeah," Dominick said, staring at Kuklinski's face on the bottle of scotch. "Mister Softee."

On hot, sticky summer evenings on the urban streets of northern New Jersey, an incongruous sound mingles with the rumble of traffic and the raucous rhythms blasting from boom boxes. By August it becomes so familiar people hardly notice it anymore. It's an innocent singsong tune played on a celeste that is very reminiscent of the theme song from *Mister Rogers' Neighborhood*, and the recorded sound track is played over and over again, often late into the night. It comes from the Mister Softee ice-cream trucks that trawl the inner-city neighborhoods, enticing children outside with that familiar strain, inviting them to come down and buy a cool, sweet treat. Inevitably anyone who drives one of these ice-cream trucks becomes known to his patrons as Mister Softee, but in the early 1980s there was one driver from North Bergen who was known to Richard Kuklinski as Mister Softee, and he was into more than just Dixie cups and Eskimo Pies. His real name was Robert Prongay.

Just as Agent 007, James Bond, had Q, the technical wizard who supplied him with deadly gadgets and high-tech weaponry, the Iceman had Mister Softee. Although he was ten years younger than Kuklinski, Prongay was the Iceman's instructor in the various methods of assassination. While mobster Roy DeMeo showed Kuklinski that murder could be profitable, Prongay showed him that it could also be interesting. Kuklinski considered Mister Softee both a madman and a genius.

When Robert Prongay was a student at Auburn University in Alabama, he channeled his creative energies into pornographic filmmaking. He transformed his room at the Magnolia Dormitory into a studio and rigged a bunk bed over a water bed, installing a two-way mirror in the mattress of the upper berth so that he could film sequences from overhead. His works were shown on campus in dorms and fraternity houses, where admissions were charged. When the administration got wind of this, the campus police were sent to raid Prongay's room at 6:00 A.M. on May 14, 1974. In their search, they found eight porno films that appeared to have been processed "in New York or New Jersey." Prongay was eventually expelled from the university for his transgressions.

But by the time Robert Prongay became associated with Richard Kuklinski several years later, Mister Softee was into more than just making movies. Prongay had become an expert in arcane killing techniques.

Kuklinski first learned about the ways of cyanide from Prongay, who mysteriously seemed to have no trouble obtaining the poison. To prove the efficiency of putting cyanide into a spray mist, Prongay took him along on a job. They drove to a bank in Pennsylvania early one morning and waited for a certain bank officer to show up for work. When the man arrived, Kuklinski watched from the car as Prongay strolled over to his target, feigned a sneeze, and sprayed cyanide into the man's face from a small nasal spray bottle. The man collapsed to the asphalt, struggled briefly, then keeled over and died. It took about fifteen seconds, start to finish. From that moment on, Kuklinski became a true believer in the wonders of cyanide.

But cyanide wasn't the only poison in Mister Softee's arsenal. He had developed a concoction that worked particularly well in crowded bars where a killer could pretend to be intoxicated and carry a glass of the toxin as if it were a cocktail. The "drunk" would pass by his intended victim, stumble, and spill the liquid onto the person's pants. The killer would apologize profusely, but by the time he started to walk away, the man would already be having trouble breathing as the poison penetrated his skin and entered his system. In the panic caused by the dying man's collapse, the "drunk" would escape unnoticed.

Mister Softee experimented with other poisons as well: chloral hydrate, succinylcholine, ricinine. But these didn't hold a candle to cyanide.

Also an army-trained demolitions expert, Prongay was equally adept with explosives. One of his inventions was called the Seat of Death. A shotgun shell was glued to a square of plywood and surrounded with flash powder. The board was surreptitiously placed under the driver's seat of the intended victim's car with a small cup of ignition fluid positioned next to the shell. When the victim drove the car, he would inevitably hit a bump big enough to upset the cup of fluid, which would ignite the flash powder and fire the shotgun shell up through the car seat.

One time Kuklinski and Prongay had been given a contract murder, and their Mafia employer stipulated that only the target was to be killed, no innocent bystanders. This was a problem because the gregarious gentleman was seldom alone. Prongay rigged a bomb to the man's car with a remote-control detonator, but they hadn't counted on their target's conviviality. The man must have *hated* to be alone because he always had someone with him—his wife, one of his kids, friends, business associates, anyone. Kuklinski and Prongay had to follow him in their van for three days before the man was alone in the car. It was like an orgasm for Mister Softee when he was finally able to flip the switch on the remote control and feel the vibrations of the explosion.

On another murder for hire they found that they couldn't get close to their victim or his car because of the cadre of bodyguards he kept. Taking a tip from a movie he saw, Mister Softee strapped some C-4 plastic explosive and a detonator to a toy remote-control car. They waited a block away, watching the man's limousine. When the man finally came out and got into the car, Mister Softee sent the toy car on its way, maneuvering it underneath the limo. When he hit the switch, the C-4 turned a hundred-thousand-dollar stretch into scrap metal.

Though he savored the unorthodox methods, Prongay, an avid reader of *Soldier of Fortune* magazine, wasn't at all averse to doing things the old-fashioned way. When he and Kuklinski were sent to collect on a bad debt from the owner of an adult bookstore outside Chicago, the man refused to pay them. Mister Softee simply told the man it was too bad he felt that way because he was going to have to go out of business now. The bookstore owner looked puzzled as the two men from New Jersey started walking out of his store. Then Prongay lobbed a hand grenade over his shoulder from the doorway. It was the last thing the man saw.

Together Kuklinski and Prongay did "jobs" all over the country. One job took them to Canoga Park, California, the pornography capital of the country. A porno distributor owed someone in New York a lot of money, and he was making it plain that he didn't intend to pay up. He was making his shylock look like a fool, and that couldn't be tolerated.

Prongay and Kuklinski shipped their guns to Los Angeles via air express, then flew out themselves. They took their time scouting out the man's home in Canoga Park, which to their annoyance was built like a fortress. Posing as a deliveryman who required the man's signature in order to leave a package, Prongay rang the doorbell and waited by the heavy metal door, peering through the peephole. After a long wait Prongay was told through the intercom that the man wasn't at home, that he was on vacation. But after watching the house day and night, Prongay and Kuklinski were convinced that the man was inside hiding. Prongay wanted to bomb the whole place to kingdom come, but Kuklinski reminded him that the wiseguy who had sent them would not be pleased if he found out the man's family had been hurt. So they waited and tried to think of another way. The afternoon wore on, and the man's family left the compound by car. Then, as the sun was setting on the horizon, Prongay suddenly remembered the peephole in the door.

He told Kuklinski to check his gun and follow him. At the front door, Prongay drew his weapon and motioned for Kuklinski to do the same. Then he rang the bell and peered through the peephole. Prongay had remembered that when there's a strong backlight, you can see silhouettes through a security peephole, and sure enough, he saw a dark shape coming toward him in the peephole, spears of light coming from the floor-to-ceiling windows at the end of the hallway behind. As the silhouette was just about to peer into his end of the peephole, Prongay started firing, and Kuklinski followed suit. They heard something go *thunk* against the door, then heard some moaning, but it was brief. They walked calmly back to their car and headed for Hollywood to see the brass stars embedded in the sidewalk on the Walk of Fame. Kuklinski suggested they go check out Rodeo Drive as long as they were in L.A. He bought a gift for his wife there, the satin pillow she kept on their bed at home.

It was also Mister Softee's idea to freeze Louis Masgay's body as an experiment to see if freezing could truly disguise the time of death. At the time Kuklinski and Prongay had rented adjacent garages in the same complex. Kuklinski's space did not have electricity, but Prongay's did. However, the police never found a freezer large enough to hold a man in either garage. The only freezing unit Kuklinski would have had access to was the ice-cream locker in Mister Softee's truck, which was powered by an electric generator when the truck's engine wasn't running. During the two years that Louis Masgay was missing, Robert Prongay sold ice cream out of that truck.

In many ways Kuklinski saw Mister Softee as a mentor, someone who showed him that there were better ways to kill: quiet ways, bloodless ways, foolproof ways, nearly undetectable ways. It was the perfect student-teacher relationship: One had the know-how; the other had the ambition. But in August 1984 the two men had a disagreement that led to some heated words, and the volatile Mister Softee made the mistake of his life: He threatened Kuklinski by saying that he knew where he lived.

He must not have realized that Richard Kuklinski's home was sacred. The mere suggestion that he would even think about approaching Kuklinski's wife and children sealed Robert Prongay's fate.

On August 9, 1984, Prongay failed to appear in court, where he was facing aggravated assault charges for bombing the front door of his ex-wife's home and threatening to run over both her and their teenage son. The judge issued a bench warrant, and two sheriff's detectives were dispatched to find him. The next afternoon they located his garage on Newkirk Street near Seventieth Street in North Bergen, just across the courtyard from Richard Kuklinski's garage. When the detectives opened the garage door, the first thing they saw was Robert Prongay's lifeless body hanging out the counter window of his Mister Softee truck. He'd been shot twice in the chest with a .38-caliber revolver.

Crayon drawings of turkeys and Pilgrims hung in the windows of St. Mary's Catholic School on Washington Avenue in Dumont. The leaves had turned, and the residential streets that led to Sunset Street were lined with knee-high piles. As Barbara Kuklinski turned the corner onto her street, she heard a heavy thud in the trunk of the red Oldsmobile Calais. She frowned and made a face. She'd just gone grocery shopping, and the heaviest item she'd bought was a gallon of milk. She prayed that it hadn't broken open. Who'd want to hear Richard if it had?

As she approached the house, she noticed that Matt's car was in the driveway. Richard's car wasn't there. Christen and Matt didn't hang around the house much when Richard was home.

She pulled the car into the driveway and popped the trunk, hoping she wouldn't find it flooded with spilled milk. When she lifted the trunk, she saw that the plastic gallon was out of the bag and on its side, but nothing had spilled. As she turned the bag upright and started to repack it, she suddenly heard someone calling to her from the street.

"Mrs. Kuklinski? Mrs. Kuklinski?"

She turned and saw two men in suits coming up the driveway. She couldn't imagine what they wanted. Then she noticed that one of them was holding up a badge.

"Mrs. Kuklinski, I'm Detective Volkman, New Jersey State Police. This is Detective Kane. We're looking for your husband."

"Well, I— Why are you looking for my husband?"

Barbara Kuklinski watched Detective Kane's eyes scouring the inside of the trunk. He seemed angry and suspicious.

But so was she. She didn't appreciate this sudden intrusion. Why were they confronting her out here in the driveway? Why didn't they come to the door? "Is there something wrong?" she asked. She knew her voice had a sharp edge to it, and she didn't care.

"We're looking for your husband, Mrs. Kuklinski," Detective Kane said. "We have some questions we'd like to ask him."

"About what?"

They ignored her question. "Is he at home, Mrs. Kuklinski?"

"His car's not here, so I guess he isn't home."

"Do you know where he is, Mrs. Kuklinski?"

"No."

"Is there any way you can get in touch with him?"

"I don't know where he is."

"Did he leave a phone number where you could leave a message?"

"I just told you, Detective, I don't know where he is." Detective Kane was still staring into the trunk as if he were looking for something. "What's this all about? What's the problem?"

"We'd prefer to discuss it directly with your husband, Mrs. Kuklinski," Detective Volkman said. He was passing her off, and she didn't like that.

The front door opened then. Shaba was barking. Matt stepped outside without his jacket. Christen was in the doorway, holding the big black Newfoundland by the collar.

"What's the matter, Mom?" Christen called out.

Before Barbara could answer, the two detectives moved toward Matt. "Excuse me, what's your name?"

Matt was startled by their abruptness. When he hesitated, they fired off another question. "What exactly are you doing here, sir?"

Barbara put herself between Matt and the detectives. "He's my daughter's boyfriend if that's any business of yours. Now what I want to know is what *you're* doing here."

Volkman suddenly looked grim. "I told you, Mrs. Kuklinski. We need to talk to your husband."

"No, you didn't tell me, Detective. *What* do you want to talk to him about?"

Kane answered. "We need to question him regarding a number of murders."

"What?"

"When do you expect your husband to return, Mrs. Kuklinski?"

The last question didn't register. "A number of murders" was still echoing in her ears. Those words and Shaba's barking were the only things she could hear.

"Mom? What's going on, Mom?"

The trembling in Christen's voice struck a nerve. Her family, her home was being invaded. A mother's instinct is to protect her children from harm, and Barbara immediately lashed out.

"Get out!"

"Mrs. Kuklinski—"

"Get off my property!" she demanded.

"Mrs. Kuklinski, if you let me ex—"

"Show me a warrant or get the hell out of here. *Get out!*"

"Mrs.—"

"Christen," she yelled, "let the dog go."

Shaba was agitated, barking and straining at the collar, baring his teeth. Christen could just barely control him. "But, Mom—"

"Let Shaba go, I said."

But Christen wouldn't let go of the dog's collar. The two detectives just stood there, staring at the big black dog, waiting for something to happen.

When it became obvious that the young woman wasn't going to release the dog, Detective Volkman pulled a business card out of his pocket. "Mrs. Kuklinski, when your husband comes home, please have him call me."

Barbara Kuklinski just stared at the card in her hand. Murder? She didn't believe this was happening.

The two detectives crossed the lawn then and headed for their car, which was parked across the street a few doors down.

Barbara stared at the state police seal on the business card. *A number of murders?* She knew Richard was no angel, but murder? He had a vicious temper, but not murder. She couldn't imagine.

Christen was trembling. "Were they serious, Mom?"

Barbara pulled herself together. She didn't want to upset the kids. "It's nothing, honey. It must be some kind of misunderstanding. Take in the groceries for me, will you, Matt? Christen, bring Shaba inside."

"But, Mom—" Christen started, concern in her eyes.

"Go ahead," she told her daughter. "Take him in before the neighbors complain about the barking."

Reluctantly Christen did what she was told. Barbara followed her in. She went to the dining-room table and sat down without taking off her jacket. Her heart was beating fast. Staring ahead blankly, her eyes gradually focused on the china cabinet across the room, and her stomach started to ache.

She suddenly remembered what that room had looked like the day Richard exploded in there. It had looked like a bomb site when he was through.

It had been another one of his rages, one of the long, slow, torturous sessions. She couldn't even remember how it had started. Most times she had only a vague notion of what she'd done to set him off. That time he'd made her sit right where she was sitting now as he yelled and screamed, interrogated and accused, smashing plates and cups and saucers one by one to punctuate his anger. It went on for hours, and the only way she could keep her sanity was by reciting a rosary in her head. When she finished that, she tried to remember the names of all the characters in the books she'd read in the last year. Anything to keep from focusing on the "bad Richard" raging in front of her. It had started sometime in the afternoon, and it was dark out when he finally ran out of things to break. When it was all over, a hundred thousand dollars' worth of Royal Doulton lay smashed to bits on the floor.

When Barbara Kuklinski realized where she was, her hand was in her pocket, clutching the business card in her fist. She knew she was going to have to tell Richard that those two detectives had been here to see him. There was no way she couldn't tell him. But this would definitely bring out the "bad Richard." She wished there were a way she could *not* tell him, but there wasn't. The kids were there; they had seen it. If he somehow found out that those detectives had been here and the kids didn't tell him about it— she didn't even want to consider what he might do.

No, she was going to have to tell him herself.

Barbara closed her eyes and let her head drift back as she unclenched her fist on the business card.

A number of murders. God help us, she thought.

FRIDAY, NOVEMBER 28, 1986—4:00 P.M.

The day after Thanksgiving was quiet at 169 Sunset Street. Too quiet. Barbara and the girls had gone to the mall, and Dwayne was out with his friends. Richard Kuklinski was home alone, holed up in his office. The door was closed even though there was no one else in the house except Shaba, curled up in a corner of the room, sound asleep. Richard had his feet up on the desk, staring out the window, massaging his temples. He'd had a headache since he woke up that morning.

That detective's business card was on the desk. Volkman and his buddy Kane. He wondered what the hell they really knew. And if they did know something, who told them?

Percy House and Barbara Deppner, that's who. Who else could it be? He knew the state had them in protective custody somewhere out in Pennsylvania. Someone from "the store" had happened to run into Percy by chance out there, and word had gotten back to Kuklinski. At least now he knew the general vicinity of where they were living. He glanced down at his briefcase on the floor and frowned.

Even if he did find them, getting rid of them wouldn't

be that easy. Sure, he could shoot them or knife them or even strangle them, but all those methods leave evidence. Besides, the state cops must check in on them pretty regularly if they're in protective custody. Getting them at home could be risky.

If only he could get some cyanide . . .

With cyanide he could do it anywhere. Follow them till they went somewhere, then spray them in the face as they got out of the car. Or put it in a sandwich or something. Get them to eat it, the way Gary Smith had.

If only he had some cyanide . . .

Dominick Provenzano had said he could get him some, but he never came through with it. Dominick was giving him some fugazy bullshit about his source clamming up because of that Lipton soup poisoning in Camden. But that was back in September. Things must have cooled down by now.

Kuklinski's eyes slid to the phone on his desk. Dominick said he could get it. Guys say a lot of things they don't really mean especially when they're trying to make themselves out to be more important than they really are. He hadn't heard from Dominick in almost a month. The guy was supposed to be all hot to make a deal on a shitload of arms and crap for the IRA. What happened to that? The guy was bullshit. He had to be. Unless he's found another source for what he wanted.

Dominick had been talking big money last time they discussed this deal. Half a million. If Dominick was being straight about that, ripping him off would be one sweet payday. It had been too long since Kuklinski had made a decent score, and he was getting low on cash. That had really hit home yesterday when he sat down to Thanksgiving dinner with Barbara and the kids. Christmas was coming. Barbara was out starting her Christmas shopping right now. He'd always hated the holidays, but Barbara loved this time of year. He needed money to buy her something nice. He was still feeling a little guilty about the house they hadn't bought, the one around the corner from President Nixon in Saddle River. He had gotten everyone all excited about moving; then he just dropped it because he didn't have the money. He felt he had to make it up to Barbara.

But aside from Christmas presents, he needed money anyway. Real money. Too many deals had fallen through lately. They were starting to live like everyone else in this goddamn neighborhood, and his family deserved better than that. *He* deserved better than that. He was Richard Kuklinski after all, and Richard Kuklinski was never going to be poor ever again. Never. That's why he *needed* money.

A fluttering sensation spread through his chest, and his breathing was suddenly short. It occurred to him that maybe he was losing his touch. He was going to be fifty-two in a few months. Maybe he was getting too old for all this. The panic of being stuck without cash zinged through him like an arrow. Maybe he really was losing it. Those two state police detectives were on his case, and those other two rats, Percy House and Barbara Deppner, were probably telling them anything to keep them happy, probably telling them he had killed JFK. He hadn't pulled down a single major score this year. And Dominick Provenzano, the one guy he'd thought he had on the line, didn't seem to care about him anymore. Richard Kuklinski could see Dominick's half a million dollars flying right out the window.

Kuklinski kneaded his temples and wondered what the hell was wrong with him. His head was splitting. His whole world was turning to shit. What the hell had happened? What was wrong with him?

Nothing.

Richard Kuklinski took his feet off the desk and pulled up his chair. He picked up a pen and started drawing boxes on a yellow legal pad. There was nothing wrong with him. Nothing. He was a somebody. He was somebody because he knew he had the ability to do whatever was necessary to survive. He was somebody because he knew things no one else knew, things he'd done that the cops were still trying to figure out.

He drew boxes as he ticked off his achievements in his head.

He had done Gary Smith and Danny Deppner.

He had done Louis Masgay and put him in the freezer.

He had done Paul Hoffman, the pharmacist.

He had done George Malliband, a deadbeat who pushed his luck a little too far.

He'd done Mister Softee.

Johnny, the bully at the projects.

The pool hustler in Hoboken when he was nineteen.

He'd done a few jobs for Roy DeMeo.

He'd done the guy in California through the peephole with Softee.

He'd done the Asian guy who fell out his hotel-room window in Hawaii.

He'd done the wiseguy in Manhattan on Christmas Eve, the guy who wouldn't pay up. Afterward he went home to put a wagon together for Dwayne, and he saw it on the TV news: "Mysterious Mob-Related Slaying in Midtown." He couldn't get the goddamn wheels on the wagon.

He had done one on a bet, shot the guy in the throat and waited to see if it would take at least five minutes for him to bleed to death. He'd lost the bet.

He'd done the guy who stopped at a red light and started to light a cigar. Blew the guy's head off before he even took a puff.

Then there was the kid who had cut him off on the highway. He ran the kid's car off the road, beat him to pulp with a baseball bat, then backed over his body before he left. Just because the kid pissed him off.

He'd gotten away with doing a loan shark who worked for a Gambino captain. Stiffed the guy, then whacked him after he complained to the wrong people.

There was the guy in Switzerland.

The guy in the Howard Johnson's parking lot on Route 46.

The guy who shit his pants praying to God, begging for mercy.

The guy with the wavy white hair who owed money in Oklahoma. Shot in the head by the golf course.

The contract job where they wanted the tongue cut out and shoved up the ass.

There was the guy in the garage who was working on his truck.

The guy who got it in the ear with an ice pick.

The two guys who had made the mistake of sticking up a mob-sanctioned card game.

The big black guy in that bar in Harlem, splattered his head like a watermelon with one shotgun blast.

There was the guy who looked so surprised when he suddenly realized the big Polack was holding a little two-shot derringer on him. Two dumdum bullets were more than enough.

There was the guy he'd done in Dracula's apartment, shot the top of his head right off.

The guy out walking his dog.

The guy from the video arcade, three .22s to the back of the head.

Then there were the ones in Pennsylvania, New York, Rhode Island, Florida, Georgia, the Carolinas, Tennessee, Colorado. . . .

When he finally couldn't think of any more, the page was full of boxes. A whole page of them. He smiled down at the pad. The butterflies weren't fluttering in his chest anymore. His headache was gone. He gazed at all his little secrets on the page. They were his and no one else's.

He stared at the telephone as he leaned back in his chair. Maybe it was time to give Dominick a call, he thought. He was smiling as he opened the top drawer to get his address book.

SATURDAY, DECEMBER 6, 1986—10:00 A.M.

The sky was overcast at the Vince Lombardi Service Area. Sea gulls hovered and soared, scouting the parking lot for tasty litter. Two gulls picked through the green barrel near the bank of phone booths and pulled out a discarded hamburger bun. Dominick Polifrone watched them feast, his hands jammed in the pockets of his black leather jacket, a white silk scarf tied loosely around his neck.

Out in the parking lot Bob Carroll and Paul Smith sat in the silver sedan. Another investigator was posted by the entrance to the service area. Dominick watched for the coffee cup on the silver sedan's dashboard to disappear, his signal that Kuklinski had arrived.

This meeting with Kuklinski had been hastily arranged, and they were short of manpower today, so these were the only backups Dominick had. He was also wearing only the Nagra tape recorder. They couldn't get the Kel transmitter to work, so Dominick's backups wouldn't be able to monitor what went on between him and Kuklinski today.

Standing inside a phone booth, Dominick wondered what kind of attitude his "friend" would be wearing today. They hadn't seen each other in over a month. Kuklinski had pulled back, and the task force had decided to let him be. But that had given him a lot of time to think things over. He might be happy to see Dominick, more anxious than ever to do the arms deal with him. Or he could be mad as hell that Dominick was wasting his time, that Dominick was all talk and no show. Or Kuklinski could be any shade of gray in between. There was no telling until he got there.

The gulls squawked and flapped their wings, fighting over the hamburger bun. Dominick glanced over at the silver sedan. The cup was gone from the dash. He scanned the cars pulling into the lot, looking for the blue Camaro. He wasn't expecting the white Cadillac that rolled into a space on the far side of the phone booths.

The Caddy's door swung open, and out stepped Kuklinski, dressed in a dark suit and tie under a black cashmere overcoat. Dominick was stunned. He hadn't expected this either.

Dominick extended his hand as Kuklinski approached. "Jesus, Rich, you look like the board of health here, all dressed up nice."

Kuklinski flashed a toothy smile as he shook Dominick's hand. "So whatcha been doing, guy?"

"Same shit."

"Oh, yeah?"

They moved over to the picnic table. Dominick sat on the tabletop. Kuklinski put his foot up on the bench and leaned on his knee.

Dominick lowered his voice. "You know, Rich, I gotta tell you something. I was at that greasy spoon next door to 'the store' the other day, and there were these two detectives there. From the state police, I think. They were asking questions about you."

Kuklinski shrugged. He seemed unconcerned.

"I'm just telling you to let you know, Rich. You better be careful now."

"Dom, they been on my ass since 1980, and they still haven't got me. Maybe someday they will. Who knows? But in the meantime, what the hell'm I gonna do about it?"

"Well, I'm just passing it on. I thought you'd want to know."

"Yeah, Kane and Volkman, I know all about them."

"One of them, his name was Pat something or other, he asked me if I knew you. I told him I didn't know nobody. Whatta they want you for?"

The big man tilted his head from one side to the other. "They're after me because—well, let's just say there were some people who got hurt. Some . . . problems."

"Yeah, I understand."

"Then there's this one guy who turned out to be a pointer. The police got him in protective custody now. Problem is they can't get anybody to back up his bullshit. I been trying to find him."

"Oh, yeah?"

"I hope he gets a bad cold and drops dead."

Dominick laughed. "That would be nice."

"This guy who turned out to be a pointer had a couple of friends who had accidents. I was lucky with them. But these goddamn troopers got a bug up their asses about me. They want to get me for murder."

"No shit."

"Yup. I'd love for this other guy, the pointer, to have an accident like his buddies. But like I said, they got him in protective custody." He shook his head. "Percy House," he grumbled in disgust.

Dominick couldn't believe it. Kuklinski had come right out and said he was looking for Percy House. He mentioned Percy House *by name*. But why was Kuklinski telling him this?

"Yeah, those goddamn troopers are dying to get me. I'm probably a thorn in their side, just like Percy's a thorn in mine. I mean, face it, I'm no virgin. I done a lot of shit in my time. The cop that gets me won't be getting no virgin. He'll be getting an old whore with me."

"So whattaya gonna do about this?"

"Nothing. I'll do just what I been doing. Being careful, and staying out of sight. That's why I don't go to 'the store' no more. I haven't been there in two years."

"Well, Rich, if there's anything I can help you out with, just let me know."

"There's nothing that can be done, Dom. If they get me, they get me. But they got nothing on me. If they did, they wouldn't be going around asking everybody questions about me. Right? So until they have something they can use, I intend to just go about my business and do what I have to do."

"That's all you can do, I guess. Listen, I had that stuff you wanted. You know what I'm talking about?"

Kuklinski's eyebrows rose. "The powder?"

"The special order you put in. I had it in my trunk, a little vial of the stuff. I called you a couple of times, but there was no answer. I didn't want to be carrying that shit around with me, so I brought it back and told the guy to hold it for me until I found you."

"Jeez, that's just what I could use right now."

"How come no one answers that phone, Rich?"

"When I'm not there, I unplug that line. That's my special line. If there's no answer or you get an answering machine, you know I'm not around."

"Oh. Okay."

Dominick brought up Tim then and renewed his interest in buying ten hit kits for his wiseguy customer in New York as well as completing the big arms deal for the Irish Republican Army. That morning Bob Carroll had coached him on what he should get Kuklinski to talk about, and they'd discussed how Dominick might draw him out. But Kuklinski didn't need any drawing out today. He was running on at the mouth, more talkative than he'd ever been, acknowledging his criminal career, stressing his need to get rid of Percy House, referring to the murders of Gary Smith and Danny Deppner. After a while Dominick had to keep himself from looking at his watch to see how long they'd been there. He couldn't believe this. Why was Kuklinski telling him so much? Why was he sharing all this incriminating information?

The answer was obvious, and it came as no surprise to Dominick. Kuklinski intended to kill him. Why else would he be talking so much? Dominick only hoped that the task force's assumption about the Iceman was correct, that he killed only when there was a profit to be made. As long as Dominick didn't have any large quantities of cash with him, he was safe. Nevertheless, he kept his hand on the gun in his pocket. And even with that, he paid close attention to which way the wind was blowing, so that he'd know where to move if Kuklinski tried to spray him in the face.

"So, Rich, you still interested in doing the kid with me?" Dominick said, steering the conversation toward the matter of killing the "rich Jewish kid."

"That's *your* game, Dom. You tell me when. I'm ready to do whatever you want to do with him."

"We do him with cyanide, no? The way you told me, right?"

"Okay."

"So how do we do it?"

Kuklinski frowned and shrugged. "You bring him back here. I'll have a van. You tell the kid to get in the back of the van so you can do the deal, and we'll do it there."

"And you're sure the cyanide won't show up when they find him?"

"If they do a regular zip-zap job and throw him out, it don't matter, they won't find it. If they do certain tests on him, it might show up. But like I'm saying, it all depends on how thorough the coroner is. If he's not thorough, he's in a hurry to get the fuck home and he just slaps it together, you got it made."

"How about just making him disappear completely?"

"There's some old abandoned mine shafts in Philadelphia. Drop something down there, you don't even hear the fucking thing bounce."

"All right. That's possible. And how about the car? You think we should leave it or get rid of it?"

"Either way. We could sell it for parts. I know a place—bang, bang, bang—they cut it up and get rid of the parts the same day. They don't keep anything around to get 'em in trouble."

Dominick wrinkled his face and looked doubtful. He wanted Kuklinski to talk some more about murder. "You sure about all that stuff about fooling the coroner? They got all kinds of ways to find out things, don't they?"

"Hey, you think those people are smart? Listen to me. They found this one guy, and when the autopsy was done, they said he was only dead two and a half weeks. But see, he wasn't. He'd been dead two and a half *years*. Those guys got their little nuts twisted on that one."

"Oh, yeah?" Dominick knew exactly who he was talking about.

A sly grin stretched across the Iceman's face. "In a freezer nothing changes, my friend."

"You mean, the freezer maintains—"

"Everything. It's like pulling a steak out of the fridge."

Dominick shook his head in amazement. The Iceman had just admitted to the freezing of Louis Masgay. Unbelievable.

"Cyanide?" Dominick asked.

"In that case, no."

Dominick knew that was true. Masgay had been shot. Dominick almost wanted to thank Kuklinski for his unusual cooperation. He suddenly became very aware of his Nagra. The goddamn tape recorder better be working, he thought. Kuklinski was giving him gold here.

The conversation then moved on to how they would administer the cyanide to the rich kid, and Kuklinski weighed the pros and cons of each method. Putting it in a spray was possible, but as he'd already explained, you always had to be sure you were downwind of the mist or else you could end up spraying yourself.

Putting it in cocaine could work very well, too, but when someone is sampling from a big bag of coke, slipping cyanide into his line without detection could be awkward, if not impossible.

Putting it on food was a much better bet. As long as you could get the guy to eat something thick and wet, like a sauce or a gravy, where the poison could be mixed in and disguised. If it's simply sprinkled on a piece of meat, say, it'll cake and make the food unappealing. "Don't put just a fucking sprinkle, put enough to spread it over," Kuklinski advised. "I mean as long as it's something gooky, spread it over, let it blend in, let him have enough to have a *bon appétit.*"

Ketchup was a great thing to mix cyanide with, Kuklinski said. Mix it in with the ketchup on a guy's hamburger and he'll never know it's in there. Kuklinski recounted the time he gave a guy a poisoned hamburger and he practically ate the whole thing before it affected him. "The fucker must have had the constitution of a fucking bull." He was talking about Gary Smith.

Out of the corner of his eye Dominick looked for those two gulls fighting over the ketchup-stained hamburger bun, but they were nowhere to be seen.

Kuklinski then expressed his desire to "retire into the woodwork" soon. He was ready to get out of all this dirty business, he said, and he confided that he had some money "set aside out of the country."

Dominick nodded and listened. He knew that Kuklinski had taken several trips to Switzerland in the past.

"I've got it all set up," Kuklinski said. "I'm ready. I just have some unfinished problems here I'd like to take care of. I'd like to find this one guy, and that's the end of my problems as far as that goes. It's personal, you know. I allowed it to happen, so it's my own mistake. And I hate to leave a mistake undone."

"I agree."

"I mean this guy Percy, he trapped a guy in his own crew. Wore a wire on the kid, and now the kid's in jail with a life sentence.

The kid used to work for him. That's what kind of rat this guy Percy is."

From the way Kuklinski spoke of him, Percy House wasn't just a thorn in his side; he was a public menace who had to be obliterated from the face of the earth for everyone's protection.

Before they said good-bye, Kuklinski asked one more time if Dominick was sure that the rich Jewish kid wasn't connected to the Mafia in some way. Dominick told him not to worry. "I'm the only one who's connected," he said. They agreed to stay in touch about this.

Kuklinski got back into his Cadillac, as respectable as a banker in his suit and tie, and drove out of the parking lot. Dominick got into the Shark and watched the big white car sail past the gas pumps. His head was spinning with all that he'd just heard. He started his engine and drove out of the parking lot, then got on the turnpike. He was halfway to the next exit when he finally noticed that someone was right on his tail, blowing his horn and blinking his headlights like some kind of nut.

Dominick glanced in the rearview mirror and saw Paul Smith's silver sedan. He pulled into the next rest stop, found a parking space, and shut off his engine.

Smith pulled his car in next to the Shark. His eyes were bugging out of his head as he rolled down his window and motioned for Dominick to do the same.

"Dominick, what the hell happened? You were out there an hour, the two of you yakking like a couple of old ladies. What'd he say?"

Dominick just shook his head. His face was drained. "I'm full up, Smith. I'm full. Can't hold no more." The Nagra tape recorder was in his hand. He took the lid off and checked to see if the tape had progressed from one reel to the other. It had. It was all down on tape. Dominick let out a long sigh of relief.

"But, Dominick, what the fuck did he tell you?"

Dominick kept shaking his head. "I'm full, Smith." He put the lid back on the Nagra and handed it to the investigator.

"But, Dom—"

Dominick made him take the Nagra. "Here. *Bon appétit.*"

He started up the Shark.

"Where the hell you going, Dom?" Paul Smith was having a conniption fit. "They're waiting for us back at the office to go over—"

"Later." Dominick hit the power button and closed the window in Paul Smith's face. He backed the Lincoln out of the space and got back on the turnpike. He had to take a ride and unwind.

FRIDAY, DECEMBER 12, 1986—EARLY EVENING

In the conference room at the Organized Crime Bureau offices in Fairfield, the guys from the Attorney General's Office—Deputy AG Bob Carroll, Deputy Chief Bobby Buccino, Investigators Ron Donahue and Paul Smith—all sat forward, leaning on their elbows, staring intently at the tape deck as the cassette turned around and around. The reel-to-reel Nagra recording of Dominick's latest meeting with Kuklinski at one-fifteen that afternoon at the Vince Lombardi Service Area had been transferred to a cassette.

Dominick leaned back in his chair and rubbed his eyes. He was afraid they were going to wear the damn tape out the way they were playing it.

"Listen to this," Dominick was saying on the tape. *"The Jewish kid asked me if I can get him* three *kilos. I said yeah, I got it. Eighty-five thousand, cash. Wednesday morning he's coming. He'll be here around nine, nine-thirty. Now here's the thing. I'll pick up the cyanide that morning from my guy. How long—"*

"Doesn't give me enough time," Kuklinski interrupted. *"Doesn't give me enough time. I need a couple of days to get it ready. . . ."*

Dominick got up, went to the cabinet behind Bob Carroll, and pulled out the new bottle of Johnnie Walker Black that had the picture of Kuklinski from the old bottle taped over the label. He needed a drink. He'd heard this goddamn tape a hundred times already. He knew the goddamn thing by heart.

"Too bad you can't pick the stuff up earlier, Dom, 'cause I gotta have it done up, see? I don't do it myself. I don't have the, ah, you know, the facilities to do it. I bring it to a guy who does it for me. I pay to have it done. That's something you don't want to fuck around with, ya know. A mistake on that, and you got a problem. If I fuck with it and I do something wrong, it could be my *fuckin' problem. I don't want to fuck with something like that. I have a guy that makes it up."*

"Let me ask you something, Rich. Can you just have the components, then I can just bring the stuff and your guy can tell you how much to put in?"

"I don't have the stuff to mix it with. He has *it. He mixes the stuff together perfectly. He has to see the strength of the stuff, some stuff isn't as strong as others, ya know? He has to see how strong it is. He tests it. Then he puts in these things, and he's gotta have a seal on it. You gotta make it airtight. You can't fuck around with this stuff. If it's not airtight, it could be a problem for you . . . and me."*

"Bullshit." Bob Carroll was frowning.

They'd found out from the state chemist that cyanide is water-soluble. Mixing the deadly spray should be as simple as making Kool-Aid.

Dominick was talking on the tape. *"What about the other way, Rich?"*

"What's that? Putting it in the guy's food? You sure the guy's gonna eat?"

"Yeah."

"Then we'll need a couple of hamburgers, something like that. But will the kid eat?"

"Yeah, no problem."

"Then that's great."

"Guaranteed. It'll be an egg sandwich. Every time I meet this kid, he orders an egg sandwich. We'll get him an egg sandwich."

"We can do that. Do they sell egg sandwiches here? I don't even know if they do."

As Dominick set out five plastic cups, he remembered Kuklinski blowing into his hands at the Lombardi Service Area and looking back over his shoulder at Roy Rogers. It had been cold and wet that day, and the ground was covered with dirty slush. Dominick's feet were still cold from standing outside by the phone booths with him.

"Don't worry about it," Dominick said on the tape, assuring Kuklinski that he'd get the sandwiches. *"Anything with eggs this kid'll eat. Is that okay for you?"*

"Don't matter to me," Kuklinski said. *"Once we get him in the van, he's ours—"*

Bob Carroll reached over and shut off the tape deck. He didn't look happy. None of them did.

"He's hinky," Paul Smith said. "He's getting ready to give you the runaround? Why does he sound so hesitant to commit himself all of a sudden? Why does he need a couple of days to mix the spray? He's hinky. He's gonna disappear. You watch."

Dominick poured out the scotch. There was barely enough left in the bottle to give everyone a taste. He emptied the last drops, then set down the bottle next to the small brown glass vial on the table. The vial contained fine white granules of quinine, specially prepared by a state chemist to resemble cyanide. Dominick was going to give it to Kuklinski and tell him it was the poison.

"Hey, Smith, I forgot to ask you," Dominick said as he passed the plastic cups around, "you do like eggs, don't you?"

"Too late now if I don't."

An egg sandwich was the first thing that had popped into Dominick's head when Kuklinski started to give him trouble about needing time to mix the spray. If he was going to meet the rich kid at nine o'clock in the morning, it was more logical that someone would eat an egg sandwich than a hamburger. But Dominick could tell that the guys from the state weren't exactly thrilled with his improvisational talents. Well, all he could say was he was out there and they weren't. When Kuklinski had started to hem and haw, he had to act fast to keep him from making any more excuses.

Dominick hoisted his drink. "Gentlemen, a toast." He swiveled his chair to face the larger picture of Kuklinski that was taped to the wall. "This is for you, Richie. I hope you're enjoying yourself now because your days are numbered, my friend. You are *mine*, my friend. You are fucking mine." He threw back the scotch and drained the cup.

Paul Smith lifted his cup. *"Bon appétit,* Richie."

They all laughed and downed their drinks. They had to laugh because they knew that if they didn't, they'd be climbing the walls. It wasn't a matter of cockiness or false bravado or machismo. Kidding around was a survival mechanism. If you let the tension get to you, you'd lose your edge and you'd start questioning yourself. And once you started to doubt your abilities, you started making mistakes. And you do not want to make mistakes with a mass murderer. That's why Dominick was laughing the loudest.

The deputy attorney general set down his cup and pressed his lips together. "I'm still thinking we should move the meeting indoors."

"Why?" Ron Donahue asked.

Deputy Chief Bobby Buccino shrugged and showed his palms. "Kuklinski has never wanted to meet anywhere but Lombardi. If you try to change the place, he may not go for it. Why run the risk of turning him off?"

Bob Carroll tapped his fingers on the table to make his point. "Yes, but if we can get him inside, we can videotape the whole thing."

Buccino looked confused. "We can videotape outside. We've got the equipment."

Carroll shook his head. "No, that's not what I mean. What I'm thinking is we get a three-room apartment somewhere. We set it up so that Dominick and Paul are in the living room doing the coke deal. Richie will have to go out of the room to put the cyanide in the sandwich and we'll get it all on video. Can you imagine how that would look to a jury if they could see a film of Kuklinski actually putting poison on a sandwich, getting ready to kill someone?" The deputy attorney general was almost bouncing in his seat he was so excited by his brainstorm.

Dominick shook his head. "Where'd you get that one? *America's Most Wanted?*"

"No, no, think about it. How can a jury fail to convict? How could the defense say his actions weren't premeditated?"

"Hold on, hold on," Paul Smith said. "What if Kuklinski changes his mind? What if he just pulls out a gun and shoots me?"

"Why would he do that?"

"We know he doesn't *just* kill with cyanide. If he thinks he's alone in there with Dominick and the rich kid, why mess around with cyanide? May as well just shoot the kid and get it over with, right?"

"I don't think he'd shoot you," Ron Donahue said. "He might use a knife, though."

"Or he might try to strangle you," Bobby Buccino offered. "He's done that before." Buccino was grinning at the young investigator.

"This isn't funny, Bobby. What if he really does shoot me?"

"So you'll wear a vest."

"What if he shoots me in the head?"

Dominick waved him off. "Smith, you worry too much. Look at it this way. If he kills you indoors, we'll just carry you out in a rug. But if we do it at Lombardi, he's gonna stick you in a barrel, and face it, who wants to be stuck in a barrel? Remember what happened with that guy he did in Jersey City."

"You mean Malliband?"

"Yeah, Malliband."

Paul Smith looked disgusted with the bunch of them. "At least I'll fit," he grumbled.

George W. Malliband, Jr., made a big mistake, and at the time he probably didn't even realize it. He showed up at Richard Kuklinski's house unannounced.

It was a hot summer Sunday afternoon in the late seventies, and the Kuklinskis were having a barbecue in their backyard in Dumont. The kids had some of their friends over, and Barbara's mother was there, presiding over the plenty at the picnic table, urging everyone to eat. Barbara kept going in and out of the house to fetch things while Richard tended to the grill, flipping hamburgers and turning the hot dogs.

Richard Kuklinski was relaxed that day, enjoying himself. He liked it when his family was all together, doing something together as a family. Moving back from the rising smoke, he watched the flames lick the sizzling burgers as fat dripped onto the burning coals. Another couple of minutes and the burgers would be done. He opened up a package of buns to toast on the grill just before he took the meat off.

But just as he started to separate the buns, his mother-in-law came over and grabbed him by the sleeve. She looked upset. There was a big man standing on the grass at the side of the house, staring at them, she said. She'd asked the man what he wanted, but he said he had to talk to "Richie."

Kuklinski looked up and squinted against the smoke. George Malliband was at the edge of the yard, waving him over. The three-hundred-pound, six-foot-three man wore metal-rim glasses and a bushy mustache. From the look of horror on Kuklinski's mother-in-law's face, it was as if the Blob had suddenly arrived for lunch.

Kuklinski's mood turned black. He shoved the bag of hamburger buns into his mother-in-law's hands and ordered her to watch the grill while he took care of the intruder. He strode toward Malliband, slow but purposeful. Malliband had a hell of a lot of nerve coming to his house.

But before he said a word to Malliband, he managed to put a clamp on his rage. He was furious that Malliband, a wheeler-dealer from central Pennsylvania whose main source of income was pornography, had shown up without an invitation and barged in on a family cookout. He regretted that he'd ever brought Malliband home that one time. He was just trying to be social, but that was a big mistake. He swore he'd never do that again with anybody.

But Kuklinski didn't show his anger to Malliband. He could only blame himself, really. Apparently he hadn't made it clear enough that he did not like having his family exposed to his business associates. He didn't say anything at the time, but in the back of his mind this unwelcomed visit would be a permanent black mark against Malliband. It was the kind of thing he would never forget.

Years later, at two o'clock in the afternoon on February 1, 1980, Richard Kuklinski was at George Malliband's house in Huntingdon, Pennsylvania. It was Malliband's forty-second birthday, but they weren't sticking around to celebrate. They had business to attend to in New York—serious business.

George Malliband was in big trouble. He'd borrowed money

from Roy DeMeo, and he'd fallen way behind in his weekly "vig" payments. The mobster did not like deadbeats. They were bad for business, and they made you look bad. He demanded that Malliband come to Brooklyn to see him. Since Richard Kuklinski was the one who had vouched for Malliband, he was responsible for him, and he was going to make sure that Malliband made that appointment.

That evening, when they arrived at DeMeo's hangout, the Gemini Lounge in Canarsie, Roy wasted no time with niceties. Eight of DeMeo's men hustled Malliband and Kuklinski through the back hallway into Cousin Dracula's apartment. They sat Malliband down at the kitchen table, and DeMeo put it to him straight.

"You owe me a lotta fucking money," DeMeo yelled. "You owe money to Las Vegas, too. And you owe money to Altoona. You owe all over the place. How you gonna fucking pay all this, George? Huh?"

Malliband was sweating. "Don't worry, Roy. I'm good for it."

"Is he?" DeMeo's hot glare turned to Kuklinski.

Kuklinski was taken by surprise. "I—I dunno, Roy—"

"Well, you fucking better know. You brought this fucking mutt to me and told me he was okay. You knew what was going on with him, and you never said nothing to nobody. I hold *you* responsible, Polack. If I don't get my money in three days, it's gonna be *your* problem. You understand? Now get the fuck outta here, and don't come back unless you got the green."

As they drove back to New Jersey, Malliband was frantic. He had loan sharks coming at him from all directions. He definitely didn't have enough money to pay up, and he was beyond the point of placating DeMeo with a partial payment. He didn't know what to do. He pleaded with Kuklinski to think of something. "You gotta help me, Rich. You gotta!"

Kuklinski glanced at him sideways as he drove. "Why do *I* have to help you? I didn't help you lose the money, did I?"

"Hey, c'mon, Rich. You *gotta* help me. I'm desperate. These guys'll fucking kill me."

"You're damn right they'll kill you."

Malliband slapped the dashboard in frustration. "Goddammit, don't say it like you're not involved here. You got me in with DeMeo. You're part of this. He said so himself. You gotta help me."

"I don't *gotta* do anything, my friend." Kuklinski gripped the wheel tighter. He hated when people told him what to do.

Malliband's eyes were wild with fear. "Listen, Rich. You gotta help me. I'm telling you. I know where you live. You know I do."

Kuklinski's vision blurred. "What? What're you saying here? You telling me you're gonna hurt my family?"

"If you don't help me out."

Kuklinski fell silent, and his black mood filled the cab of the van like a toxic gas. Malliband's nervous chatter eventually tapered off, and he stared out the passenger side window, lost in thought, biting his fingernails. After a long stretch of tense quiet Malliband was startled back to the present when the van suddenly pulled to a stop. The street outside his window was dark and deserted.

George Malliband frowned at the unfamiliar setting. "What're we doing here?" he asked.

Kuklinski didn't answer. He pulled a .38 revolver out of his coat pocket and pumped five bullets into the left side of Malliband's chest. The explosions were deafening inside the van. The muzzle flashes left spots in front of Kuklinski's eyes. He stared down at Malliband's body slumped over the dashboard. His ears were ringing. He thought back to that cookout at his house years before when George Malliband had the gall to walk onto his property without an invitation.

The next day Kuklinski delivered an attaché case containing fifty thousand dollars in cash to Roy DeMeo to settle Malliband's debt. He was no longer responsible for the man.

* * *

On February 5, 1980, at 10:55 A.M., the owner of the Chemitex Coated Corporation opened the rear door of the plant at 3 Hope Street in Jersey City. At the bottom of the palisades that overlooked the building, he noticed a dented steel drum turned over on its side. From where he was standing, the man couldn't quite make out what was inside the barrel, but it looked very peculiar. Walking closer, he saw what he thought he had seen: a pair of legs, one of them bloody and hacked.

The barrel had been rolled off the cliffs some sixty feet above. The lid had popped off when it hit bottom. The police determined that the victim—a three-hundred-pound middle-aged white male—hadn't quite fit into the fifty-five-gallon steel drum headfirst, so the killer cut the tendons on the back of the last leg in order to snap the knee and bend it forward, forcing him in.

Apparently George Malliband never got it. He'd made the same mistake twice, and he never even realized it. Nobody threatens Richard Kuklinski's family and gets away with it.

TUESDAY, DECEMBER 16, 1986—LATE AFTERNOON

If you put a ten-gallon hat on James "Hoss" DiVita, he would be a dead ringer for Dan Blocker, the actor who had played Hoss on the old television western *Bonanza*. But unlike the stalwart TV character, Hoss DiVita was given to grand Neapolitan gesturing. His face could switch from joviality to utter dejection, like a clown-faced Pagliacci. Perhaps, it was this comic quality that appealed to Richard Kuklinski because he had been doing business with DiVita for a long time, getting Hoss stolen cars, which he then fenced for Kuklinski. Or maybe it was just that Hoss DiVita always seemed to have what he needed. That was certainly why Kuklinski had traveled all the way up to DiVita's home in New London, Connecticut, that day. He needed a van, and the first person he thought of was Hoss DiVita. Hoss specialized in vehicles.

Kuklinski had called Hoss earlier that day and asked him to pick him up at a shopping center in New London. When they got back to the house, Hoss's wife had company over, so they went to the back room where Hoss stored the merchandise for his "wholesale business." Hoss closed the door for privacy. Kuklinski was in a strange, pensive mood, and Hoss came right out and asked what was bothering him.

Kuklinski leaned against the wall and crossed his arms over his chest. "My friend," he said softly, "in this life you never set a pattern."

Hoss looked concerned. "What'sa matter, Rich? You got trouble with the . . . ?"

Kuklinski smiled and shrugged. "I'm feeling a little heat, yeah. I have to have my car checked for bugs every day. That's why I didn't drive up here."

"Oh . . . I'm sorry to hear that." Hoss decided not to ask how Kuklinski got to New London. He knew better than to ask nosy questions. "So what can I do for you, Rich?"

"I need a van. You said you had one."

"Yeah, I got one." Hoss went to the window and lifted the dusty shade. He pointed into the backyard. "That one, over there."

Kuklinski moved to the window and peered at the van parked next to the garage. He let out a long sigh. The damn thing had too many windows.

"That one's no good. I need one with no windows."

Hoss rubbed his chin. "I might be able to get you one, Rich. How soon do you need it?"

"Today." Kuklinski had talked to Dominick that morning. Dominick would be bringing the rich Jewish kid to the Lombardi Service Area tomorrow morning to do the coke deal. He'd promised to be there with a van.

"Jeez, Rich, you should've told me. I don't know where to get one *that* fast."

"I've got cash, Hoss."

"Yeah, but I don't have a van with no windows. Getting one's gonna take a little time. I mean—"

The phone in the next room rang then, and Hoss frowned at all the noise coming from the front rooms. "Hang on, Rich." He went into the next room to pick it up.

"Rich? It's for you."

Kuklinski poked his head into the den. Hoss was holding out the receiver, the cord stretching to a phone on an end table by the couch. "Who is it?" Kuklinski asked.

Hoss shrugged. "He says his name is Tim."

Sposato. Kuklinski took the phone, and Hoss left, closing the door behind him. "Hello?"

"It's me. John."

"What's wrong?" Kuklinski didn't like the sound of his voice.

"You find a van?" Sposato asked.

"No. How about you?"

"Well," Sposato started, "I got a problem. See, I don't have any money, not even to rent one. I'm broke."

Kuklinski clenched his jaw and felt his face and neck getting hot. He'd told Sposato last week to start looking for a van. But he held his temper and didn't say a word, just breathed into the phone and let the bastard think about what he'd just said.

"Rich? You still there?"

"Get me a van, John. I don't care how. Just get it. And make sure it doesn't have any windows. No windows." He kept his voice calm and even. People took threats more seriously when there wasn't any yelling.

"But, Rich, you don't understand. I can't—"

"Just get one. I'll call you later."

Kuklinski hung up the phone. He didn't want to give Sposato the last word with his sniveling bullshit. He wanted to leave him with something to think about.

He went back into the storeroom, where Hoss was waiting for him.

Hoss started shaking his head. "I'm real sorry I can't help you with the van, Rich. Rich?"

Kuklinski went to the window and stared out at the darkening sky. "You know, these days I feel like I'm in the middle of this big circle of people and everyone is disappearing around me. Pretty soon I'll be the only one left standing."

Hoss made a face. "Wha'?"

Kuklinski turned around and looked at him. "Never mind."

Hoss changed the subject. "You ever come by any Corvettes anymore, Rich?"

"Nah. Those days are over." He was staring out the window again.

"That was nice when you used to get those. Got rid of those fast, no hanging around. Good money with those things."

Back in 1982, when Kuklinski had Percy House, Danny Deppner, and Gary Smith stealing brand-new Corvettes, Hoss DiVita fenced them for him. They usually got one quarter of the sticker price, about six thousand dollars. Hoss would get two thousand, and Kuklinski would take the rest. Sometimes Hoss went down to Kuklinski's warehouse in North Bergen to pick up the cars, and sometimes Kuklinski drove them up to Connecticut.

On one occasion Kuklinski had delivered a new white Corvette to DiVita. Danny Deppner drove the stolen sports car while he followed in his own car. They met Hoss at a diner in New London, and when they went inside, Hoss noticed that Deppner wouldn't say boo in front of Kuklinski. He asked Kuklinski why his guy was so quiet, but Kuklinski didn't really give him an answer. Hoss thought it was awfully strange that "the quiet guy" wouldn't even smoke until Kuklinski gave him permission. When the waitress came to take their orders, "the quiet guy" didn't do that for himself either. Kuklinski ordered for him.

Six months later Kuklinski had met DiVita at the Dunkin' Donuts across from Teterboro Airport in New Jersey. In the course of conversation, Hoss had asked about "the quiet guy."

"He's gone," Kuklinski had said. "He was running off at the mouth, so I had to take care of him."

In that same conversation over coffee and doughnuts, Kuklinski had mentioned to Hoss that there was a guy in protective custody who could mess him up, a possible "pointer." He'd even mentioned the pointer's first name, Percy. In hindsight, that wasn't very smart.

Kuklinski turned back from the window and stared at Hoss. He was thinking about that circle of people and how it was shrinking. Maybe he'd told Hoss too much.

He glanced out the window at the van again. The wooden sash bars were like crosshairs in a rifle scope. Kuklinski had done a few jobs with rifles, but he always preferred small handguns—.22s, .25s., 380s. Big handguns like 9mms, .45s, and .357s were for intimidation. Small pieces were what you brought when you meant business. His favorite gun was a two-shot derringer loaded with dumdum bullets that expanded on impact and could rip a hole as big as a hubcap as it exited the body. When he was fully armed for a job, his weapons of choice were two derringers—one in each pocket—a larger gun in an ankle holster for backup, and his hunting knife in his belt.

Kuklinski sucked his teeth as he squinted down an imaginary scope, taking aim at the van outside.

"Is there anything else you need, Rich?"

Kuklinski didn't turn around. "I don't think so, Hoss." He kept the windshield of the van in his crosshairs.

WEDNESDAY, DECEMBER 17, 1986—8:45 A.M.

It was cold and damp at the Vince Lombardi Service
Area, and Dominick Polifrone's feet were freezing as he
stood by the bank of phone booths, waiting for Richard
Kuklinski to arrive. He switched the white paper bag he
was holding to his other hand so he could blow into his
fingers. The bag contained the three egg sandwiches with
lots of ketchup that he'd just bought at a diner on his way
over here. In the left-hand pocket of his leather jacket
was a brown paper bag containing the small brown glass
vial of simulated cyanide. In his right-hand pocket was
his gun. Concealed on his body were the Nagra tape recorder and a Kel transmitter. Dominick scanned the access roads that led to the parking lot, looking for the blue
Camaro, the red Oldsmobile Calais, or the white Cadillac.
His squinting gaze swept the rows of parked cars in the
lot. Today was the day. They were ready to take him
down.

He hadn't gotten much sleep last night. He was too
pent up to sleep. Around midnight he called his old partner, Margaret Moore, at home.

"Did I wake you up?"

"Yes."

"Sorry."

"I figured it was you."

"We're gonna take him down tomorrow."

"Be careful."

"I'm always careful."

"Be more careful."

Dominick chuckled.

"Don't laugh. Now I'm gonna be up all night worrying about you."

"Don't worry. We've got everything covered. Nothing will happen. I promise."

"Yeah, sure."

"Go back to sleep. I'll call you tomorrow and tell you how it went." He was about to hang up.

"Dominick?"

"What?"

"Seriously. Be careful."

Dominick didn't like hearing the concern in her voice. He was sorry that he'd made her upset. "I'll be careful, Margie. I promise."

The worry in her voice was still bothering him as he stood out in the cold, waiting for the Iceman.

A few minutes later the red Oldsmobile Calais cruised down the access road and pulled into the parking lot. The driver's oversized frame behind the wheel was unmistakable.

"There he is," Dominick said.

The transmitter broadcast his words to the entire arrest team. He wanted them all to know that he'd spotted the Iceman.

Kuklinski pulled his car into the closest available space to the bank of telephone booths. He emerged from the car, and Dominick saw that he was wearing his street clothes—gray leather jacket over a navy blue shirt, a yellow T-shirt, and pressed blue jeans. He was wearing his dark glasses, too. The big man walked toward Dominick, avoiding the puddles and stepping over the slush at the curb. They shook hands when they met.

"How ya doing, big guy?" Dominick said.

"Not bad."

Dominick wished he could see Kuklinski's eyes behind the glasses. He handed Kuklinski the white paper bag. "Here's the sandwiches. The kid called me last night and again this morning. There's no problem."

Kuklinski took the bag. "You sure?"

"Yeah, yeah."

"Where's your friend now?"

"He's not far from here. I'm gonna go get him." Dominick couldn't read Kuklinski. He seemed reluctant, annoyed, something. Maybe this was the way he got when he was getting ready to kill. Or else he was suspicious. Dominick hoped that wasn't the case. Just stick with the program, Rich, he thought. No improvising. Just stick with the program.

No one wanted the Iceman to start improvising.

"I'll go get the kid and be back in like fifteen minutes."

Kuklinski nodded. "Okay. I'll go get the van. It isn't far from here. Just down the next exit. It's just a ten-minute ride."

"What color is it, so I'll know?"

"Blue."

"Now where are you gonna park it so I can bring him right there?"

"Right here. We might as well do it over here out of the way of everybody." Kuklinski seemed to be getting into it. He didn't seem so reluctant now. Dominick relaxed a bit.

"I'll be sitting in the driver's seat," Kuklinski continued. "You can't miss it."

Dominick lowered his voice. "Okay, I'm gonna bring him right into the back of the van to let him test the coke."

"Okay."

"Here." Dominick took the crumpled brown paper bag out of his pocket. "Here's the cyanide."

Kuklinski took the bag and shoved it into his pocket. "Okay."

"You got enough shit there to take care of Hackensack and Paterson. Now I'm gonna bring him back in his car, so afterward I'll take care of the car while you get rid of him. Where you gonna put him?"

"I'm gonna put him away . . . for safekeeping."

Dominick wished to hell he could see Kuklinski's eyes. He couldn't tell if the Iceman was being funny or evasive or what.

"Okay, everything's all set, right?" Then Dominick made believe he just remembered something. "You got a pair of gloves for me? I didn't bring none."

"Don't worry. I'll give you a pair." He nodded toward his car, and they started walking across the slushy lot.

"Fucking cold," Kuklinski commented as he zipped up his jacket.

"I know." Dominick was thinking about Bob Carroll's last instructions. He should try to get Kuklinski to *say* that he intended to commit murder. Dominick looked at the bag with the sandwiches in Kuklinski's hand. "Whattaya gonna do? Put it on the food—"

"Yeah."

Dominick wanted Kuklinski to elaborate, but he wasn't going to push it. Not at this point. Not when he couldn't see his eyes.

Kuklinski pulled out his keys and unlocked the trunk of his car. He put the sandwiches and the brown bag with the bottle of quinine in and started poking around, looking for a pair of gloves for Dominick. He couldn't find any. "I'll get you a pair. Don't worry."

"Okay. I'll tell you what. When you come back with the van, go get three coffees. I'll pull up back over here somewhere." Dominick pointed to a row of empty slots on the far side of the telephone booths.

Kuklinski shut the trunk. "You'll see the van right away. It's a conversion van, all dressed up. Two-tone blue. Light blue and dark blue. You won't miss it."

"Okay, how long will it take you to get back here?"

"Twenty minutes."

"All right. I'll be back in exactly half an hour."

"When I see you come in, I'll go in and get the coffees. Then I'll come out and . . ." Kuklinski let his words trail off.

"Right."

Dominick wished Kuklinski would come right out and say it, but he knew from experience that bad guys rarely do that. He didn't think Kuklinski was on to him, though. This just seemed like his normal degree of caution. Normal for a killer, that is.

Kuklinski got back into his car and started the engine as Dominick walked toward his black Lincoln. As Kuklinski backed out of his space, Dominick waved, then turned away as he spoke out loud for the transmitter. "All right, boys, you got the choice here. You can take him now or wait till he comes back and take him with the van. I suggest we let him go and come back. Let him go get the van."

Arresting him with the sandwiches and the simulated cyanide would be fine, but it would be much better if they waited until he actually put the "poison" *on* the sandwiches. Dominick got into his car and looked at his watch. It was five of nine.

Through the windshield Dominick saw a heavyset man in his early fifties inside one of the phone booths. It was Deputy Chief Bobby Buccino. He was pretending to be on the phone, but in fact, he had an earplug in his covered ear, and he was listening in on Dominick's transmissions. A folded newspaper was taped over his hand. Inside the newspaper he was holding a 9mm automatic. He'd been there the whole time Dominick and Kuklinski had been there.

In the rearview mirror Dominick could see the unmarked black van where three heavily armed troopers—Detectives Ernie Volkman, Pat Kane, and Dennis Vecchiarelli—were waiting. Ron

Donahue was also back there somewhere in another car. Other investigators from the Attorney General's Office and agents from the Bureau of Alcohol, Tobacco, and Firearms were scattered around the area. Dominick's best friend, Lieutenant Alan Grieco of the Bergen County Homicide Unit, was back there, too. A plainclothes trooper with a shotgun and another one with an assault rifle were at separate positions nearby. Uniformed state troopers were parked along the turnpike near the entrance ramps in case additional backups were needed. When Kuklinski returned, they'd hit him hard and fast. If it all went down the way they'd planned it, there'd be no opportunity for accidents or unpredictable behavior. No improvising.

Dominick turned the key in the ignition and put the Shark into gear. He had to go get the "rich Jewish kid." It wouldn't be long now.

9:45 A.M.

An hour later, as the arrest team waited for Richard Kuklinski's return at the Vince Lombardi Service Area, Barbara Kuklinski sat in her living room, her eyes closed and a hand over her forehead. She felt miserable. She had a headache and a fever, but she didn't think it was the flu or a cold. The damp, chilly weather had probably aggravated her arthritis, and fever was usually the first symptom. She'd already called her doctor and made an appointment to have her SED rate taken to check for signs of infection in her bloodstream. It would confirm what she already suspected.

She opened her eyes and stared blankly at the unlit Christmas tree, the colored balls and tinseled garland shining dully in the gray morning light. She didn't want to be sick for Christmas. The kids always got so excited, even now that they were older. It was the one holiday she loved most.

She got up and went to the window. Looking through the curtain, she saw Richard outside, hunched over the open trunk of the Calais. He was doing something in the trunk, but she couldn't see what because the lid was blocking her view. She wondered why he'd decided to come back home. He had left the house early that morning, and normally he would have been gone for at least a few more hours.

Richard had called her a little while ago from the Grand Union on the other side of town to ask her if she wanted to go out for breakfast. He'd said he was picking up a few things that Dwayne had wanted, pasta and cookies. She'd told him how awful she felt and that she'd called the doctor, so he offered to make breakfast for them at home instead. He'd hung up before she could object. When Richard cooked, he cooked for an army. The cleanup after he was through was hardly worth the effort. Hanging up the phone, she'd changed her mind and decided to go out to breakfast despite her fever. She could go straight to the doctor's office from there. The thought of dealing with Richard's mess in the kitchen made her weary. Sometimes it was just easier to go along with what he wanted than to argue with him.

She parted the curtain for a better view but saw only the top of her husband's head behind the open trunk. Whatever he was doing, he was awfully busy doing it. She sighed and closed her eyes. Whatever it was, she wasn't going to ask. She was in no mood for a fight.

While Barbara Kuklinski watched her husband from her living-room window, Detectives Thomas Trainor and Denny Cortez of the New Jersey State Police were also watching him. They had been assigned to monitor the Kuklinski residence in Dumont that morning. At 9:20, Detective Cortez had driven their unmarked car past the house at 169 Sunset Street. Sitting in the passenger seat, Detective Trainor saw no sign of Richard Kuklinski or the red Oldsmobile Calais at that time. Cruising the neighborhood and staying out of sight so as not to be obvious, they returned twenty-five minutes later and could now see Richard Kuklinski standing in the driveway, leaning over the open trunk of the red Oldsmobile he'd been driving that morning. Not wanting to be spotted by Kuklinski, they circled the block and parked far enough up the street from the cedar shake split-level so as not to be seen. Trainor radioed the arrest team at the Vince Lombardi Service Area to report that Kuklinski was back home, doing something they could not identify in the trunk of the red car.

The Shark was parked at a rest stop on the New Jersey Turn-pike, a mile north of the Lombardi Service Area. Dominick Polifrone was standing outside at a pay phone, the receiver clamped on his shoulder so he could keep his hands warm in his pockets. He was talking to Deputy Chief Buccino, who was still at the service area. "So where the hell is he, Bobby?"

"We don't know yet, Dom. I'm waiting to hear."

Buccino was in charge of the arrest, and he was the one calling the shots. Dominick had worked with him before, and he knew that Bobby Buccino was the kind of no-nonsense field commander who led from the front lines. With twenty-five years in law en-forcement under his belt, he was no one's jolly uncle at times like this. The deputy chief's goal for the day was clear: Arrest the suspect and make sure no one gets hurt.

"Where's Paul?" Dominick asked.

"He's on the road, waiting to hear. Just like the rest of us."

"You think Richie knows?"

"I don't know." Buccino's voice was terse. If he was frustrated, he wasn't showing it.

Dominick was trying not to be frustrated. He kept telling him-self that this really wasn't a problem, that they'd catch up with Kuklinski later on, no problem. Still, he was worried. Kuklinski was improvising, and that could mean trouble. Sure, they already had a mountain of evidence to use against him: the Nagra tapes of him talking about killing with cyanide; his intentions to kill the pointer, Percy House; his admission that he had frozen one of his victims and kept him on ice for more than two years as an experi-ment; his plan to set up an illegal arms sale with "Tim." They also had the .22-caliber pistol fitted with a silencer that Kuklinski had sold to Dominick. They had plenty of evidence to nail this guy, so it really didn't matter whether or not they caught him red-handed with a "poisoned" egg sandwich. So what if they didn't get the big finale the way they'd planned it? That didn't matter. What was really bothering Dominick was the fact that Kuklinski was out there improvising. There was no telling what he was up to now.

"Why don't I call him up?" Dominick suggested. "I'll find out what went wrong and try to set it up again for tomorrow—"

"Do you really think he'll go for the rich kid thing again? How will you explain it to him? Logically how long could you keep this kid hanging? It doesn't make sense."

"Yeah . . . You're probably right." Dominick stuck his free hand under his armpit. He was freezing out there in the cold.

Then something suddenly occurred to him. He remembered Kuklinski talking about the nest egg he had stashed overseas. Probably in Switzerland. What if he really was on to them? He could hop on a plane and flee to Switzerland and live happy as a clam off his nest egg.

"Bobby, have you checked the airports—"

"Hang on a minute, Dom."

Dominick heard other voices on the other end of the line, but he couldn't make out what they were saying. All he could hear was Buccino's voice giving orders. He was telling them to go, go, the arrest was on.

"Bobby! Bobby, what happened?"

"Kuklinski's at home. Trainor and Cortez just spotted him. They just called it in. We're gonna take him down there."

"What about the van? Does he have the blue van with him?"

"I don't think so. I gotta go now, Dom."

"Okay, I'll meet you at the house—"

"No," Buccino ordered. "You go back to the courthouse in Hackensack and wait for us."

"But, I can—"

"No," Buccino barked. "I don't want you at Kuklinski's house.

You're not supposed to know where he lives. If he spots you there, he'll know something's up, and I don't want a shoot-out in the middle of the street. You stay away."

Bobby Buccino hung up, and Dominick was left listening to the dial tone. He knew Buccino was right, he should stay away, but he couldn't help feeling left out. After all the time he'd put into this thing, he was going to miss the arrest. It wasn't that he wasn't going to "get the collar." That was television bullshit. This was a shared operation, and that had been understood from the very beginning. The glory belonged to everyone. What he regretted was that he wasn't going to see the look on Richie's face when he found out that "Dominick Provenzano" was really a cop. Dominick knew it was going to be a priceless moment, but unfortunately he was going to have to find out about it secondhand.

As he walked back to the Shark and blew into his cold fingers, he could see the flashing dome lights on the highway in the distance as the arrest team sped off toward Dumont. He got into the car, started the engine, and just sat there for a moment, thinking, wondering where Richie had the blue van stashed, wondering why he hadn't come back, wondering what the hell he was up to.

As he put the car into reverse and backed out of the space, he realized that all that didn't really matter because in a half hour they'd have him in handcuffs. He still wished he could see Richie's face when they took him down, though, even if it was from the back of the crowd. He could stay out of sight. No one would ever know he was there. It would be a shame to miss the arrest after all he'd gone through with this investigation. A *damn* shame . . .

10:45 A.M.

The only thing Barbara Kuklinski could think about as she got into the red car was getting through breakfast and getting to the doctor. She felt weak and listless, and the fever wasn't going away.

Richard got in on the driver's side and looked at her. "You sure you don't want to stay home and let me make something?"

She shook her head. "No. Let's just go, so I can see the doctor."

He started the car but didn't put it in gear right away. When she looked up, she caught him staring at her. His expression was strange. She couldn't tell if he was concerned or angry at her. "Let's go, Rich," she said gently. "I've got an appointment."

He put the Calais into gear and backed out of the driveway. She glanced sideways at his profile. She couldn't figure out if this was the good Richard or the bad Richard.

As he pulled out onto Sunset Street and headed toward the end of the block, she noticed the Christmas decorations on the neighbors' houses and worried about the upcoming holidays. Richard hated Christmas. It always made him surly and suspicious because it reminded him of all the things he hadn't had as a child. She worried that he wouldn't keep his black mood to himself this year and that he'd ruin the holidays for her and the kids.

She looked at him again as he signaled to turn left at the end of the block. "Rich?" she said.

"Yeah, babe?"

"Do you want—"

Suddenly a big black shape appeared right in front of them. A black van was coming straight at them.

"Rich! Look out!"

The van's brakes screeched, and it swerved right into their path, blocking the road ahead. Barbara felt the pull of their car as her husband stomped on the brakes. Her heart was pounding. Her only thought was that the driver had just had a heart attack, that he'd lost control of the van and was going to plow right into them. But when she saw three men jumping out of the van with weapons drawn and pointed at them, she didn't know what to think.

"Oh, God! Rich! What's going on?"

Her husband grumbled something under his breath, but she was too scared to understand what he was saying.

Investigator Paul Smith didn't wait for ATF Special Agent Ray Goger to stop the car they were in before he jumped out. They had just cruised by the Kuklinski house and seen Richard Kuklinski getting into the red Oldsmobile. Smith, who was in constant radio contact with the black van, had given the order: "Go! Take him! Take him down!"

As more cars arrived on the scene and plainclothes officers spilled into the street, Paul Smith drew his gun and led the pack running down the street toward the black van to assist with the arrest. His boss, Deputy Chief Bobby Buccino, was a few feet behind him.

Suddenly Smith heard the unexpected screech of spinning tires.

Up ahead the red Oldsmobile Calais was mounting the curb, doing an end run around the black van. The Calais ran over a lawn, then bounced back into the street, metal scraping the pavement and tires smoking. The engine roared.

Standing in the middle of the street, the red car coming right at him, Paul Smith could see Kuklinski's large frame behind the wheel. The options flew through Smith's mind: He could either jump out of the way and hope he wouldn't get run over, or he could shoot. But as he gripped his weapon, he could see that there was someone else in the car with Kuklinski. Maybe one of the kids, he thought. If he touched off the shooting, the gunfire would be so heavy the person in the passenger seat would die for sure. Then there was the matter of stray bullets ricocheting off the vehicle. This was a residential neighborhood; someone could get hit. But the red car was bearing down on him now, and it wasn't going to hit just him. Kuklinski was going to mow down every man in his way, men Smith had known and worked with for years. Paul Smith's finger tightened on the trigger. The red car kept coming. He started to squeeze the trigger, resolved to shoot, but then suddenly the red car bucked and started to slow down. It was moving forward but very slowly as if Kuklinski had taken it out of gear and just let it roll under its own momentum.

The three state troopers from the black van—Detectives Pat Kane, Ernie Volkman, and Dennis Vecchiarelli—were running toward the car from behind, shouting as they came, but Paul Smith, who was now the closest man to the car, kept his eye on Kuklinski at the wheel. As he rushed up to the car, leading with his weapon, he couldn't see the big man's eyes behind the dark glasses. Smith whipped the door open, and Kuklinski leaned forward. He appeared to be reaching under the seat for something. Before he could get his hand back up, Paul Smith jammed his gun into Kuklinski's ear and pinned the Iceman's head to his other shoulder.

"Freeze! Police officer! Put your hands on the dash or I'll blow your friggin' head off," Smith yelled into Kuklinski's face as loud as he could.

Kuklinski didn't move a muscle; then slowly he brought his hands up and put them on the steering wheel. There were at least four muzzles pointed at Kuklinski's head now.

Investigator Smith grabbed the Iceman by the shirtfront, keeping the gun in his ear, and started to pull him out of the car. Kuklinski said nothing and put up no resistance at all. Smith tipped him over on his side, and Pat Kane grabbed a fistful of Kuklinski's jacket, hauling him all the way out of the car and onto the ground. The Iceman just let it happen.

On the other side of the car Deputy Chief Buccino, who had just come as close to pulling the trigger and shooting someone as he ever had in his entire career, had his arm across Barbara Kuklinski's chest, pinning her against the seat back to get her out of his line of fire in case he had to shoot. When her husband was out of the car, he pulled her out, too, and held her to the ground, still concerned that there would be gunfire.

Barbara Kuklinski did not understand that these men were policemen, and she had no idea why this man with a gun was holding her down. In her panic and confusion she screamed out to her husband.

"Rich! Rich! Help me!"

Detective Kane had just managed to get the handcuffs on Kuklinski's huge wrists—and it had been a struggle just to get them to click on the last notch—when all of a sudden the ground seemed to shake. Hearing Barbara's cries, Kuklinski erupted, bursting to his feet and bulling his way through the crush. He let out an ungodly roar as he lunged for the roof of the car, trying to get to his wife.

"Leave her alone!"

Members of the arrest team jumped on his back and tried to secure him, but he turned on them and shrugged them off. More men converged on him, and he shrugged them off, too. Finally enough men came so that they were able to wrestle Kuklinski back to the ground. It took five men to hold him down. Pat Kane was ready with a pair of the largest leg irons he could find. Unfortunately they didn't fit around Kuklinski's ankles. Unwilling to risk letting Kuklinski get back to his feet without leg restraints, they carried him horizontally to the black van.

Barbara Kuklinski, crying and still confused, was also handcuffed and then handed over to a female officer, who took her away to another car.

Paul Smith, in the meantime, searched the red Oldsmobile and found a .25-caliber Beretta automatic pistol under the driver's seat. This was what Kuklinski had been reaching for under the seat.

In the trunk of the car they found the three egg sandwiches, each one wrapped in butcher's paper and placed in the white paper bag. In a plastic bucket filled with rolled coins and loose change, they found the brown paper bag containing the brown glass vial of quinine. The vial was not full.

Later that morning Kuklinski's house was searched, but the two-tone blue van he had told Dominick about was not found in either the driveway or the garage. Officers searched the areas around Kuklinski's home and the Vince Lombardi Service Area for days, looking for an abandoned blue van. They never found one.

While Richard Kuklinski was being read his rights, Dominick Polifrone was in Hackensack, pacing the floor, wondering what the hell was going on at Kuklinski's house. He had fought the urge to go see the arrest for himself and had gone back to the Bergen County courthouse complex to wait. When the word finally came in that Richard Kuklinski was under arrest and was being brought in, Dominick rushed from the offices of the Bergen County Homicide Unit, where he'd been waiting, to the Sheriff's Department next door.

The Bergen County courthouse complex is a stately building with marble columns and a huge domed rotunda, but the Sheriff's

Department is housed in a small addition to the courthouse that is tucked away on the parking lot side. Its designer must have had a dark sense of humor because the structure has a decided medieval facade complete with crenellated battlements along the roofline. In the Sheriff's Department Dominick found an empty office off the main staircase that leads up to the holding cells. If he couldn't see Kuklinski's face, maybe he'd at least be able to hear the big son of a bitch when they brought him in. He left the door partway open.

Dominick watched from a window as the caravan of vehicles returning from the arrest pulled up to the entrance to the Sheriff's Department. From that window he couldn't see them bringing the Iceman out of the van, but he had no trouble hearing Kuklinski after they had him inside.

Kuklinski's arrogant voice carried up the stairwell. "You know what your trouble is? You guys been watching too many movies."

Dominick furrowed his brow. He thought he could hear a woman crying in the midst of a jumble of male voices.

"Hey! I told you guys to leave my wife alone," Kuklinski bellowed. "She didn't do nothing. This has nothing to do with her. Now get those fucking cuffs off her."

The sound of shuffling feet carried up the stairwell.

Dominick wondered if Kuklinski was really giving them a hard time or just mouthing off. He couldn't tell for sure. He was dying to go down and see Kuklinski's face, but he figured he'd better stay out of sight just in case Kuklinski got out on a technicality and he had to approach him again as "Michael Dominick Provenzano."

Dominick strained to hear what was going on down there, but it was hard to tell. He had already heard that they couldn't get Kuklinski in leg irons, and he had imagined the big man struggling to get free, kicking and thrashing his head and swinging his shoulders. But it was pretty quiet down there now. Dominick listened to the scrape of shoes on the steps as the pack passed by on its way upstairs to the holding cells. Kuklinski wasn't talking.

But when the cell door upstairs finally slammed shut, that's when Kuklinski started. He yelled and roared, taunting and threatening the police who'd brought him in, demanding to know what they were doing to his wife.

"Hey! What're you gonna do with my wife? You let her go. She didn't do nothing. Let her the fuck go or I'll kill somebody."

His bellowing was so loud Dominick was certain they could hear it in all the courtrooms next door. They could probably hear it across the street.

Dominick sat down at a desk and just shook his head. It was finally over. The Iceman was behind bars. After all this time it was hard to believe.

"Dominick. What the hell did you do?" Lieutenant Alan Grieco, Dominick's best friend, was standing in the doorway. His tie was askew, and his eyes were wide.

"What do you mean?"

"Your friend Kuklinski is up there shaking the bars like he's King Kong. I can't believe you went undercover with that animal. You *must* be crazy."

Dominick could only shrug. "Hey, Alan, you do what you gotta do in this business. You know that."

Grieco was about to say something when the Iceman's roar rang through the building.

"I'll kill you bastards! I'll kill all of you!"

The two men just looked at each other and shook their heads.

After his arrest Richard Kuklinski appeared before New Jersey Superior Court Judge Peter Ciolino and was charged with nineteen offenses, including five murder counts for the killings of George Malliband, Louis Masgay, Paul Hoffman, Gary Smith, and Danny Deppner. The Attorney General's Office decided not to charge him for conspiracy to murder the "rich Jewish kid," so the question of what Kuklinski's real intentions were on the morning of his arrest would have to wait. The state was more interested in building a solid case against him for the five murders at hand. Kuklinski's bail was set at two million dollars, and he was transferred to the Bergen County Jail.

When Kuklinski's home on Sunset Street in Dumont was searched, two more firearms were discovered in addition to the .25-caliber Beretta that was found under the driver's seat of the red Oldsmobile Calais. A 9mm Walther automatic pistol, model P-38, was recovered from the master bedroom, and a neglected Mossberg twelve-gauge bolt-action shotgun was wedged behind some garden tools on a garage wall.

The Newark office of the Bureau of Alcohol, Tobacco,

and Firearms ran a trace on these weapons, but both handguns were too old to yield any information. The rusty Mossberg shotgun, however, was traced to a firearms wholesaler in Mahwah, New Jersey, who had sold the gun to the Two Guys department store in Hackensack on August 2, 1979. On the day before Christmas 1979, the gun was purchased by a Robert Patterson of Bergenfield, New Jersey. When the police questioned Mr. Patterson about the shotgun, he told them that he'd bought it for his brother, Rich, who was now living in Jupiter, Florida.

Rich Patterson was very nervous when he returned to New Jersey to answer questions about the shotgun, but his nerves didn't keep him from talking. In fact, the young man had quite a bit to get off his chest when he sat down with state investigators who wanted to know how his gun had gotten into Richard Kuklinski's garage.

The answer was simple: Rich Patterson had lived with the Kuklinskis from 1983 to early 1986. He had been engaged to Merrick, the Kuklinskis' older daughter. Richard Kuklinski had liked him, and he had wanted them to get married.

But before moving in with the Kuklinskis, Patterson explained, he had briefly had an apartment of his own, a small studio just a few miles from Dumont at 51-1 Fairview Avenue in Bergenfield. Patterson swallowed hard and paused before he continued with his story. He seemed suddenly shaken. When he finally collected himself, he told the state investigators about the weekend in February 1983 when he and Merrick Kuklinski and a group of friends went away to a hunting lodge in upstate New York. He wasn't sure which weekend it was, but he did remember that one of the other boys in the group had fallen onto a wood-burning stove and burned himself so badly he had to be taken to the hospital in Ellenville, New York. (Hospital records later confirmed that the young man Patterson mentioned had been brought to the emergency room with severe back burns on Saturday, February 5, 1983.) Other than that trip to the emergency room, the weekend had been pretty uneventful. He and Merrick returned home late Sunday night, and Patterson spent the night at the Kuklinskis'.

The next morning Richard Kuklinski asked "young Rich," as the family called him, to give him a hand with something. They got into Kuklinski's white Cadillac, and Kuklinski let young Rich drive. It had just snowed, and the roads were slippery. Kuklinski told Patterson to head toward the Blazing Bucks Ranch in West Milford. Patterson knew the way. The family had taken him there many times to go horseback riding.

On the way Richard Kuklinski told the young man that something had happened at his apartment that weekend. Kuklinski, who had a set of keys to the place, had let a friend stay there. The friend had been living at a motel on Route 46 because he was in some kind of trouble. Kuklinski had been helping him, bringing him food so he wouldn't have to go out and risk being seen. But when Kuklinski had gone to Rich Patterson's apartment to check on his friend sometime during the weekend, he found the man dead. He'd been shot. The body, Kuklinski said, was in the trunk. He said he wanted to dispose of it in the woods so that young Rich wouldn't have to go through the hassle of having to explain to the police how someone had gotten killed in his apartment.

Gripping the steering wheel with bloodless fingers, Patterson followed Kuklinski's directions to an old logging road near the ranch. He pointed to a place at the side of the road and told Patterson to pull over. Other than the reservoir there was nothing but woods on this road. Kuklinski told him to shut off the engine and pop the trunk. Young Rich obeyed, but he couldn't bring himself to get out of the car. Driving there with the body in the trunk had already given him the creeps. Touching the thing was unimaginable.

Sitting behind the wheel of the Cadillac, staring into the rear-view mirror, Patterson heard a few thumps in the trunk. The trunk lid slammed shut, and Patterson saw Richard Kuklinski, his future father-in-law, dragging something wrapped in dark green plastic garbage bags through the snow. Knowing what it was, Patterson could imagine the shape of the dead man inside. Richard Kuklinski disappeared into the trees with his bundle.

A few minutes later Kuklinski returned and got into the car. He told Patterson to head home. On the way back Kuklinski said it would be best if they just forgot that this had ever happened.

Young Rich was afraid to go back to his apartment, and he was certainly never going to sleep there again. Two days later he did return, though, to collect his things. Richard Kuklinski went with him. While Patterson gathered his belongings, Kuklinski got down on his hands and knees and scrubbed the red-brown stain on the gold-colored carpeting where he said the dead man had bled after he was shot. As Kuklinski worked on the bloodstain, Patterson noticed a few pieces of Tupperware on the kitchen counter that weren't his. They looked as if they had been laid out to dry after being washed. He was pretty sure he'd seen these containers before at the Kuklinskis' house.

The investigators asked Patterson if Richard Kuklinski ever mentioned the dead man again after that.

Only once, Patterson said, and he didn't exactly mention it. That spring the family was up at the Blazing Bucks Ranch, and once again he had gone with them. Kuklinski, who never rode himself, had been reading the local West Milford newspaper. He pointed to an article and told Patterson to read it. The article was about a body that had recently been found in the vicinity by a man out riding his bicycle.

Young Rich and Merrick eventually broke off their engagement, and Patterson moved out of the house. The dead man was never mentioned again.

With the information provided by Rich Patterson, Investigators Paul Smith and Ron Donahue went to the studio apartment at 51-1 Fairview Avenue in Bergenfield with a photographer and a state police chemist to look for the stain in the carpet. The current resident, a flight attendant who lived there only part of the time, told them that she remembered there being some discoloration in the rug when she moved in, but she couldn't recall exactly where it was, and she definitely didn't remember its being red or brown. She said she had had the entire carpet professionally cleaned before she moved in several years ago.

With the resident's permission, Smith and Donahue moved the furniture and proceeded to pull up the carpeting, hoping to find some trace of blood on the canvas backing and foam rubber padding. They started with the edge closest to the window, which was where Patterson had remembered seeing the stain. Dust flew into their eyes and the odors of former tenants filled the air as they yanked at the old carpeting. They pulled up four feet worth and folded it back.

There was no sign of any staining on the canvas backing.

They ripped up the foam padding and folded that back.

Nothing.

Paul Smith was disappointed. Rich Patterson had been definite about the bloodstain being near the window. If there had been a stain, there should have been some trace of it on the underside. Even professional cleaning doesn't clean that well.

"C'mon, Paulie, let's put it back and get outta here," Ron Donahue said. "I told you this was gonna be a waste of time."

Paul Smith tapped his foot on the bare wood floor. "Why don't we pull up a little more? What the hell, we've come this far." He avoided the gaze of the woman who lived there. He'd promised her that they wouldn't make a mess.

Donahue frowned at the young investigator. "This is a waste of time, I'm telling you. If there was a bloodstain here, Kuklinski would've gotten rid of the whole goddamn carpet. He's no dummy."

"Ronnie, we're here, for chrissake," Smith said under his breath so the woman wouldn't hear them argue. "What's it gonna hurt to do a little more?"

Donahue smirked and shook his head. "If it'll make you happy, Paulie. But don't listen to me. I've only been doing this friggin' job since you were in short pants."

"Just give me a hand, will ya, Ronnie?"

Coughing and blinking, they pulled up four more feet of carpeting and padding.

Still no stains.

Paul Smith cursed under his breath.

"See, Paulie? What'd I tell you? Now let's put it back so we can get outta here."

"Hang on a minute. Let's just pull up a little bit more. I got a feeling."

The older investigator looked at Smith as if he were crazy. "You got a *feeling*? What're you, a friggin' psychic now?"

"C'mon, Ronnie, just a little more."

Ron Donahue looked to the woman who lived there and shrugged, giving her a helpless look.

Paul Smith glanced at her waiting in the doorway. Her arms were folded, and all of a sudden she didn't look like a nice, accommodating flight attendant anymore. She was scowling at him. "You told me you wouldn't make a mess."

Paul Smith coughed into his fist. "I'm sorry, ma'am, but this is a murder investigation. Don't worry, though. The state will reimburse you for any damages."

She rolled her eyes, exasperated. "Go ahead then. Do what you have to."

"Thank you. We'll put it all back the way it was. I promise." Smith and Donahue moved her table and chairs onto the exposed wood floor and tipped her foldout couch up on one end to make room.

"There'd better be a something under here," Ron Donahue whispered to Paul Smith. "This lady's gonna call the governor if there isn't."

"Just shut up and help me, will you, please?"

They heaved the carpeting back over on itself with a dusty *whomp*. The padding was stuck to the canvas backing, and they had to tear it away to get a look.

Paul Smith blinked back the grit in his eyes, then beamed at what he saw. It was as if he'd found the pot of gold at the end of a long rainbow.

Ron Donahue's jaw dropped.

"I told you I had a feeling, Ronnie."

A large brown blob-shaped stain was on the canvas backing, and its twin was on the foam padding. The stain had even soaked through the padding and penetrated the hardwood floor. Paul Smith took out a tape measure to get the exact location of the stain. It was twelve feet seven inches from the window.

While the photographer started to take pictures, Herbert Heany, the state police chemist, tested the dried stains on the carpeting, the padding, and the floorboards. He tested four separate areas for the presence of human blood.

Paul Smith hovered over him like an expectant father. "Well? Is it or isn't it?"

Heany took his time and made sure of the results before he looked up at Paul Smith. "It's positive," he said. "Four for four. It's all blood."

Smith slapped Donahue on the back. "See? What'd I tell you, Ronnie? The Patterson kid was right about the stain. His geography was just a little screwed up, that's all."

The flight attendant coughed to get their attention. She wanted to know when they were going to put her apartment back together.

"Soon." Paul Smith put on a straight face and tried to contain his glee and project a more professional image for the citizen whose home they'd just torn apart. "Just as soon as we finish up here, ma'am. As I mentioned, this *is* a murder investigation."

As Deputy Attorney General Bob Carroll proceeded to assemble the evidence against Richard Kuklinski, the matter of Danny

Deppner's death remained a problem. They had Rich Patterson's statements that he'd witnessed Kuklinski dumping a body in the woods. They knew that Danny Deppner must have died in Patterson's Bergenfield apartment, and the bloodstains found under the carpeting supported that contention. They had Patterson's statement about seeing the Tupperware in his kitchen that didn't belong to him. It was possible that Kuklinski had brought cyanide-laced food to Deppner in those plastic containers. They had the medical examiner's report describing the pink lividity on Deppner's chest and shoulders, which *could* have been caused by cyanide poisoning. Focusing on the deaths of Gary Smith and Danny Deppner, Bob Carroll wanted to draw a line between these two cases to show that both men were killed in the same manner and that these two murders formed a pattern. By proving a consistent method of killing, he could bolster the state's case against Kuklinski.

In his heart Bob Carroll had no doubt that Kuklinski had gotten rid of Deppner the same way he'd gotten rid of Gary Smith, by poisoning his food, but *proving* it would be difficult. Cyanide isn't the only toxin that causes pink lividity on the skin. According to Patterson's statement, Kuklinski had told him that *someone else* had killed the man who'd died in his apartment. And even though disposing of a body is a crime in itself, it does not necessarily prove murder. But that was what Bob Carroll needed to prove if he was going to nail the Iceman. He hoped that Dr. Geetha Natarajan, the forensic pathologist who'd done the autopsy on Deppner, might be able to help him.

The air was warm and moist with the coming of spring when the deputy attorney general drove to the Office of the Medical Examiner in Newark. He entered the two-story brick building through the bays where the bodies were brought in, signed himself in with the guard, and walked down the long marble hallway past the "work room." The smell always caught him by surprise whenever he came here. It smelled like a very ripe pet shop.

Pushing through the metal door at the end of the hall, he entered the offices where a secretary was handling the phones while technicians in lab coats rushed in and out of the warren of small offices that lined the outer wall. He found Dr. Natarajan's office. The door was open, but he knocked anyway to get her attention.

The attractive woman who usually had a ready smile for everyone snapped her head up from her cluttered desk and pushed the hair off her forehead. Her dark eyes flashed at him. "I'm mad at you," she huffed.

Investigator Paul Smith was already sitting in the chair opposite her desk. He had his hand over his mouth.

Bob Carroll showed his palms. "What did I do now?"

Dr. Natarajan whipped an eight-by-ten color photograph from her desk and held it up for him to see. It was one of the photos taken of Danny Deppner's body when it was found in the woods. The toe of someone's shoe had gotten into the picture on the left side, a bright red pump.

"Paul says you won't crop out my foot," she said. She was smiling mischievously now.

"You know I can't do that, Geetha. That's tampering with the evidence."

"But what if the defense attorney gets me on cross and he pulls out this picture and says, 'Doctor, is this your red shoe in this picture?' That will destroy my credibility with the jury. What kind of doctor wears silly red shoes like this? You tell me. It looks like I'm walking through Oz." She was laughing.

Her laughter was so infectious Bob Carroll couldn't help but smile. It put him at ease as he settled into the other chair in her minuscule office. Putting this case together was turning out to be a monster, and he'd been putting in long, tedious hours. He was going to prosecute it himself, so he wanted everything to be perfect, no room for error. That's why he was happy to have Geetha working on this one. She was an excellent pathologist and very difficult to discredit on the stand. He got right down to business.

"Have you guys come up with anything on Deppner that we can use?"

"Well," Paul Smith said, "it's pretty much the way we thought. Danny Deppner's death is consistent with cyanide poisoning, but we just don't have as much as we have with Gary Smith."

The attorney looked at the doctor. "How about the hemorrhaging you found on his neck? Isn't that indicative of strangling?"

"It could be, but trauma like this could also have been caused by several other things. With Gary Smith, the ligature marks were very clear. The neck trauma on Deppner is open to a great deal of interpretation, I'm afraid. It's a shaky premise for trying to prove that the man was strangled."

"What about the stain on the rug?"

She shook the ice in an empty soda cup. "Pulmonary edema. After death the lungs fill with fluid, and the gravitational flow sends it out the mouth and nose." She sucked on the straw. "All it tells us is that Deppner was left facedown on the rug after he was killed."

Paul Smith had his chin in his hand. He looked glum. "All that work pulling up that goddamn carpet . . ."

Bob Carroll leaned back and linked his fingers behind his head. The pictures of Smith and Deppner in death ran through his mind as he searched for a connection between the two murders, something they hadn't considered yet. He remembered the close-up of the deep ligature mark on Gary Smith's neck and started thinking out loud.

"There were no defense wounds found on Gary Smith, right?"

Dr. Natarajan shook her head. "Not on the neck or the hands. Usually in strangulation asphyxia, you find scratches and cuts indicating that the victim struggled to save herself. But in some cases there is no sign of struggle because the victim was impaired by drugs or alcohol."

"Or cyanide," Paul Smith added.

Bob Carroll's brows were knit. He leaned forward and looked at

Dr. Natarajan. "Why did you say 'herself'? 'The victim struggling to save *her*self.' "

"Because healthy adult men are rarely strangled to death. It's much more common with women and children who can be overpowered by a stronger person."

"And a man can't be overpowered by another man?"

"Not a healthy adult, not usually. A man under attack, even by another man, will struggle successfully and prevent the strangulation."

"Do you have statistics on that?"

"I can get them for you. Give me a minute."

Dr. Natarajan swiveled to her computer terminal. Bob Carroll and Paul Smith were on the edges of their seats. It took several minutes for the doctor to weed through the data bases and pull up the information.

"Here we go," she finally said. "I've gone back ten years and searched for all the healthy, unimpaired adult males who died by strangulation in the state of New Jersey. There were none."

Paul Smith bounced in his seat. "None! Out of how many strangulation murders in this state over that time period?"

Dr. Natarajan rolled her eyes. "Oh, several hundred, at least."

But Bob Carroll wasn't ready to celebrate yet. "Just for the sake of argument, Geetha, if there had been any strangulations of healthy, unimpaired men, how would you say they would have died?"

The doctor shrugged. "They probably would have been bound, handcuffed, something like that. Or perhaps in the case of an exceptionally small man, he might have been overpowered by a stronger person. Perhaps."

"Okay, so what do have now?" Carroll was thinking out loud again. "Healthy adult males do not die by strangulation unless they are impaired in some way. There were no defense wounds on Danny Deppner—"

"His stomach was practically full," Dr. Natarajan added. "No gastric emptying, which indicates that he died shortly after eating a meal." She shuffled through her notes on Deppner. "Stomach contents included . . . pinkish beans, some partly burned on one side. I would say this food was homemade. What restaurant could get away with serving burned beans?"

"And the Tupperware on the counter," Paul Smith said. "The Patterson kid said he remembered seeing that stuff at Kuklinski's house."

Bob Carroll picked up the train of thought. "So Kuklinski brought the food from his home and gave it to Deppner. Food poisoned with cyanide because Deppner showed pink lividity on his skin and he died right after he ate."

"And pulmonary edema would be consistent with cyanide poisoning," Dr. Natarajan threw in, "which would account for the stain on the carpeting."

"So whether Kuklinski strangled him or not is almost beside the point. The circumstances are the same as with Gary Smith's poisoning. It shows a pattern of behavior, a pattern of poisoning his victims' food."

Paul Smith's eyes lit up. "Which was what he was going to do to me, the rich Jewish kid. Cyanide in the egg sandwiches."

Bob Carroll grinned. "And we've got that all down on tape, thanks to Dominick. Kuklinski gave him a lesson in how to put cyanide in someone's food. It all fits."

Smith pounded on the desk in triumph. "I think we've got him on Deppner."

Carroll nodded, faintly grinning as he tried to find a hole in their reasoning. But he couldn't come up with one. "I think you're right, Paul. I think we've got him on Deppner. I do."

Dr. Natarajan beamed at the two men, her eyes sparkling. "See? I've solved another case for you." She pointed to the photo on the edge of her desk. "*Now* will you take my shoe out of the picture?"

FOUR

On January 25, 1988, thirteen months after the arrest, jury selection began on the case of the *State of New Jersey* v. *Richard Kuklinski*. The counts against Kuklinski were divided so that there would be two trials. The first was to try him for the murders of Gary Smith and Danny Deppner; the second for the murders of George Malliband and Louis Masgay. The state's position was unequivocal: They were seeking the death penalty.

Without Paul Hoffman's body, the state did not have enough evidence to win a conviction on that murder. They offered instead to let Kuklinski plead to those counts in the hope that he would reveal the location of the pharmacist's body so that the family could give the man a proper burial. After giving several false leads, Kuklinski eventually told state investigators about the steel drum abandoned next to Harry's Corner, but despite exhaustive efforts to trace that barrel, Paul Hoffman's body was never found.

The prosecution team consisted of Bob Carroll and Charles E. Waldron, another deputy attorney general from the state. Chuck Waldron's litigation skills complemented Bob Carroll's investigative talents. Tall, fit, and prematurely gray, Waldron was a long-distance runner in his spare time, and this case had already required a marathoner's stamina just to prepare it for trial.

The defense was handled by Public Defender Neal M. Frank. Given the enormity of the charges against his client and the negative publicity that the Iceman nickname had generated, Frank had his work cut out for him. He planned to give Richard Kuklinski no less than his best effort to get an acquittal, but in reality, the attainable goal was keeping his client out of the gas chamber.

Presiding over the trial was the Honorable Frederick W. Kuechenmeister, a stern, compact sixty-one-year-old man who wore large metal-frame glasses and combed his thin hair straight back. Around the Bergen County Courthouse in Hackensack, Judge Kuechenmeister had a nickname: they called him the Time Machine. When it came to sentencing, the maximum allowed by law was the minimum allowed by Kuechenmeister. Lawyers who had defended cases in his court knew that he also believed in swift justice. According to Judge Kuechenmeister, a murder trial should take no longer than three days. He had once completed a murder trial in half that time. He also believed that the bench should not be used as an instrument for social work. A judge's primary responsibility is to protect the public, and if that means getting a criminal off the street forever, so be it. He did not approve of the so-called country club prisons, and on many occasions he had stated for the record that if the penal system were under his control, he'd have prisoners "pounding boulders into rocks, rocks into stones, stones into pebbles, and pebbles into *sand.*"

It must have been a happy day at the Attorney General's Office in Trenton when they learned that the Iceman's fate would in the hands of the Time Machine.

The prosecution began presenting its case on February 17, 1988. Through a series of police witnesses, the events leading up to Gary Smith's death were unfolded: the stolen car ring that specialized in Corvettes; the arrest of Percy House, the foreman of the gang; the subsequent flight and search for the two workers, Gary Smith and Danny Deppner.

Danny Deppner's ex-wife and Percy House's current companion, Barbara Deppner, was then called to the stand. The painfully thin woman trembled visibly in the presence of Richard Kuklinski. Even though she was living out of the state with a new identity under protective custody and Kuklinski had not seen freedom since the day of his arrest, her fear of the accused flashed in her eyes as she testified. Under Bob Carroll's questioning, she told of Kuklinski's efforts to hide Smith and Deppner in one motel after another. She told of going to the York Motel just before Christmas 1982 and meeting her ex-husband, Danny, who told her that Kuklinski had made up his mind to get rid of Gary Smith because he was too much of a risk.

Bob Carroll asked her what Danny Deppner had told her on the evening of Gary Smith's murder.

"Richard Kuklinski was bringing back hamburgers from someplace," Barbara Deppner testified, "and Gary Smith's was going to have a drug on it. They knew which one Gary's would be because his didn't have pickles on it."

She was later asked to recount the description of Smith's death as told to her by her ex-husband after it had happened.

After Gary had eaten his hamburger, "he had fallen back on the bed and they [Danny Deppner and Richard Kuklinski] were laughing at him because his eyes were so goofy."

Kuklinski's lawyer, Neal Frank, tried to discredit this testimony with allegations that the state's Division of Criminal Justice had improperly interfered with efforts made by the New Jersey Division of Youth and Family Services to take Barbara Deppner's minor children away from her and her allegedly abusive live-in companion, Percy House. Frank's contention was that the Division of Criminal Justice wanted to keep its star witnesses happy so that they'd cooperate fully in this trial. A Division of Youth and Family Services legal counsel, a woman who happened to be a deputy attorney general just like the two prosecutors, testified that she had been approached by another lawyer from the Division of Criminal Justice who had asked her to drop the legal actions against Barbara Deppner concerning her children.

But the heartbreaking sight of that pale, frightened mother of nine trembling on the stand proved to be a hard image to shake from the minds of the jurors.

Percy House was called to the stand next. Gruff and burly, House made no attempt to sugarcoat his involvement with Richard Kuklinski. His attitude was blunt: He was what he was, take it or leave it. Under questioning by Chuck Waldron, House admitted to ordering Gary Smith's execution from his jail cell because he was afraid Gary would rat on him, but he also revealed that Richard Kuklinski had admitted to him at a later meeting that he had eliminated both Smith and Deppner for the exact same reason.

Given House's involvement in Gary Smith's death, his previous involvement in another unrelated murder, and the fact that he was granted immunity in exchange for his testimony, Neal Frank had a golden opportunity to trash this witness's credibility—until his client cut his legs out from under him.

As court broke for lunch and Percy House was leaving the stand, prosecutor Waldron saw Kuklinski glare at his former associate as he pointed his finger and cocked his thumb as if he were firing a gun at House while mouthing the words "You're dead." The jury was still in the courtroom when this happened, and Waldron immediately brought it to Judge Kuechenmeister's attention. The end result was that the jury accepted the prosecution's contention that as bad as Percy House was, he was only the foreman in the gang. Richard Kuklinski was the boss.

Gary Smith's wife, Veronica Cisek, testified to the events on the night of December 20, 1982, when her husband arrived home unexpectedly while he was on the run. He had been hiding out from the police, but he had risked coming back to see his daughter one last time. She testified that when her husband walked in the door,

"He was very upset. He was very nervous. He couldn't relax or even sit still. In fact, he walked into my daughter's room and just stood there and looked at her and stood there crying."

"How long was he in your daughter's room?" Chuck Waldron asked.

"Oh, about three or four minutes."

"And when he came out, how did he look?"

"He was crying. He had tears rolling down his face. . . ."

Veronica Cisek later testified that her husband felt he couldn't escape from Richard Kuklinski, even though he knew Kuklinski intended to kill him, "for the simple reason that Richie had told him that he was going to kill our daughter if he ran."

Even the severely impartial Time Machine was moved by this testimony.

James "Hoss" DiVita willingly told of his role as the fence for the stolen Corvettes. He also told of conversations he'd had with Kuklinski in which the Iceman had admitted to killing Danny Deppner, "the quiet guy," and spoken of his desire to eliminate Percy House. Questioned by Bob Carroll, DiVita paraphrased the Iceman's statement to him the day before the arrest: Richie Kuklinski "said that everybody was disappearing around him. He felt like he was in this big circle and he was the only one left standing."

Rich Patterson was a bundle of nerves when it was his turn to testify about the trip he had taken to the woods of West Milford with Richard Kuklinski to dump Danny Deppner's body. But despite his distressed appearance, he held to his statements under vigorous cross-examination. As with Barbara Deppner, the jury did not take his nervousness as a symptom of guilt or lying. They saw it as fear of the Iceman.

Darlene Pecoraro, the flight attendant who had taken over Rich Patterson's studio apartment in Bergenfield years after the murder, gave testimony on the condition of the gold-colored carpeting in that apartment when she moved in, and Investigator Paul Smith followed with a description of how the bloodstain was discovered on the reverse side.

Dr. Geetha Natarajan then provided expert testimony on the autopsies of Smith and Deppner. Her statements were precise and detailed, intentionally loaded with medical terminology.

"If a person were to ingest a quantity of cyanide," Bob Carroll asked her, "what would be the possible symptoms that could be manifested?"

"The symptoms of cyanide poisoning will depend primarily on the dosage. The lethal dose—the amount that is necessary to kill a human being—of sodium or potassium cyanide is from thirty milligrams to about sixty or seventy milligrams.

"Now if a smaller amount is consumed orally, smaller than thirty milligrams, the person will have a burning sensation on the roof of the mouth and the food pipe, and he will then have dizziness, headaches, confusion, depending on how hypoxic he gets or how much of the cyanide there is in the material he consumed and how much of it has blocked the cellular respiration. . . ."

"How long does cyanide typically remain in a body after death?" Carroll then asked.

"Cyanide is metabolized premortem. . . . The cyanide is broken down and converted in the liver. The person's liver converts the cyanide which is lethal to an inert compound called thiocyanate which is nonlethal and it's done by an enzyme reaction in the liver. The enzyme is rodense. . . ."

It was Dr. Natarajan's policy to bombard the jury with her technical knowledge whenever she testified in court. In her experience she had found that explaining medical issues in lay terms often lessened her credibility because juries tend to regard women doctors as somehow inferior to men. It was all right if they didn't understand everything she said, just as long as they believed that she knew what she was talking about.

Defense attorney Neal Frank repeatedly tried to poke holes in her testimony regarding Danny Deppner, pointing out that the cause of death was officially listed as "unknown" until it was determined that the deceased had been associated with Richard Kuklinski. It was only then that the cause of death had been amended to murder by poisoning. The defense presented other pathologists who raised other possibilities for the presence of pink lividity on the bodies of Smith and Deppner, but Dr. Michael Baden, medical examiner for the New York State Police and former ME for the city of New York, testified for the state and buttressed Dr. Natarajan's findings in clear, unequivocal statements that did not go over the jurors' heads.

Yet despite all this condemning evidence, no one had actually *witnessed* Richard Kuklinski committing murder. As damning as all this testimony was, it was largely circumstantial. The prosecution's job now was to prove that its contention—that Richard Kuklinski had killed Gary Smith and Danny Deppner with the help of cyanide—was *consistent* with the facts presented so far. Consistent. It was a word that Bob Carroll would hammer home in his summation. And to prove that these crimes were consistent with Richard Kuklinski's regular pattern of behavior, he called the state's most important witness, Special Agent Dominick Polifrone.

On the afternoon of March 2, 1988, Dominick Polifrone sat in the front row of the courtroom, ready to take the stand. As the accused was brought in, their eyes locked. He hadn't seen Richard Kuklinski face-to-face in more than a year, not since that December morning at the Vince Lombardi Service Area when they'd made their final plans to murder the "rich Jewish kid." Though he was slightly nervous about testifying before the judge and jury, Dominick narrowed his eyes and met Kuklinski's gaze without flinching. Just as at their first meeting at the doughnut shop, Dominick would not allow the Iceman to intimidate him.

Kuklinski's stare was cold. He was playing his intimidation game. But Dominick knew that he was playing with an empty hand.

On the stand Dominick told of his undercover assignment, how he had worked to establish a relationship with Kuklinski, then, once that relationship had been established, how he had secretly recorded their conversations. Portions of the Nagra tapes were played in court, and the jury heard Richard Kuklinski in his own voice connect himself to the crimes of which he was accused.

He was accused of using cyanide to kill Smith and Deppner. On tape he had explained to Dominick in great detail how to kill with cyanide, how to mix it in someone's food, how you have to make sure to mix it in with something "gooky" so that it's palatable to the intended victim.

Richard Kuklinski was accused of putting cyanide on a hamburger and giving it to Gary Smith. On the tapes he had told Dominick Polifrone that he had put cyanide on a guy's hamburger once and that the guy must have had "the constitution of a fucking bull" because it took him so long to die. This was consistent with the testimonies of Dr. Natarajan and Dr. Baden, who said that Gary Smith had been strangled probably because the cyanide didn't appear to be working. It must have seemed that the dose wasn't big enough. But in fact, Richard Kuklinski and Danny Deppner had just been impatient. Had they waited a few more minutes, the cyanide would have certainly killed Gary Smith.

All through Dominick Polifrone's testimony, Richard Kuklinski's words came back to haunt him time and time again. The tapes played on and on, and for Richard Kuklinski *this* burden of proofs accumulated by the prosecution got heavier and heavier. On tape Kuklinski had spoken of his need for cyanide to take care of "a couple of rats." In one conversation he had told Dominick about "the pointer" who could send him to jail, and in another he had mentioned Percy House by name. From the testimonies of House and Barbara Deppner, it was already obvious to the jury that these two knew too much.

The tapes rolled on, and the jury heard Richard Kuklinski lend his unique expertise to the plan to kill the "rich Jewish kid." They heard about the egg sandwiches that Kuklinski would lace with cyanide. They learned how to dispose of a body in a fifty-five-gallon drum. They heard all about sealing a barrel and dumping it. They heard about disposing of the rich kid's car after he was dead, selling it for parts and making it disappear. They heard Kuklinski's warning to Dominick not to go back to the kid's apartment more than once after they'd killed him because that was how guys got caught. The jury heard the expert advice of an old hand at murder.

When it was all over, Dominick Polifrone had been on the stand for a day and a half, and Richard Kuklinski was buried under a landfill of his own words.

Defense attorney Neal Frank attempted to paint a different picture, suggesting that all this talk was nothing more than that, just talk. He offered the possibility that his client was "blowing smoke" at the undercover agent, that he saw Dominick as a bad guy and felt that he had to project an equal image in order to do business with him. When you deal with people like "Dominick Provenzano," as Frank admitted his client sometimes did, you *had* to brag, you *had* to inflate yourself and show that you could be bad, too.

The jury didn't buy it.

After four weeks of testimony the jury took a total of four hours to reach its verdict.

Richard Kuklinski was found guilty on all counts.

On the murder charges, however, the jury did not find him guilty of murder *by his own conduct.* In the absence of eyewitness testimony on the murders and given the fact that Danny Deppner was the one who had actually strangled Gary Smith, the jurors did not feel that they could go all the way. In this sense the defense achieved its goal. This conviction could not carry the death penalty in New Jersey. Neal Frank had succeeded in saving his client's life.

After prolonged posttrial negotiations Richard Kuklinski returned to Judge Kuechenmeister's courtroom on May 25, 1988, for sentencing. As he was led into the courtroom, Kuklinski spotted

Dominick Polifrone sitting in the spectators' section. "Hello, Dominick," he said with a smile. "How ya doing?"

"Good," Dominick replied. "How're *you* doing?"

Even as he was about to face sentencing, Richard Kuklinski would not let on that any of this bothered him. He wouldn't give Dominick Polifrone the satisfaction.

The judge emerged from his chambers, and the proceedings began with Bob Carroll outlining the terms of an agreement Richard Kuklinski and his attorney had reached with the state. At the arrest Barbara Kuklinski had been charged with possession of an illegal weapon because she had been in the red Oldsmobile when the .25-caliber handgun was found under the seat. Kuklinski's son, Dwayne, had also been facing a minor marijuana possession charge in an unrelated incident. In exchange for dropping these charges against his family, Richard Kuklinski agreed to confess to the murders of George Malliband and Louis Masgay, thereby saving everyone the agony of a second trial.

Standing before Judge Kuechenmeister, Richard Kuklinski stated for the record, "I shot George Malliband five times." When asked why, he replied, "It was . . . it was due to business."

As for Louis Masgay, "On July 1, 1981, I shot him once in the back of the head."

Judge Kuechenmeister then pronounced sentence. Citing the futility of commenting on the "depths of depravity reached in these cases," the Time Machine imposed two life sentences on Richard Kuklinski—one for Smith and Deppner, the other for Malliband and Masgay. For Smith and Deppner, a mandatory sixty years would have to be served before parole could be considered—thirty years for each slaying, one consecutive to the other. For Malliband and Masgay, the same penalty was imposed. The two sixty-year terms would run concurrently.

Richard Kuklinski was transferred to the Trenton State Prison in the state capital. From the north end of this maximum-security facility, inmates can see the sharp angles of the nearby Richard J.

Hughes Justice Complex, where Deputy Attorney General Bob Carroll's office is located.

After sentencing was passed, Dominick Polifrone was asked to comment on the Iceman's future.

Dominick looked down and showed a weary but satisfied smile before he answered. "For twenty-one months the last thing I saw at night before I shut my eyes and the first thing I saw in the morning when I opened them was Richard Kuklinski's face. But now, for the rest of his life, every time Richie goes to bed at night and every time he wakes up in the morning, he's gonna be seeing mine."

Richard Kuklinski will not be eligible for parole until he is one hundred and eleven years old.

In many ways Richard Kuklinski remains a locked box. At his arraignment Deputy Attorney General Bob Carroll referred to Kuklinski as a "killing machine," but the exact number of people he has killed is unknown. Kuklinski no longer maintains that he is an innocent man, and he has estimated his personal body count to be around a hundred victims. From time to time he will allude to murders he *may* have committed, refusing to give whole names, being deliberately vague about dates and places. His only complaint with his conviction is that he wasn't tried for the "right things," and therefore, the state didn't get him "fair and square."

As for the plan to kill the "rich Jewish kid," he claims that he never intended to go through with it. He also claims that he never intended to murder "Dominick Provenzano." Yet in a statement made to the police two days after Kuklinski's arrest, John Sposato, who had represented himself as Tim, the arms dealer, said that Kuklinski did indeed intend to kill Dominick that very Saturday when they would have lured him down to a warehouse in Delaware to complete the big arms deal for the Irish Republican Army. Sposato had been arrested on the same day as Kuklinski, but he chose to cooperate with the state and willingly confessed to his involvement with Kuklinski. Charges against him were dropped, and he was released. He later assisted the Secret Service and the New Jersey State Police with an investigation into an international arms sales and currency counterfeiting scheme.

Exactly what was going on in Kuklinski's mind on the morning of December 17, 1986, may never be known. When the three egg sandwiches were recovered from the trunk of Kuklinski's red Oldsmobile, the contents were combined so that the state chemist could accurately measure the amount of quinine present in the sandwiches against the total amount he had previously put into the square brown glass vial. But in doing this, the number of sandwiches that were poisoned was never determined.

If only one sandwich had been poisoned, it's possible that Kuklinski did intend to go back and fulfill his part of the bargain with Dominick. But if two sandwiches contained the simulated cyanide, perhaps Kuklinski had decided to kill *both* the rich kid and Dominick. The promise of the big arms deal had been dangled in front of his face for months, but nothing had materialized. Perhaps he had lost faith in Dominick and decided to settle for the bird in the hand, killing these two and taking the entire eighty-five thousand dollars that the rich kid was supposed to be bringing to buy three kilos of cocaine.

Or it may have been that Richard Kuklinski's obsessive love for his wife overruled his desire to make the score. When he learned of Barbara's illness that morning, returning home to take care of her may have become his paramount concern. Though he did prepare the sandwiches, perhaps he changed his mind. Getting her to the doctor may have become the only thing that really mattered to him that morning.

The police never found the two-tone blue van Kuklinski had told Dominick he had waiting just down the turnpike from the Vince Lombardi Service Area. He did not get a vehicle from Hoss

DiVita in Connecticut the day before, and John Sposato was apparently so broke that day he couldn't even afford to rent one.

Kuklinski has also reasoned, "Who would eat a cold egg sandwich?" No one, not even a cocaine addict, would eat something that had been hanging around as long as those three sandwiches had.

But if in fact, he did not have a van that morning, perhaps he never intended to kill the "rich kid" at all. But he had poisoned at least one of the sandwiches, so who *did* he intend to kill?

Perhaps the sandwich was actually intended for John Sposato. Kuklinski had never forgiven him for showing up at his house with his two goons. Overweight and slovenly, Sposato was hardly a picky eater. The fact that an egg sandwich was cold and a little stale might not have mattered that much to him.

Another possibility is that Richard Kuklinski was just lazy that day. Why bother killing the rich kid for half of eighty-five thousand dollars when all the while he intended to rip off Dominick later in the week for half a million? Kuklinski knew the police were after him for murder. Why add another killing to his résumé for a relatively paltry amount of money? He didn't know who this rich kid was, and he had always been very cautious when he killed. Despite Dominick's assurances that the kid wasn't connected to the mob, Kuklinski may have feared that their intended victim could very well have had Mafia ties. A spoiled rotten cokehead with money to burn was just the kind of friend a wiseguy would want. Perhaps Kuklinski figured killing this kid simply wasn't worth the risk.

But only Richard Kuklinski knows why he didn't show up to kill the "rich Jewish kid" that morning. It is one of many items in the locked box.

Though he admits to freezing Louis Masgay's body and keeping it on ice for more than two years, Kuklinski will not say *where* he kept the body all that time. A freezer big enough to hold a man would have to have left some kind of mark on the floor of his rented garage in North Bergen, but the police found no hard evidence that a unit that large had ever been there. The refrigerated lockers inside Mr. Softee's ice-cream truck would have been big enough to hold a body with room to spare, but when asked about all this, Richard Kuklinski just smiles.

Richard Kuklinski claims that one of his favorite weapons was the compact derringer pistol and that he carried two when he was fully armed. But no derringers were found when his house and cars were searched. He says that he had been carrying a one-shot firearm shaped like a fountain pen in his shirt pocket when he was arrested. It was lost in the scuffle at his arrest, he says.

International currency exchange was Richard Kuklinski's supposed legitimate business, but many questions remain unanswered on that aspect of his life. He claims to have made a great deal of money selling Nigerian currency at a discount to American companies that had factories in that country. He has implied that he had obtained the Nigerian money through arms deals. But how would he have made a profit if he had to sell the currency at a discount in order to get American dollars? Were these arms deals deadly rip-off scams like the one he had planned for Dominick Polifrone in which the weapons never actually existed?

Only Richard Kuklinski knows.

The hunting knife that he kept in his briefcase had ten notches on the handle. He claims to have killed with knives, but none of the murders that the police have connected to him were stabbings. Who were *these* victims?

Only Richard Kuklinski knows.

The locked box may open up someday, but until then we can only speculate on what else is in there. Only Richard Kuklinski knows for sure.

Judge Kuechenmeister has observed that most of the convicted criminals who face sentencing in his courtroom seem impassive and even relieved when their punishment is handed down. The average offender cannot structure a life for himself, and so he falls into a life of crime. Prison will provide a structure that these criminals have never had, and in that sense they are relieved of the burden of having to figure out what to do with themselves every day, day after day.

Criminals like Richard Kuklinski are the exception. They have structured their lives. This is why Kuklinski was so hard to catch. He was careful, he was methodical, and he was disciplined. He knew how to separate the various aspects of his life, and he tried not to let his emotions overtake his "business" decisions. But it is this ability to structure a life that has made prison so difficult for him. He doesn't like other people telling him what to do and when to do it. Looking back on the morning of his arrest, he often wishes that he had died in a shoot-out with the police. If his wife had not been in the car with him, he says there definitely would have been some bloodshed.

Richard Kuklinski now works in the prison library and keeps to himself as much as possible. His brother, Joseph, is imprisoned at the Trenton State Hospital in a ward for the criminally insane, two miles from the Trenton State Prison. The brothers have not seen each other in more than twenty years, and Richard has no interest in reestablishing communication.

Kuklinski has made no friends in prison, only acquaintances. At one point convicted murderer John List tried to win his friendship. List is the New Jersey man who killed his wife, children, and mother in a bizarre ritual, then fled to Virginia and created a new life for himself, which he maintained for fourteen years before he was caught. But Richard Kuklinski wants no part of List. To him, anyone who would harm his own family is beneath contempt. He has said repeatedly that the only friend he has ever had and ever will have is his wife, Barbara.

Barbara Kuklinski says she remained in this destructive relationship that fluctuated between extreme abuse and extreme abundance because she deeply feared that her husband would have turned his rage on their children if she had ever tried to leave him. Besides, she says, the notion of "just walking out the door" is a simpleminded solution offered by people who don't know the half of it. Barbara Kuklinski compares herself with Hedda Nussbaum, the woman who lived with Joel Steinberg, the abusive, drug-addicted New York lawyer who was convicted in the beating death of his adopted daughter, Lisa Steinberg. That trial was televised, and Ms. Nussbaum's battered face, her vague, hoarse voice, and her obvious internal scarring riveted audiences all through her testimony. Seeing what her mate had done to her, people winced and asked why in God's name Nussbaum hadn't just left that monster. Barbara Kuklinski says she knows why. An outsider can never begin to understand what a woman goes through in that kind of relationship. It makes no sense, she says, unless you're there.

The house on Sunset Street was sold, and Barbara Kuklinski no longer lives in Dumont. Both her daughters are married, and her son lives on his own, but the family remains close. Barbara Kuklinski's main concern now is keeping her children and grandchildren from being branded as the Iceman's family, but she sometimes doubts that that stigma will ever heal.

Bob Carroll, Bobby Buccino, Ron Donahue, and Paul Smith still work together, making cases for the New Jersey State task force. Over the years their combined efforts have brought thousands of criminals to justice, yet Operation Iceman remains by far their most memorable case.

Dominick Polifrone is now resident agent in charge of the Bureau of Alcohol, Tobacco, and Firearms office in Fairfield, New Jersey. He still lives in the same house in northern Bergen County with his family, and he still likes to unwind on his deck with a cigar and a glass of scotch. But he has yet to relive the tension he experienced during his prolonged undercover assignment with the Iceman.

To this day Richard Kuklinski has expressed no remorse for the lives he has taken. He insists that his victims were all "players," and they got what they deserved.

The only thing he regrets is the pain and suffering he has caused his family. When he thinks about them and the life they once had together, the Iceman sometimes cries.

ACKNOWLEDGMENTS

In writing this book, I was extremely fortunate to have been given a generous amount of support and cooperation from a variety of people who all deserve recognition for their efforts.

First, I would like to thank Jim Thebaut, who brought this project to me and whose seventeen-hour videotaped interview with Richard Kuklinski provided a unique look into the mind of a killer.

Thanks to John Mumford of the Juniata College Library, Fred Ney of the *Wilkes-Barre Sunday Independent*, and Marilyn Thomas of the Ralph Brown Draughon Library at Auburn University for helping me with my research; and to Superintendent Howard Beyer for facilitating my visit to Trenton State Prison to interview Richard Kuklinski. I would also like to thank Donna Kocubinski of the New Jersey Division of Criminal Justice, whose helpfulness is surpassed only by her patience.

I am grateful to all those who gave me their time in order to be interviewed for this book: Dr. Michael M. Baden, director of the Forensic Sciences Unit of the New York State Police; Dr. Geetha Natarajan, assistant New Jersey state medical examiner; Dr. Frederick Zugibe,

Rockland County chief medical examiner; and Dr. Michael Schwartzman, Ph.D.;

Former Attorney General for the State of New Jersey W. Cary Edwards; Director of the New Jersey Division of Criminal Justice Robert T. Winter; Deputy Chief Robert T. Buccino, Investigator Ron Donahue, and the late Investigator Ronald Jivins of the New Jersey Organized Crime and Racketeering Bureau; Deputy Attorney General Charles E. Waldron;

The Honorable Frederick W. Kuechenmeister;

Lieutenant Ernest Volkman and Detective-Sergeant Pat Kane of the New Jersey State Police;

Deputy Chief Ed Denning and Lieutenant Alan Grieco of the Bergen County Prosecutors Office;

Deputy Chief Margaret Moore and Special Agent Ray Goger of the Bureau of Alcohol, Tobacco, and Firearms;

Neal M. Frank, Barbara Kuklinski, and Richard Kuklinski.

Special thanks to the guys from the "A-Team" whose enthusiasm for this project and willingness to provide me with information made them a writer's dream: Deputy Attorney General Bob Carroll, Supervising State Investigator Paul Smith, and ATF Resident Agent in Charge Dominick Polifrone.

And as always, I am eternally indebted to the people who turn my manuscripts into books: my editors, Brian DeFiore and Mitch Horowitz; my agent, Al Zuckerman of Writers House; and my wife, Judith Sachs, who reads and critiques them first (and who also endures more tales of murder and mayhem at the dinner table than any spouse should).

ABOUT THE AUTHOR

ANTHONY BRUNO is the author of eleven crime novels and four true-crime books, including *Seven* (based on the hit movie starring Brad Pitt and Morgan Freeman). His nonfiction work, *The Seekers: A Bounty Hunter's Story*, was nominated for the Edgar Award for best fact-crime book. His novel *Bad Apple* was adapted for television in 2004.

anthonybruno.net